ENDORSEMENTS

The interdisciplinary approaches to the themes found in the Book of Proverbs, which are articulated well in this fine volume by Tiberius Rata, Kevin Roberts, and Knute Larson, offer insightful and helpful complementary on this treasured book of sacred wisdom. Providing symphonic observations and perspectives from the fields of biblical studies, psychology, and counseling, as well as pastoral ministry, the three authors work in a collaborative way to offer fresh understanding and application for the twenty-first-century reader. Exploring various and important themes such as the fear of the Lord, faithfulness, parenting, patience, generosity, humility, and others, readers are given multi-sided reflections to enable and guide them in their spiritual journeys. I am delighted to recommend *Sacred Wisdom: An Interdisciplinary Commentary on the Book of Proverbs.*

David S. Dockery, Ph.D.
President and Distinguished Professor of Theology
Southwestern Baptist Theological Seminary
Fort Worth, Texas

Proverbs is an Old Testament book written for the church and to make us wise. As such it attracts Old Testament scholars, pastors, and counselors, but seldom in one place. Until now. Tiberius Rata exegetes the biblical text, Kevin Roberts analyzes its psychological significance, and Knute Larson applies it to the church. The result is a lush, interwoven study of Proverbs: what it means, how it speaks to our deepest longings, and how it shapes our communal life. *Sacred Wisdom* is a wise and friendly conversation that invites us to participate. Read it with your wise friends.

Michael Wittmer, Ph.D.
Professor of Systematic Theology
Cornerstone Theological Seminary

Personally and corporately, Christians need wisdom, God's wisdom. In this interdisciplinary commentary Rata (the exegete) mines the biblical text for divinely revealed wisdom. Using selected topics and accompanying word studies he highlights key themes in the Book of Proverbs. Then Roberts (the counselor) shapes those golden nuggets to our personal lives, helping us understand our need and the impact of God-given wisdom on how we think, feel, and live. Building on those two interactions with the biblical text, Larson (the pastor) fits our setting within a collection of gems, the local church. In that context we find a supportive and nurturing context within which we might develop God's wisdom in interpersonal relationships and corporate worship. *Sacred Wisdom* offers a refreshing and realistic approach to biblical wisdom. It can serve as a study manual for small groups in the church, for individual families, or for personal spiritual growth.

William D. Barrick, Th.D.
Emeritus Professor of Old Testament (Retired)
The Master's Seminary, Sun Valley, Calif.

It is a pleasure to recommend this brand new commentary on the book of Proverbs, so few books of the Bible are needed as desperately today as this book of Proverbs. At a time when the Fear of the LORD has fallen into such shambles and the concept of what is a man and what is a woman is so needed from a Biblical perspective; here is a wonderful answer for a whole new generation. I found this work to be solidly Biblical and full of practical application. I urge its wide distribution for it will be a needed blessing for our nation.

Walter C. Kaiser Jr., Ph.D.
President emeritus
Gordon Conwell Theological Seminary
Boston, Mass.

Sacred Wisdom at the outset by its insightful title declares that true wisdom begins in the mind and heart of God. This thoroughly biblical perspective gives the volume a rich spiritual nourishing for readers. The volume is distinctive by its interdisciplinary approach that is creative and holistic, acknowledging the whole person, individually and in community. The authors in each one's discipline present an academically sound study written in a clear, understandable style. In accord with Proverbs' genre of practical wisdom, the volume highlights practical insights and offers application questions for readers promoting readers' self-evaluation. It is excellent for pastors, teachers, and group studies.

Kenneth Mathews, Ph.D.
Professor of Divinity Emeritus
Beeson Divinity School
Birmingham, Ala.

Did you hear the one about the pastor, the theologian and the psychologist? It's no joke! Something amazing happens when those three combine their passion, scholarship, and insights to the book of Proverbs. That's precisely what Rata, Roberts, and Larson have accomplished in *Sacred Wisdom, an Interdisciplinary Commentary on the Book of Proverbs.* This book is destined to be a classic. Beginning with the rich theological insights, *Sacred Wisdom* adds psychology perspective along with pastoral discernment giving the reader a wholistic grasp of wisdom literature.

Rata, Roberts, and Larson mine out the deep truths of Proverbs while providing rich practical application. Biblical orthodoxy filled with workable orthopraxy makes *Sacred Wisdom* a valuable resource for every student of the Word.

Dave Engbrecht
Pastor at Large, Nappanee Missionary Church
Nappanee, Ind.

I was on a beach at the Jersey Shore recently and a plane flew overhead advertising a concert by a group called "Gypsy Wisdom." I wish the banner waving behind that plane had advertised this book. It's a concert of "Sacred Wisdom" and the three who put it together are themselves pretty smart. Definitely worth a read, even on a beach.

Robert E. Larson, Jr., D.Min.
Retired Pastor
Presbyterian Church (USA)

SACRED WISDOM

SACRED WISDOM

An Interdisciplinary Commentary on the Book of Proverbs

Tiberius RATA
Kevin ROBERTS
Knute LARSON

Published by BMH Books, Winona Lake, IN
bmhbooks.com
paperback 978-0-88469-260-7
ebook 978-0-88469-271-3

CONTENTS

CHAPTER 1—AN INTRODUCTION

Wisdom Literature and the Proverbs: *Dr. Tiberius Rata* 3

CHAPTER 2—THE FEAR OF THE LORD

The Wise Have the Fear of the LORD: *Dr. Tiberius Rata* 19

Reflections on the Fear of the LORD: *Dr. Kevin Roberts* 27

The Fear of the LORD at Church: *Pastor Knute Larson* 35

CHAPTER 3—FAITHFULNESS

The Wise Are Faithful: *Dr. Tiberius Rata* 41

Reflections on Faithfulness: *Dr. Kevin Roberts* 57

Faithfulness at Church: *Pastor Knute Larson* 65

CHAPTER 4—WISE PARENTING

The Wise Are Godly Parents: *Dr. Tiberius Rata* 73

Reflections on Wise Parenting: *Dr. Kevin Roberts* 89

Wise Parenting at Church: *Pastor Knute Larson* 103

CHAPTER 5—PATIENCE

The Wise Are Patient: *Dr. Tiberius Rata* 111

Reflections on Patience and Self-control: *Dr. Kevin Roberts* 121

Patience at Church: *Pastor Knute Larson* 135

CHAPTER 6—GENEROSITY

The Wise Are Generous: *Dr. Tiberius Rata* 143

Reflections on Generosity: *Dr. Kevin Roberts* 153

Generosity at Church: *Pastor Knute Larson* 161

CHAPTER 7—HUMILITY

The Wise Are Humble: *Dr. Tiberius Rata* 169
Reflections on Humility: *Dr. Kevin Roberts* 183
Humility at Church: *Pastor Knute Larson* 191

CHAPTER 8—SPEAKING TRUTH

The Wise Speak Truth: *Dr. Tiberius Rata* 199
Reflections on Speaking Truth: *Dr. Kevin Roberts* 209
Speaking Truth at Church: *Pastor Knute Larson* 217

CHAPTER 9—SPEAKING KINDLY

The Wise Speak Kindly: *Dr. Tiberius Rata* 223
Reflections on Kindness: *Dr. Kevin Roberts* 233
Speaking Kindly at Church: *Pastor Knute Larson* 243

CHAPTER 10—LIFELONG LEARNING

The Wise Are Lifelong Learners: *Dr. Tiberius Rata* 251
Reflections on Lifelong Learning: *Dr. Kevin Roberts* 261
Lifelong Learning at Church: *Pastor Knute Larson* 269

BIBLIOGRAPHY 275

DEDICATIONS AND ACKNOWLEDGMENTS

DEDICATION

"The wise woman builds her house." I dedicate this work to my beautiful and wonderful wife Carmen, who embodies the wise woman in Proverbs 14:1. I can see her genuine piety in the wisdom of her thoughts and actions towards me and our children.

ACKNOWLEDGMENTS

I want to thank my teaching assistants who have helped with this work over the years: Halley Krochta, Matthew Lingren, Caleb Voth, Jordan Weimer, Malachi Koch, and Blake Burns.

Tiberius Rata

DEDICATION

To my children, Isaac and Rachel Roberts. May the wisdom found in the book of Proverbs help you grow in faith and wisdom and serve as a guide to your life's choices, as you seek to glorify God with your life.

ACKNOWLEDGMENTS

I would like to express my deepest gratitude to my wife Heather, for her keen eye for detail and her unwavering commitment to helping me finish this project. I am truly blessed to have such an intelligent, talented, and loving partner in life who always pushes me to be the best version of myself. I want to express limitless gratitude as we attempt to sojourn our time on Earth together. I also wish to thank Jenna Ellinger for her assistance in the research aspect of this book.

Kevin Roberts

DEDICATION

"Proverbs Goes to Church" section dedicated to Jeanine Larson, wife of 61 years and model for Proverbs 31.

ACKNOWLEDGEMENT

With thanksgiving for the two churches I served, Grace Church and The Chapel, and their strong love for wisdom from God's Word and efforts to live it in a daily way! Also, in memory of my mother, Fae Ann, who through the pain of divorce and the tragic death of the 14-year-old daughter she cherished, fought cancer and pain with the struggle to trust the Lord as the Proverbs direct.

Knute Larson

CHAPTER 1

An Introduction

Wisdom Literature and the Proverbs

Dr. Tiberius Rata

What Is Wisdom Literature?

Wisdom literature is a literary genre that informs us about the principles of God's moral universe. God is not just the Creator; He is also the Moral Legislator who puts in place universal moral principles that are not bound by cultural norms. The wise person lives in accordance with these principles, while the fool rejects them.

We find wisdom literature in the books of Job, Proverbs, Ecclesiastes, and Psalms.[1] Absent, or mostly absent, from wisdom literature are concepts dealing with the law, covenant, idolatry, Israel as a nation, and the sacrificial system. However, principles dealing with timeless truths that transcend boundaries abound, including living responsibly or recklessly, human pain and suffering, justice, kingship, marriage, the discipline of children, wealth and poverty, industriousness, integrity and truth, and fear of the LORD.

Wisdom-type literature is not unique to Israel, however. It appears in other Ancient Near Eastern traditions, yet it lacks teaching about the fear of the LORD. And because the fear of the LORD is the beginning of wisdom, people cannot be identified as wise apart from a correct relationship with Yahweh, Creator

1 Psalms 1, 14, 37, 73, 91, 112, 119, and 128 are considered to be wisdom psalms.

God. Subsequently, wisdom literature that is concerned with creation theology cannot be understood apart from understanding the Creator.

We know that Solomon, one of the central authors of the book of Proverbs, is compared with other wise men of Mesopotamia, Canaan, and Egypt. We read in 1 Kings 4, that "Solomon's wisdom surpassed the wisdom of all the people of the east and all the wisdom of Egypt. For he was wiser than all other men, wiser than Ethan the Ezrahite, and Heman, Calcol, and Darda, the sons of Mahol, and his fame was in all the surrounding nations" (1 Kings 4:30–31). Solomon had asked God for "a discerning heart to govern your people and to distinguish between right and wrong," which God granted to him and more (1 Kings 3:9, 12–13). The book of Proverbs reflects this God-given wisdom.

Extra Biblical wisdom literature includes maxims about life in general, similar to what we find in the book of Proverbs. One of the earliest wisdom texts from Egypt is attributed to Ptahhotep, vizier of King Izezi of the Fifth Dynasty (around 2450 BC). "If you are a man of standing, you should found your household and love your wife at home as is fitting. Fill her belly; clothe her back. Ointment is the prescription for her body. Make her heart glad as long as you live."[2]

Wisdom literature dealing with the mystery of innocent suffering was recorded around 1000 BC in what is known as Babylonian Theodicy. "I am finished. Anguish has come upon me. When I was still a child, fate took my father; my mother who bore me went to the Land of No Return."[3]

Egyptian Wisdom Literature that closest resembles the material in the book of Proverbs is attributed to Amenemope, an Egyptian official. "Do not associate to yourself the heated man, nor visit him for conversation. Preserve your tongue from answering your superior, and guard yourself against reviling him."[4]

---

2 Bill T. Arnold and Bryan E. Beyer, *Readings from the Ancient Near East* (Grand Rapids: Baker, 2002), 184.

3 Arnold and Beyer, 180.

4 Arnold and Beyer, 188.

The appeal of the book of Proverbs comes from the fact that it is very practical and relevant. The principles outlined in the book keep one from violence (1:10–19), slothfulness (6:6–11), wickedness (6:12–15), and immorality (5:3–20; 6:23–35; 7:4–27). Because we are emotional beings, the book is valuable because it teaches us how to deal with our emotions. Wisdom also teaches us not to befriend angry people (22:24–25), that a soft answer turns away wrath (15:1), and that "a man of quick temper acts foolishly" (14:17).

Authorship and Date

Three names are mentioned in the book of Proverbs in relation to its authorship: Solomon, Agur, and Lemuel. Internal evidence suggests that Solomon, the son of David, is the primary author of the vast majority of the material found. Solomon's name is mentioned at the beginning of Proverbs 1:1–9:18, 10:1–22:16, and 25:1–29:27). This fits with the 1 Kings 4 narrative, where the chronicler stated,

> God gave Solomon wisdom and understanding beyond measure, and breadth of mind like the sand on the seashore, so that Solomon's wisdom surpassed the wisdom of all the people of the east and all the wisdom of Egypt. For he was wiser than all other men, wiser than Ethan the Ezrahite, and Heman, Calcol, and Darda, the sons of Mahol, and his fame was in all the surrounding nations. He also spoke 3,000 proverbs, and his songs were 1,005. He spoke of trees, from the cedar that is in Lebanon to the hyssop that grows out of the wall. He spoke also of beasts, and of birds, and of reptiles, and of fish. And people of all nations came to hear the wisdom of Solomon, and from all the kings of the earth, who had heard of his wisdom. (1 Kings 4:29–34)

Notice that Solomon wrote 3,000 proverbs and yet we only have 800 verses in the book of Proverbs, meaning we don't have the complete works of Solomon. Either way, the proverbs date back to the reign of Solomon (970–931 BC).

The superscript to 22:17 and 24:23 attributes a number of proverbs to "wise men." We are not told who these men are, but 1 Kings 4:31 compares Solomon with other wise men, such as Ethan the Ezrahite, Heman, Calcol, and Darda, the sons of Mahol. Chapter 30 is attributed to Agur son of Jakeh and chapter 31 is attributed to King Lemuel. Both Agur and King Lemuel are enigmas since we don't have any historical, geographical, or ethnic background for them.[5]

Outline

1–9	The proverbs of Solomon, son of David, king of Israel
10:1–22:16	The proverbs of Solomon[6]
22:17–24:22	The sayings of the wise
24:23–34	More sayings of the wise[7]
25–29	More proverbs of Solomon collected by the officials of Hezekiah, king of Judah[8]
30	The sayings of Agur son of Jakeh, from Massa
31	The sayings of Lemuel, king of Massa, which his mother taught him

Genres

The book of Proverbs contains several subgenres that follow the generic Hebrew parallelism pattern and poetry.

5 The name Agur appears on Sabean inscriptions, but it is not found anywhere else in the Bible. Some have identified Agur as Solomon. See William McKane, *Proverbs,* OTL (Louisville: Westminster, 1970), 643 and C. F. Keil and F. Delitzsch, *Commentary on the Old Testament: Proverbs, Ecclesiastes, Song of Solomon,* vol. VI (Grand Rapids: Eerdmans, 1963), 260–72. As with Agur, some suggest that Lemuel is none other than Solomon. But why would Solomon use other names such as Agur and Lemuel after his own name is used throughout? Using a pseudonym does not make much logical sense.

6 Chapter 10:1 seems to start a new section with the heading, "The proverbs of Solomon." Unlike chapter 1:1, the longer title, "son of David, king of Israel" is missing. It is possible that this section was added later, even though it has Solomonic authorship.

7 This section starts with the explanation, "More sayings of the wise." As with 1:1 and 10:1, this section could be a later addition.

8 Hezekiah (741–687 BC) ruled the southern kingdom of Judah and witnessed the destruction of the northern kingdom of Israel.

Proverb (māšāl)

The Hebrew word translated "proverbs" is the plural form of māšāl, which comes from the root that means "to be like." A proverb is a comparison or analogy usually expressed in a pithy sentence that makes one see what the proverb is about. Usually employing the preposition of comparison "like," proverbs paint clear and understandable pictures. Kovacs affirms that a wise person "possesses the faculty to understand each situation and apply the proverb in a skillful and successful manner."[9] Mieder notes the timelessness of the wisdom found in Proverbs when he notes that "proverbs are not passé and definitely not dead…Proverbs, those old gems of generationally tested wisdom, help us in our everyday life and communication to cope with the complexities of the modern human condition."[10]

> *Example:*
> *The purpose in a man's heart is like deep water,*
> *but a man of understanding will draw it out. (Proverbs 20:5)*

Better-than Saying

Another great didactic tool in the hand of the wise is the better-than saying. Like with a proverb (māšāl), the better-than saying employs a comparison but uses the comparative "better than" to show the superiority of the wise person. One of my favorite verses that I memorized as a child (in Romanian) is found in the example below. "For three transgressions of Israel, and for four, I will not revoke the punishment" (Amos 2:6).[11]

> *Example:*
> *A good name is be to chosen rather than great riches,*
> *And favor is better than silver or gold. (Proverbs 22:1)*

---

9 B. W. Kovacs, "Sociological-Structural Constraints upon Wisdom" (PhD diss., Vanderbilt University, 1978), 302.

10 Quoted in Craig G. Bartholomew & Ryan P. O'Dowd, *Old Testament Wisdom Literature: A Theological Introduction* (Downers Grove, IL: InterVarsity Press, 2011), 73.

11 See also Amos 1:3, 6, 9, 11, 13; 2:1, 4.

Numeral Saying

The x, x + 1 formula is not unique to wisdom literature. It appears in the prophets, too, with the same idea, namely, to show the multitude of things. The prophets used it primarily to show the vast number of sins. It appears a few times in the Agur section. Waltke and de Silva noted that the numerical sayings in Proverbs are "rhetorically and thematically unified. Rhetorically, the seven numerical sayings are arranged into two groupings" with each group "introduced by a one-verse saying."[12]

> *Example:*
> *Three things are too wonderful for me;*
> *four I do not understand:*
> *the way of an eagle in the sky,*
> *the way of a serpent on a rock,*
> *the way of a ship on the high seas,*
> *and the way of a man with a virgin. (Proverbs 30:18–19)*[13]

Rhetorical Question

Rhetorical questions have always been part of world literature. Questions that draw obvious answers are meant to teach the reader by inviting them to reflect and answer themselves. Agur is asking these to point to God's creative power and the human limitation.

> *Example:*
> *Who has ascended to heaven and come down?*
> *Who has gathered the wind in his fists?*
> *Who has wrapped up the waters in a garment?*
> *Who has established all the ends of the earth?*
> *What is his name, and what is his son's name?*
> *Surely you know! (Proverbs 30:4)*

Figures of Speech

Poets employ figures of speech rather than propositional statements to communicate truth. The book of Proverbs is no excep-

12 Bruce K. Waltke and Ivan D. V. de Silva, *Proverbs: A Shorter Commentary* (Grand Rapids: Eerdmans, 2021), 418.

13 See also Proverbs 30:21–23, 24–28.

tion. Figures of speech generally paint word pictures that are easier to see and understand.

Simile

Figures of speech employ a transfer of a word from a foreign semantic field in order to evoke an appropriate thought or feeling to the reader. Some figures of speech use comparison, some substitution, some addition or amplification, and some omission or suppression.[14] The simplest figure of speech to recognize is the simile because it uses the words "like" or "as" to compare two things of unlike nature.[15]

> *Example:*
> *Gracious words are like a honeycomb,*
> *sweetness to the soul and health to the body. (Proverbs 16:24)*

Metaphor

The metaphor differs from the simile in that the two things compared have something in common. In Hebrew, the preposition "like" or "as" does not appear, so it is an implicit comparison.

> *Example:*
> *(Like) a gold ring in a pig's snout,*
> *(is) a beautiful woman without discretion. (Proverbs 11:22)*

Allegory

An allegory is an extended metaphor. It is used in chapter 27 to point to wealth's short lifespan.

> *Example:*
> *Know well the condition of your flocks,*
> *and give attention to your herds,*
> *for riches do not last forever;*
> *and does a crown endure to all generations?*
> *(Proverbs 27:23–24)*[16]

---

14 The nineteenth-century work of E. W. Bullinger still stands as a masterpiece on figures of speech in the Bible as it has been reprinted twenty-three times. See E. W. Bullinger, *Figures of Speech Used in the Bible* (Grand Rapids: Baker, 2003).

15 The Hebrew preposition כ can be translated both "like" or "as."

16 The allegory continues through verse 27.

Anthropomorphism

Another figure of speech that employs comparison is one that describes God by giving Him human qualities.

Example:
Do not rejoice when your enemy falls,
and let not your heart be glad when he stumbles,
lest the Lord see it and be displeased,
and turn away his anger from him. (Proverbs 24:17–18)

Personification

Also employing comparison, personification gives human qualities to non-human subjects. In Proverbs, both wisdom and folly are described as women who are inviting people to follow them.

Examples:
Wisdom has built her house;
she has hewn her seven pillars. (Proverbs 9:1)
The woman Folly is loud;
she is seductive and knows nothing. (Proverbs 9:13)

Hyperbole

An exaggeration to make a point is a figure of speech involving amplification.

Example:
Surely I am too stupid to be a man.
I have not the understanding of a man. (Proverbs 30:2)

Key Terms

The vocabulary employed in the book of Proverbs is not unique to wisdom literature, but some of the terms outlined below are used in Job, Proverbs, and Ecclesiastes with much more frequency than anywhere else in the Old Testament.

Wisdom (ḥokmâ)

The word *ḥokmâ* is used to describe a variety of skills. Skilled tailors create priestly vestments (Exodus 28:3), and craftspeople are given wisdom by God to build the tabernacle (Exodus 31:6–7).

Other skills that are associated with God's wisdom involve metal, stone, wood (Exodus 25:31–33), spinning (Exodus 35:25–26), embroidery (Exodus 35:35), the ability to lead people well (Deuteronomy 34:9, 1 Kings 2:6), and sailing (Psalm 107:23–30). Most of the occurrences of the word "refer to the intellectual manifestations of wisdom."[17] In Proverbs, wisdom helps one live in accordance with God's moral universe (Proverbs 10:8). A wise person shows their wisdom in a willingness to learn (Proverbs 1:5–6) and actively avoiding sinful and wicked situations (Proverbs 14:16). Subsequently, the wise person can teach others the ways of God (Proverbs 13:14; 15:2).

Figure 1.1 The word "wisdom" in the Old Testament[18]

Knowledge (dāat)

The word "knowledge" appears for the first time in the Bible in Genesis 2 in reference to the tree of the knowledge of good and evil (2:9, 17). Humans are blessed with knowledge about historical information (1 Kings 5:3), how to hunt (Genesis 25:27), how to make music (1 Samuel 16:16–18), how to read (Isaiah 29:12), how to speak (Jeremiah 1:6), and how to make laws (Esther 1:13). In Proverbs, knowledge appears forty times, and it's used interchangeably with wisdom (*ḥokmâ*) and understanding (*tebû*nâ or *bînâ*). The wise (Proverbs 10:14), the righteous (Proverbs 11:9),

17 Gerald H. Wilson, חכם in *New International Dictionary of Old Testament Theology & Exegesis,* vol. 1 (Grand Rapids: Zondervan, 1997), 133.

18 All word graphics come from "Logos Bible Software Bible Word Study Guide." Logos Bible Software, Computer software. Bellingham, WA: Faithlife, LLC.

and the prudent (Proverbs 13:16) possess knowledge, and those who have knowledge love discipline and instruction (Proverbs 12:1; 23:13). "The fear of the LORD and the knowledge of God are two sides of the same reality (Proverbs 1:29; 9:10); fear of God is reverential awe, finding expression in uprightness and devotion; knowledge of God means a fullness of relationship with God and walking in his ways."[19] Such knowledge of God can only be possible via a relationship with Him and cannot be achieved apart from faith (Hebrews 11:6).

Figure 1.2 The word "knowledge" in the Old Testament

Understanding (tebûnâ or bînâ)

Used mostly in wisdom literature, the concept appears for the first time in Deuteronomy in connection with God's commandments (Deuteronomy 4:6). In many instances, it is used in conjunction with wisdom or insight (1 Chronicles 22:12; Proverbs 2:2, 6; 3:13, 19; 5:1; 8:1; 23:23). Isaiah uses the term to describe the Spirit of God (Isaiah 11:2) and the faithful remnant (Isaiah 29:24; 33:19). The wicked have no understanding (Isaiah 27:11) or discernment (Isaiah 29:14). Steinmann suggests that the term is "most often used to describe the overall conceptual framework of one's reason and knowledge (Proverbs 23:4; 30:2).[20] The book of Proverbs affirms that understanding is attainable (Proverbs 4:5), but it must be pursued (Proverbs 4:7) and is only available to those who fear the LORD (Proverbs 2:5).

---

19 Terrence E. Fretheim, "דעת" in *NIDOTTE*, vol. 2 (Grand Rapids: Zondervan, 1997), 411.

20 Andrew E. Steinmann, *Proverbs* (St. Louis: Concordia, 2009), 26.

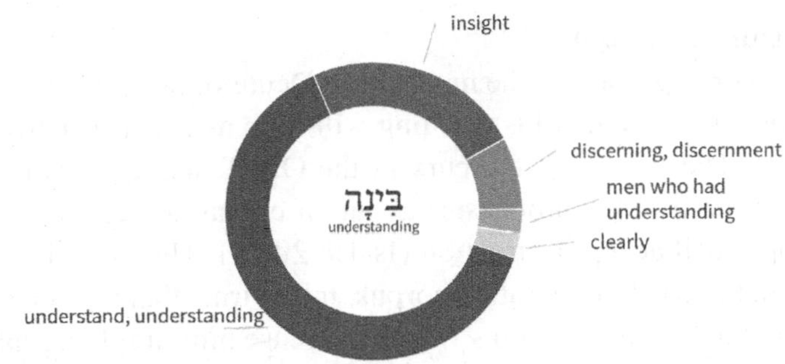

Figure 1.3 The word "understanding" in the Old Testament

Advice/Counsel (ēṣâ)

The word occurs for the first time in Deuteronomy to refer to a nation lacking wisdom (Deuteronomy 32:28). In the historical books, it refers to people giving and receiving advice (Judges 20:7; 2 Samuel 15:31; 1 Kings 12:8; 2 Chronicles 10:8). In the book of Job, God is the One who possesses wise counsel (Job 12:13), while the counsel of the wicked needs to be rejected (Job 21:16; 22:18) because it ultimately leads to their downfall and destruction (Job 18:7). The psalmist affirms that the wise do not follow the counsel of the ungodly (Psalm 1:1), but the counsel of the LORD stands forever (Psalm 33:11). In the book of Proverbs, the noun "advice" occurs ten times and the substantival participle translated as "advisor" appears four times (Proverbs 11:14; 12:20; 15:22; 24:6).

Figure 1.4 The word "counsel/advice" in the Old Testament

Instruction (léqaḥ)

The word appears for the first time in Deuteronomy, where Moses sings his desire that his teaching will drop as rain (Deuteronomy 32:2). The last time it occurs in the Old Testament is in Isaiah when the prophet prophesies about an eschatological time when people will accept instruction (Isaiah 29:24). The other instances are in the wisdom literature corpus. Job affirms that his doctrine is pure, but Zohar uses Job's words to accuse him, implying that his doctrine is not pure and is why he suffers (Job 11:4). In the book of Proverbs, the word is used in connection with the wise who will increase learning (Proverbs 1:5; 9:9) and the father imparting good precepts to the son (Proverbs 4:2). As a result, the wise will be prudent and persuasive in speech (Proverbs 16:23). The word is used negatively one time in the description of the immoral woman who tries to seduce the young man to sin with her persuasive speech (Proverbs 7:21).

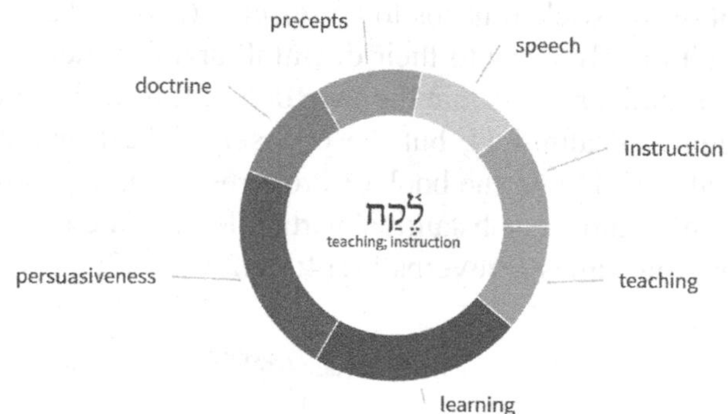

Figure 1.5 The word "instruction" in the Old Testament

Discipline (mûsar)

This word occurs thirty times in the Old Testament, once in the Pentateuch, thirteen times in the prophets, and the rest in the wisdom books. It has a wide semantic range, but in most cases, it can be translated "instruction" or "discipline." In Deuteronomy, it appears in construct relationship with Yahweh. Moses exhorts the

Israelites who will enter the Promised Land to obey Yahweh by considering the "discipline of the LORD" (Deuteronomy 11:2). In the prophets, the word is used primarily to point back to Israel's rejection of God's instruction or discipline (Isaiah 26:16; Jeremiah 2:30; 5:3; 7:28; 17:23; 32:33; 35:13). In the book of Proverbs, the word is best translated either "instruction" or "correction." Instruction and wisdom are used interchangeably several times (Proverbs 1:2, 3; 15:33; 19:20; 23:23). The wise who fear the LORD are contrasted with the fools who despise both wisdom and instruction (Proverbs 1:7). The ones who hate discipline will pay the penalty dearly for it either by going astray, by experiencing poverty, or by paying the ultimate price (Proverbs 5:12, 23; 10:17; 13:18). Lady Wisdom invites all to "take my instruction instead of silver" (Proverbs 8:10, 33) and the wise accept discipline and instruction (Proverbs 13:1). Wise parents discipline their children (Proverbs 13:24; 22:15; 23:13), and wise children receive their parents' instruction (Proverbs 13:1).

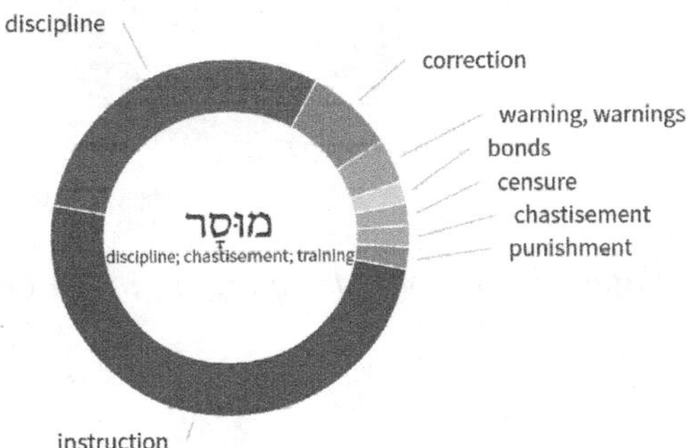

Figure 1.6 The word "discipline" in the Old Testament

Upright (yōšer)

The adjective "upright" or "righteous" is a derivative of the verb that means to be straight, level, or right. The verb is used as an expression in conjunction with "in the eyes of" (Numbers 23:27; Jeremiah 18:4). In the book of Proverbs, the word appears as a plural adjective and is mostly translated "upright" or "righteous."

In most cases, it is used to contrast those who reject God's wise ways. The upright are in God's confidence, while the crooked is an abomination to the LORD (Proverbs 3:32). The upright walk in integrity, while the unfaithful are destroyed by their own treacherous ways (Proverbs 11:3). Furthermore, the upright are contrasted with the wicked (Proverbs 11:11; 12:6; 14:11; 15:8; 21:18), the fool (Proverbs 14:9), and the sluggard (Proverbs 15:19). The upright benefit from divine blessings, such as inhabiting the land (Proverbs 2:21), divine guidance (Proverbs 11:3), deliverance (Proverbs 11:6), domestic flourishing (Proverbs 14:11), prayer acceptance (Proverbs 15:8), and a good inheritance (Proverbs 28:10).

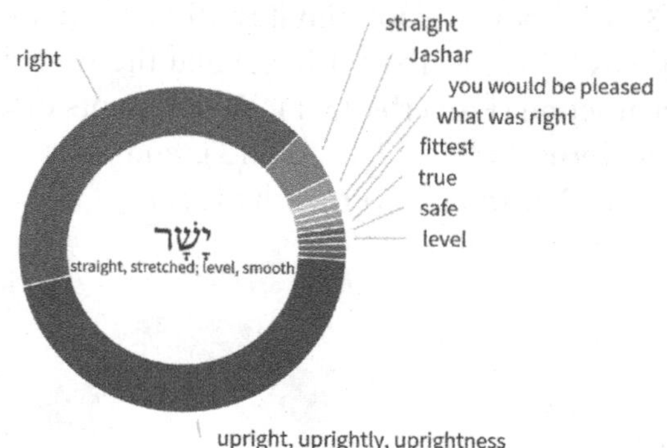

Figure 1.7 The word "upright" in the Old Testament

CHAPTER 2

The Fear of The Lord

A Theological Perspective

The Wise Have the Fear of the LORD

Dr. Tiberius Rata

Behold, the fear of the LORD, that is wisdom,
and to turn away from evil is understanding.
—Job 28:28

The Fear of the LORD in the Old Testament

The fear of the LORD is not a concept that begins and ends with the book of Proverbs. In the Law, Moses commanded the Israelites, "You shall fear the LORD your God. You shall serve him and hold fast to him, and by his name you shall swear" (Deuteronomy 10:20). From the beginning, the fear of the LORD had a very practical side to it.

Those who feared the LORD served Him. Those who feared the LORD stayed close to Him. Those who feared the LORD trusted Him and trusted in Him. Crenshaw notes that the "fear of the LORD consists of the ancient covenantal obligations, and no genuine conflict exists between wisdom and sacred history."[21] Job, a man whose name is synonymous with suffering, is introduced as a man who feared God and turned away from evil (Job 1:1). Later in the book, the fear of the LORD is associated both with wisdom and separation from evil. "Behold, the fear of the LORD, that is wisdom,

21 James L. Crenshaw, *Old Testament Wisdom: An Introduction* (Louisville, KY: Westminster John Knox, 1998), 79.

and to turn away from evil is understanding" (Job 28:28). In the book of Psalms, the fear of the LORD continues to be associated with wisdom (Psalm 111:10) and the one who fears the LORD is considered blessed (Psalm 128:1). Because the fear of the LORD is pure (Psalm 19:9), the psalmist commands his hearers to "Fear the LORD, you his saints, for those who fear him lack nothing" (Psalm 34:9). At the end of Ecclesiastes, Solomon exhorts us to "fear God and keep His commandments" (Ecclesiastes 12:13).

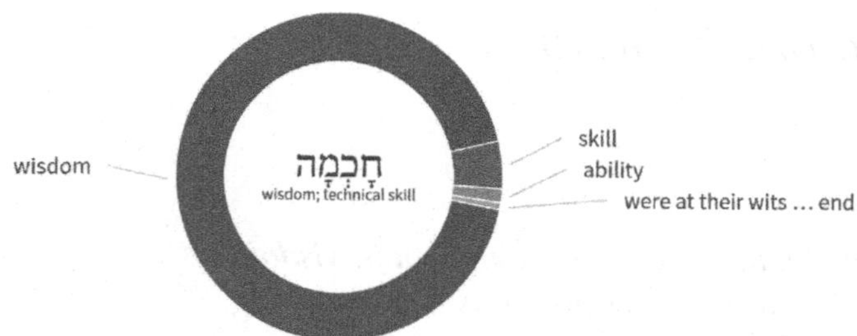

Figure 2.1 The semantic range of the word "wisdom"[22]

The Fear of the LORD in the New Testament

The first-century church grew because of believers who were walking "in the fear of the LORD" (Acts 9:31), and the fear of the LORD led believers to share the gospel (2 Corinthians 5:11). Indeed, those who fear the LORD are characterized by generosity and piety (Acts 10:2). Even Cornelius, a Roman centurion, is described as a God-fearer and as a result is well-spoken of by the whole Jewish nation (Acts 10:22). Fearing God is a prerequisite to being accepted by Him (Acts 10:35). Paul uses the phrase to command attention when speaking to those in the synagogue of Antioch of Pisidia (Acts 13:14). In the middle of his speech, he uses the concept of fearing God interchangeably with "sons of the family of Abraham" since he knows how to exegete his audience

22 The word appears 149 times in the Old Testament with 139 times being translated "wisdom." Nine times it refers to skill or ability (Exodus 28:3; 31:3, 6; 35:26, 31; 36:1, 2; 1 Chronicles 28:21), and one time it is translated "at their wits' end," referring to people in distress who ultimately cry out to the LORD (Psalm 107:27–28).

well (Acts 13:26). "Fear God and give him glory" is the command given to earth-dwellers at the end of history (Revelation 14:7). Here we have a parallel to Daniel 4 where Nebuchadnezzar is instructed by an angel to serve and give glory to the Most High (Daniel 4:34 LXX). In each context, we see that the fear of the LORD is not an abstract concept but a very practical one that is associated with one's way of life.

The Fear of the LORD in the Book of Proverbs

Solomon establishes that to have the fear of the LORD is foundational for a life of wisdom. The seventh verse of the first chapter declares that "The fear of the LORD is the beginning of knowledge; fools despise wisdom and instruction" (Proverbs 1:7). The expression "the fear of the LORD" appears fourteen times in the book of Proverbs and only seven times in the rest of the Old Testament. Those who possess knowledge then, absent the fear of the LORD, are fools no matter how intelligent or business-savvy they might be. There is no middle ground on the way to wisdom. Either one is on the path of wisdom or the path of foolishness.

"The wisdom of Proverbs" is introduced as "godly wisdom flowing from a positive relationship with Yahweh."[23] The tenth verse of the ninth chapter emphasizes this point. Solomon writes, "The fear of the LORD is the beginning of wisdom, and the knowledge of the Holy One is insight" (Proverbs 9:10). Garrett is right in that "believers must teach their children that in their pursuit of wisdom they will be surrounded by others going the opposite direction who will be encouraging them to do likewise. In this fashion, the polarity of the entire book of Proverbs—the way of the wise and the way of the fool—is introduced. The reader faces the alternatives and is challenged to attain wisdom through the fear of God."[24]

But how can fear be something good? We dread fear, we avoid fear, we try to prevent fear. That is because we fear people, we

---

23 Steinmann, *Proverbs,* 55.

24 Duane A. Garrett, *Proverbs, Ecclesiastes, Song of Songs*, vol. 14, The New American Commentary (Nashville: Broadman & Holman Publishers, 1993), 68.

fear circumstances, and sometimes we even fear things that have not yet happened. The fear of the LORD is different. The fear of the LORD "captures both aspects of shrinking back in fear and of drawing close in awe. It is not a trembling dread that paralyzes action, but neither is it a polite reverence."[25] Easton asserts, "It is a fear conjoined with love and hope, and is therefore not a slavish dread, but rather filial reverence."[26]

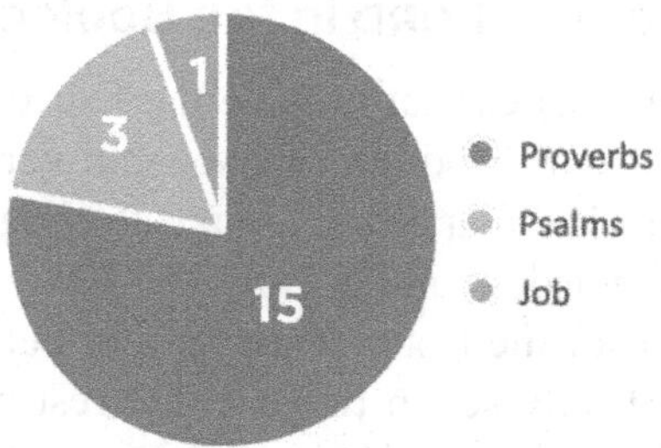

Figure 2.2 The occurrences of "Fear of the LORD" in poetic literature[27]

The Fear of the LORD Is Attainable

For believers, having the fear of the LORD is not beyond our grasp. "My son, if you receive my words and treasure up my commandments with you…then you will understand the fear of the LORD and find the knowledge of God" (Proverbs 2:1–5). Knowledge of God cannot be separated from God's Law. Indeed, the word "commandment" is associated with God's Law by Moses in the first five books of the Bible.[28] Longman affirms that "the fear of the LORD inevitably leads to obedience. The ones who fear God

25 Allen P. Ross, *Proverbs,* Expositor's Bible Commentary, vol. 5 (Grand Rapids: Zondervan, 1991), 907.

26 M. G. Easton, *Illustrated Bible Dictionary and Treasury of Biblical History, Biography, Geography, Doctrine, and Literature* (New York: Harper & Brothers, 1893), 254.

27 Job 28:8; Psalms 19:10; 34:12; 111:10; Proverbs 1:7, 29; 2:5; 8:13; 9:10; 14:26, 27; 15:16, 33; 16:6; 19:23; 22:4; 23:17; 31:30.

28 Genesis 26:5; Exodus 16:28; 24:12; Leviticus 27:34; Numbers 36:13, and Deuteronomy 30:10.

will follow the advice that God imparts through the sages."[29] On the other hand, by rejecting the fear of the LORD, fools will suffer the consequences of their choices. "Because they hated knowledge and did not choose the fear of the LORD, would have none of my counsel and despised all my reproof, therefore they shall eat the fruit of their way, and have their fill of their own devices" (Proverbs 1:29–31). Sometimes, "the worst judgment God may ever pronounce this side of eternity is to allow us to have the full impact of the ways we choose (Romans 1:24–28). The guarantee of God is that we will reap what we sow (Galatians 6:7)."[30] Garrett is right in that "wisdom is not abstract, or secular, or academic but personal and theological. To reject wisdom is to reject God."[31]

The Fear of the LORD Is Valuable

The fear of the LORD will help believers know God better and love Him more, while at the same time, it will lead us to hate evil. "The fear of the LORD is hatred of evil. Pride and arrogance and the way of evil and perverted speech I hate" (Proverbs 8:13). A wise person cannot be proud or arrogant, but a fool is both. A wise person does not use perverted speech, but a fool uses perverted speech while walking on the way of evil. Kidner notes that "what is repugnant to godliness is repugnant to wisdom: there is no conflict of interests."[32]

Another benefit of the fear of the LORD is that it prolongs life. "The fear of the LORD prolongs life, but the years of the wicked will be short" (Proverbs 10:27). The apostle John affirms that life can indeed be cut short due to unwise living (1 John 5:16–17). The

---

29 Tremper Longman III, *The Fear of the LORD is Wisdom: A Theological Introduction to Wisdom in Israel* (Grand Rapids: Baker, 2017).

30 John Kitchen, *Proverbs: A Mentor Commentary* (Ross-Shire, Scotland: Christian Focus, 2006), 53.

31 Garrett, *Proverbs, Ecclesiastes, Song of Songs,* 72.

32 Derek Kidner, *Proverbs: An Introduction and Commentary*, Tyndale Old Testament Commentaries, vol. 17 (Nottingham, England: Downers Grove, IL: InterVarsity Press, 2008), 73.

fear of the LORD is one's source of life and gives one confidence. Its value has trickle-down benefits to those who follow, not only by giving life but also by avoiding death. "In the fear of the LORD one has strong confidence, and his children will have a refuge. The fear of the LORD is a fountain of life, that one may turn away from the snares of death" (Proverbs 14:26–27). As Kidner observes, "Godliness protects the soul by its solidity (26) and its vitality (27). Both aspects are necessary, since evil not only attacks but attracts us; therefore the man of God must know (and show his family, 26b) something both stronger and better."[33]

The fear of the LORD helps one see life in the right perspective. In the world's eyes, having riches might be considered beneficial, but according to Scripture, "Better is a little with the fear of the LORD than great treasure and trouble with it" (Proverbs 15:16). Indeed, contentment is a treasure that is much more valuable than a treasure that can be eaten by rust. The apostle Paul instructs young Timothy that "godliness with contentment is great gain" (1 Timothy 6:6). From God's perspective, "the greatest possessions are a pious life, a loving home, and personal integrity."[34] Steinmann observes that "prosperity is not an unmixed blessing if it is accompanied by situations that can embitter one's existence. It is better to have less material wealth and dine on a relationship with Yahweh by grace, so that one has the love of God, family, and friends."[35]

Reeves argues that "the fear of God is not a state of mind you can guarantee with five easy steps."[36] He goes on to argue that "the fear of the LORD is the reason Christianity is the most song-filled of all religions...Christians instinctively want to sing to express the affection behind their words of praise."[37]

---

33 Kidner, *Proverbs,* 104.

34 Garrett, *Proverbs, Ecclesiastes, Song of Songs*, 154.

35 Steinmann, *Proverbs,* 348.

36 Michael Reeves, *What Does It Mean to Fear the LORD?* (Wheaton: Crossway, 2021).

37 Reeves, *What Does It Mean to Fear the LORD?*

The Fear of the LORD Leads to True Heroism

At the end of the book of Proverbs, King Lemuel affirms that the woman who fears the LORD is to be praised. "Charm is deceitful, and beauty is vain, but a woman who fears the LORD is to be praised" (Proverbs 31:30). Indeed, some of the terms used to describe this God-fearing woman are military terms. "The heart of her husband trusts in her, and he lacks no plunder" (Proverbs 31:11). Plunder is something one gets after the war. "She rises while it is yet night and provides food for her household" (Proverbs 31:15). The word translated "food" is literally "prey," another military term. "She dresses herself with strength," another term used for mighty warriors (Proverbs 31:17). Lastly, the last verb employed in verse 29 is a verb that is used in other places to signify going into battle. "Many women have done excellently, but you surpass them all" (Proverbs 31:29), portraying the woman as a victorious hero. The conclusion is this: true heroism is domestic, and the woman who fears the LORD is a true hero.

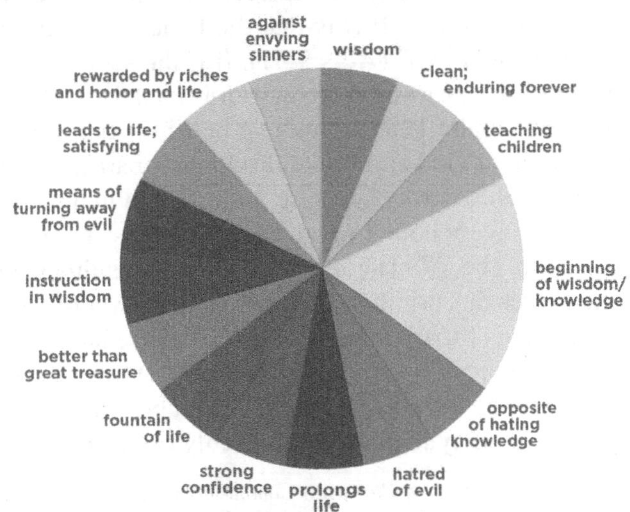

Figure 2.3 The semantic range of "The Fear of the LORD" in poetic literature

A Lesson from Church History

The second-century church father Tertullian commented on Proverbs 9:10, "The fear of the LORD is the beginning of wisdom."

> Discipline is an index to doctrine. [The heretics] say that God is not to be feared. So everything is free to them and unrestrained. But where is God not feared, except where he is not present? Where God is not present, there is no truth either; and where there is no truth, discipline like theirs is natural. But where God is present, there is the fear of God, there are decent seriousness, vigilant care and anxious solitude, well-tested selection, well-weighed communion and deserved promotion, religious obedience, devoted service, modest appearance, a united church, and all things godly.[38]

A Christological Reading

The believer saved by Christ and indwelled by the Holy Spirit walks in the fear of the LORD. Describing the growth of the first-century church, Luke affirms that the believers "were walking in the fear of the LORD" (Acts 9:31). It is the same fear of the LORD that made Job turn away from evil (Job 1:1), that blesses Old Testament saints (Psalm 128:1), and that helps the believer to expand the kingdom of God and make disciples. Apart from Christ, we cannot do it. That is why we sing with the old hymn, "I need Thee every hour, every hour I need Thee; Oh, bless me now, my Savior, I come to Thee."[39] The apostle Paul affirms this when he reminds the church at Corinth that Christ is the power of God and the wisdom of God (1 Corinthians 1:24). And since the fear of the LORD is the beginning of wisdom (Proverbs 9:10), we need Christ as Savior in order to have the wisdom from above that we need every day as we journey toward our heavenly Canaan.

---

38 Thomas C. Oden, ed. *Ancient Christian Commentary on Scripture: Proverbs, Ecclesiastes, Song of Solomon,* vol. IX (Downers Grove, IL: InterVarsity Press, 2005), 76.

39 "I Need Thee Every Hour," lyrics written by Annie S. Hawks and Robert Lowry, 1872.

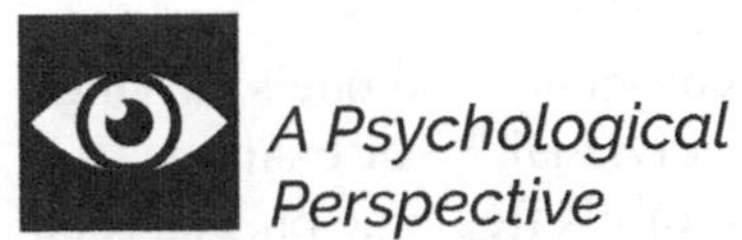

Reflections on the Fear of the LORD

Dr. Kevin Roberts

The remarkable thing about God is that when you fear God you fear nothing else.
—Oswald Chambers

The fear of the LORD is the beginning of all wisdom. Why is fear of an omnipotent and omniscient God the starting point for wisdom? Solomon, in his vast wisdom, contrasts the righteous path of the wise and the crooked path of the fool. As we grow and change throughout life, Solomon encourages us to consider our choices, paths, and what we are striving to obtain. This chapter examines how our strivings drive us toward goal-oriented behavior. It also examines how our choices are influenced by things like power, control, and fear. We see how the fear of the LORD can serve as a powerful mechanism to realign our motives, choices, and, ultimately, the path of our lives.

Striving toward Goals

What do we know about human striving and desire for growth? Adlerian Psychology, also known as Individual Psychology, is an approach to counseling based on the work of Alfred Adler. Adler maintained that you can understand much about a person based on their striving behavior. He believed that all human behavior is goal-oriented, although not always conscious, and one's strivings and effort give us insight into the individual.[40] For example, if I have an adolescent who spends most of his free time on YouTube watching baseball training videos, then we can safely assume that his effort points toward a goal of being better at baseball.

Adler further asserted that this human striving could point in one of two directions.[41] He felt the individual could strive toward perfection (for believers, that would be Christ) and the betterment of others. In contrast, Manaster and Corsini described a second type of striving as one for superiority. "Striving for superiority means to move in a vertical direction, toward personal superiority in relation to others for personal gain within one's own biased apperception not coherent with the interests of others and the common sense of social living."[42] Adler, therefore, believed that there is both a productive striving and a useless, unproductive striving. But the question remains, which type of striving are we pursuing? Are we moving toward perfection and being like Christ, or toward personal superiority and control? Proverbs talks about sinful ways as being crooked paths that people choose to take, but why do we choose these paths? Is it just for the purpose of hedonistic pleasure? Or does it go far deeper than that?

From the beginning of time, Satan has used a bait-and-switch strategy that tempts our sinful nature. Satan promises that there will be no immediate consequences, only immediate gratification. In the garden of Eden, Satan promised Eve, "You will not surely die. For God knows that when you eat of it your eyes will be opened, and you will be like God, knowing good and evil" (Genesis 3:4, 5). This promise insinuates that you can have immediate gratification without any consequences, and you can simultaneously get your human needs met on your own (life under your control). Satan is insinuating that you do not need God, but instead, you can take control and make life work apart from God.

---

40 Guy J. Manaster and Raymond J. Corsini, *Individual Psychology: Theory and Practice* (F. E. Peacock, 1982).

41 Manaster and Corsini, *Individual Psychology*.

42 Manaster and Corsini, *Individual Psychology*, 75.

It is the false promise of having your cake and eating it, too. Sadly, we have been falling for this same bait-and-switch trick since the beginning of time.

Many of Satan's promises offer immediate gratification, no consequences, and the promise to get our needs for love, meaning, and purpose answered apart from God. Solomon knew this all too well. In the second chapter of Ecclesiastes, we see all the ways Solomon sought to find pleasure and satisfaction. Yet, in the end, none of them satisfied the God-shaped void in his soul. Instead, Solomon found that all his strivings and pursuits were vanity, and his desire to control and get satisfaction from these strivings was meaningless in the end. We love the idea that we can meet all our needs for love, meaning, and purpose apart from God. But in reality, it is like trying to catch the wind. Oftentimes, when we face a crossroads in our lives, we will face Satan's bait-and-switch strategy. We must decide if we will choose the wide but crooked path, seeking personal control apart from God, or if we will follow the narrow path that leads toward God.

The Fear of the Lord and Humility

As each of us approaches forks in the road, we have the opportunity to choose our path. We must be willing to listen to the wisdom of God's teaching. The fear of the Lord, demonstrated by our humility, helps guide us toward wisdom. As illustrated in Proverbs 2, the fear of the Lord is within our grasp. "My son, if you receive my words and treasure up my commandments with you…then you will understand the fear of the Lord and find the knowledge of God" (Proverbs 2:1–5).

To hear God's Word, we must recognize our desperate dependence on Him, and this requires a measure of humility. A lack of humility is a hallmark trait of those who follow the crooked and wide path. Proverbs 22:4 states it this way, "The reward for humility and fear of the Lord is riches and honor and life," and we are warned in Proverbs 18:12, "Before destruction a man's heart is haughty, but humility comes before honor." These verses illustrate that throughout our lives, we will reach many decision points. We must choose to walk humbly before our God seeking His direction because in this way, we deepen our dependence on Him.

Jesus teaches, in Matthew 7:13–14, "Enter by the narrow gate. For the gate is wide and the way is easy that leads to destruction, and those who enter it are many. For the gate is narrow and the way is hard that leads to life, and those who find it are few." Sadly, many times we choose to pursue our own haughty ways and attempt to get our needs and desires met apart from God. We seek immediate gratification through the wide gate, failing to realize that it only leads to pain and destruction.

Following the Crooked Path

In psychology, we understand that human beings will often seek a perceived sense of control over their lives. We often do this by pursuing options that give us more choices, or we seek power to gain control. Inesi and Botti looked at workplace behavior in their research and found that power and choice are both forms of personal control.[43] They discovered that power, choice, and personal control have a dynamic relationship.[44] In other words, when a person has little choice in the workplace, they will often seek power. In contrast, if a person has little power over their workplace environment, they will often seek to be given more choices. If employees have neither power nor control, then they are often disgruntled.[45]

We seek control and often choose many of life's crooked paths because we are seeking to make life work apart from God. We are often seeking control because of our natural inclination toward selfishness and a sinful, stubborn nature. This act of independence to gain power from the Creator of the universe illustrates our deep desire to make life work apart from God. In fact, we are hoping to find a shortcut to meaning and satisfaction without experiencing the consequences of our crooked paths. Thus, we fall prey to

43 M. Ena Inesi et al., "Power and Choice," *Psychological Science* 22, no. 8 (2011): 1042–48.

44 Inesi et al., "Power and Choice."

45 Inesi et al., "Power and Choice."

Satan's age-old bait-and-switch tactic because we lust for both power and control.

This is especially true of people who score high levels of internal control. Those individuals who have a high level of control believe they have a great deal of control over the outcomes of their lives and therefore seek to pursue their own paths and expect to be successful. When we experience life's undulations, pain, and suffering, it is difficult to trust in the LORD. Instead, we tend to pursue our own desire for relief from these feelings. We often seek to gain power and control to avoid these feelings of vulnerability.

To remain trusting in God and walking in His ways while fearing the LORD is not an easy path. Proverbs states it well, "There is a way that seems right to man, but its end is the way to death" (Proverbs 14:12). In His infinite wisdom, God gives us the ability to choose the path of our lives, and then He uses our pain, His Word, and the Holy Spirit to try and draw us back to Him. But if God can use our personal pain, the Bible, and the Holy Spirit, then why would He use fear to motivate us?

Figure 2.4 Following the crooked path

Looking through the Lens of Fear

A few years ago, my eyesight began to change, and I realized that I was going to need glasses for the first time in my life. I tried to ignore the problem by rearranging where my screens were located on my desk, and when that didn't work, I broke down and got reader glasses. The first time I used the readers in front of my screen, I remember being shocked by the clarity! I realized how foolish it was to try and ignore this problem. In this instance, it was my pride that blinded me to my own limitations, and only through improved clarity did I realize how bad off I had let my eyes get. Often, *fear* provides clarity to our lives. Whether it is fear of a recent diagnosis or of being caught by your parents, fear can serve as a powerful motivator to clarify our vision about what is most important in life. In moments of fear, we biologically respond and prepare our bodies for action in an attempt to manage or control the stressor we are facing.

The human eye is truly an amazing creation by God. It is through our eyes that we see, gain perspective, and learn. Our eyes guide and protect us from the dangers that lie ahead. Through this function, we seek a unique relationship with the fear of the LORD. When we encounter fear, our sympathetic nervous system is forced to kick into high gear and mobilizes our resources, including our eyesight. In fearful moments, our eyes widen to improve our scanning ability, all while improving our focus on the most pertinent danger in front of us.[46] It is in these moments of fear that we narrow our focus to the most important dangers and then, with improved scanning, see any other potential pitfalls that might lie ahead.[47] In this same way, the fear of the LORD helps us improve our scanning of the paths we have chosen and all of the potential pitfalls in those paths. The fear of the LORD often helps us clarify

---

46 Justin Storbeck, Jessica Dayboch, and Jordan Wylie, "Fear and Happiness, but Not Sadness, Motivate Attentional Flexibility: A Case for Emotion Influencing the Ability to Split Foci of Attention," *Emotion* 19, no. 4 (2019): 655–64.

47 Storbeck, Dayboch, Wylie, "Fear and Happiness, but Not Sadness, Motivate Attentional Flexibility."

our vision of what really matters in our lives if we are humble enough to receive it. For instance, "Better is a little with the fear of the Lord than great treasure and trouble with it" (Proverbs 15:16), and it is in turning from these paths that one can find the fountain of life (Proverbs 14:26–27).

The fear of the Lord is a powerful reminder of who God is. We are both to fear Him and be humble in front of the God of the universe. It is in humility and fear of the Lord that we can begin to receive understanding, insight, and wisdom. The Lord has given us the freedom and responsibility to make our choices, but in making these choices, we must also own up to the consequences of our decisions. We see Solomon illustrate this point at the end of Ecclesiastes 12:13–14, "The end of the matter; all has been heard. Fear God and keep his commandments, for this is the whole duty of man. For God will bring every deed into judgment, with every secret thing, whether good or evil."

In the life of Christ, we saw Jesus tempted in the wilderness to get His needs met, and eventually, He was offered control over all the earth (Matthew 4:1–11). But in Christ, we see the trust and faithfulness in God's purposes that we are called to demonstrate in our own lives. We further see the ultimate sacrifice of Christ dying on the cross. However, in choosing the paths of our lives, we are asked to die to self, control, and our own agenda, and to put our trust in Him instead.

Application Exercises and Questions for the Fear of the Lord

1. Do you have any areas of your life that you try to keep from God? Solomon was prone to wander down the crooked paths himself at times, despite all his wisdom. Does the fear of the Lord compel you to choose a different path?
2. Does the fear of the Lord lead you toward humility, or do you become stiff-necked, as indicated in Proverbs? If so, why?
3. Have you recently looked at your personal behaviors and relationships and asked if these glorify God? If they don't, what are you doing to rectify this situation?

The Fear of the Lord at Church

Pastor Knute Larson

We in the church have not always displayed the fear of the Lord and His wisdom. If we were to go around the circle in any group of people and ask what they don't like about the church, we would hear too many stories of hurt and mistakes and sheer selfishness—the opposite of the fear of the Lord. This would be true in a church group or at the local bar or restaurant.

Church services vary greatly, and though we will not impose personal tastes on this assessment, a church with the fear of the Lord would surely demonstrate a sense of reverence for God's position and power in a church service. Members would be compelled to follow through with what they heard when the Bible was taught or preached at a church meeting.

Fearing the Lord at church looks like a group of people and leaders who count on God to give them wisdom to make decisions. They seek His wisdom rather than answers to all their questions. Such a group of people would be a praying church and asking for wisdom in their daily prayers, at their board meetings, and at family mealtimes. The same humble seeking of His wisdom would be clear in the pastoral prayers during the morning worship services. The fear of the Lord in the church starts with the pastor, the church leaders, and the board, who honestly want to please Him first and not each other. They care about doing His will, as revealed in Scripture. They never catch themselves saying, "I know the Bible says that, but…"

People who fear the LORD do not always worry about if they like the song they're singing at church but care more about setting their hearts to worship God and celebrate Him together. These people care about keeping things clean with each other because they know God speaks pretty clearly about divisions and factions in the church. They fear Him for that. Those who fear God do not just *go* to church. They are the Church, the body of Jesus Christ. They see worship times as rather serious, directed toward an audience of One. They build community in their groups, seeking to encourage each other rather than tear them apart. They fear and love their LORD enough to do what they can as a team to represent Christ and His grace, one on one with friends and through local and global mission work.

Why the Fear of the LORD Is So Important

The church is a body of people who probably heard that old commercial that tells you to fetch its product by saying, "You only go around once." We carry a book that agrees with this idea and even says that life goes very quickly. But our conclusion is to confess that we need to fear the Lord and worship Him, to glorify Him now and forever. If that is not the goal of the church, we are wasting our time. We say we know and follow the Son of God. We teach that He lived a perfect life of obedience to His Father, whose will He did with love and reverence. We must follow Him!

The church of all groups is to be known for its careful and loving ways, motivated by wisdom, pointing toward goodness, based on reverence for the Lord. We fear Him and honor His word. Without this distinction, we are just a local club of people taking up space in the schedules of singles and families, claiming some property in the town. Nice, but not all that significant. But when we are people who seek wisdom and fear God and keep His commands, our love for each other and for the world around us is evident in our schedule and our mission, as well as our mood. People know us by our love—for God, for each other, and for the people who are not yet part of us. All of that is what makes the Church unique in its mission and reason for existence.

Why the Fear of the Lord Doesn't Always Show Up

Sometimes people in the church fear the old guard at church or the new people who are coming more than they fear the Lord. All too easily, we fear what people might think more than what God tells us what He thinks in His Word. There are people who would rather keep digging the same old traditions into the ground instead of trying to think of new ways to fear God by obeying His mission to reach the lost or heal old wounds. Selfishness and traditions can keep us from honest obedience to our Lord Christ and the Scriptures, which both call for such care for others and a mission to the unbelievers. Somehow, the weekend worship might include moments of reverence and reminders rather than be all about our joy or experience. Teaching and songs may refer to our experiences, but surely some of both will feature strong worship and reverence before God. As a pastor, I recall a man who knew prophecy details like few others. He had charts and could teach eloquently. But his relationships with people were tarnished. I think he shows that we can easily embrace the content of the Bible but miss fearing the Lord who gave it to us.

The pastor who shepherds in the manner of our loving and candid Good Shepherd will carefully call out traditions that go nowhere and habits that breed death. Part of the anatomy of any church that has dwindled and died is a fear of breaking traditions that did not change lives or reach unbelievers. An alive church is a church that fears the Lord to the point of obedience to His Great Command to love and His Great Commission toward the world.

What We Can Do Personally to Fear the Lord

Pray for wisdom and a proper fear of the Lord that pushes us to love each other and care about the world outside. Never say what I have heard multiple times while pastoring: "I know the Bible says that, but..." Pray for our church leaders and encourage the pastors and boards of oversight to keep us on mission and in love with our

Savior—a love which is not so buddy-buddy that our songs and conversations sound like we are dancing with Him, but that we are honoring Him as our King and Lord of the daily and the church services and the board agendas and the small-group conversations. Do your part. Be faithful to the mission of the local church as first given in Scripture, all the while stepping carefully and sometimes kindly, cautioning those who seem like they believe the church is about them. Commend people when they show reverence for the Lord and His purposes for the church. Welcome the new and help them catch the flavor of fear of the Lord with love and joy. We can easily consider this insignificant, but the witness of a public worship service to a guest is related to the obvious sincerity and involvement of worshipers.

A Personal Prayer for the Fear of the Lord

Our suggested prayers will follow the format of P-R-A-Y: Praise, Repent (or confess), Ask, Yield.

Praise: Praise our God for the whole idea of the Church, the body of Christ. Praise Him for giving us the indwelling Holy Spirit.

Repent: For ways you have not acted like His body, for acting as Jesus Christ would.

Ask: For help to live out His commands, to honor Him with your thoughts and actions, and to walk in the manner of Jesus Christ, who defined Himself as kind and see. For help to obey.

Yield: Submit to His ways and authority and be a faithful servant at the church, showing you fear and respect our Lord.

CHAPTER 3

Faithfulness

A Theological Perspective

The Wise Are Faithful

Dr. Tiberius Rata

We are called upon not to be successful, but to be faithful.[48]
—Mother Teresa

In wisdom literature, being faithful points to one who is consistently obedient to the LORD and one whose reliability is proven by words and actions.

Faithfulness in the Old Testament

The Hebrew word ʿĕmet is generally translated as "faithful," "faithfulness," "trustworthy," or "truth."[49] It comes from the root ʻmn which has five forms that are of theological significance.[50]

48 Harold J. Sala, *Heroes: People Who Made a Difference in Our World* (Uhrichsville, OH: Promise Press, 1998), 36. Mother Teresa's last words were, "Jesus, I love You. Jesus, I love You."

49 The concept of "truth" will be covered separately in a subsequent chapter. This chapter deals particularly with the idea of "faithful" and "trustworthy."

50 R. W. L. Moberly, אמן in *NIDOTTE* vol. 1, 428. 'āmēn is a word of response to what is said so it's primarily used in a liturgical sense (Psalm 41:13 [14]; 72:19; 89:52 [53]; 106:48). The second use of 'āmēn is used as a marker of conclusion, we know it in present day use as "Amen." The most common use is ʿĕmeṯ, which is often used of speaking the truth (1 Kings 10:6; 2 Chronicles 9:5). Another derivative is ʿĕmûnâ, which is also associated with Yahweh's character (Psalm 33:4; 92:2[3]: 143;1) and is often linked with the language of steadfast love and righteousness (Deuteronomy 32:4; Lamentations 3:21–23).

The most important one is ʿĕmet, which is frequently used to describe Yahweh's character. Faithfulness is a primary characteristic of God Himself, and we see many examples of this throughout the Old Testament. Jacob recognizes that Yahweh treated him with faithfulness (Genesis 32:10). When He appears to Moses, God describes Himself as "a God merciful and gracious, slow to anger, and abounding in steadfast love and faithfulness" (Exodus 34:6). When Moses speaks of God to the new generation that will enter the Promised Land, he reminds them that God is "the faithful God who keeps covenant and steadfast love" (Deuteronomy 7:9).

However, the word ʿĕmet is also used of humans and is generally translated "faithful" or "trustworthy." The word first appears in Genesis 24:48–49 when Abraham's servant is asking for steadfastness and faithfulness from Laban and Bethuel as he is looking for a wife for Abraham's son, Isaac.

Figure 3.1 Faith/faithful/faithfulness in the Old Testament[51]

God seems to be bragging on Moses when He says that Moses is "faithful in all My house" (Numbers 12:7). In his last instructions to Israel, Joshua commands the Israelites to "fear the LORD and serve him in sincerity and in faithfulness" (Joshua 24:14). Faithfulness toward God means putting away "the gods that your fathers served in the region beyond the River and in Egypt, and serve the LORD" (Joshua 24:14).

51 The word ʿĕmet has a wide semantic range. 127 times it's translated as faith, faithful, or faithfully, forty-five times as truth/truthful, twenty-one as true, three times as security, three times as sure, two times as truly.

We see that faithfulness is a key characteristic of God-ordained leadership. After the failed leadership of Eli and his sons, God promises to "raise up for myself a faithful priest, who shall do according to what is in my heart and in my mind" (1 Samuel 2:35). That faithful priest is none other than Samuel who God uses during the reigns of Saul and David. Indeed, Samuel stands as a portrait of faithfulness even though both Saul and David are unfaithful to God during their reigns. As he spares Saul's life, King David reminds him that it is God's sovereignty that constrains David to be faithful to both the earthly king and the heavenly One. "The LORD rewards every man for his righteousness and his faithfulness, for the LORD gave you into my hand today, and I would not put out my hand against the LORD's anointed" (1 Samuel 26:23). In his farewell address, Samuel exhorts the people to "fear the LORD and serve him faithfully" with all their heart (1 Samuel 12:24).[52]

After David is anointed as king over Judah, he blesses the men of Jabesh-gilead, asking for God's steadfast love and faithfulness over them (2 Samuel 2:5–6).[53] David's instructions to Solomon include wailing before the LORD in faithfulness (1 Kings 2:4), and Hezekiah appeals to God's faithfulness when he is sick (2 Kings 20:3; Isaiah 38:3). As he makes much-needed reforms in the kingdom of Judah, the ninth-century BC king Jehoshaphat also correlates the fear of God with faithfulness. "Thus you shall do in the fear of the LORD, in faithfulness, and with your whole heart" (2 Chronicles 19:9). The fear of the LORD and faithfulness are also paired up in the description of Hanani, Nehemiah's brother. "I gave my brother Hanani and Hananiah the governor of the castle charge over Jerusalem, for he was a more faithful and God-fearing man than many" (Nehemiah 7:2). In the Psalms, David recounts God's faithfulness (Psalm 25:10) and appeals to His faithfulness to guard his royal throne (Psalm 61:7).[54] The prophets speak of God's faithfulness in the past (Jeremiah 4:2) and prophesy it for the future

52 Samuel is listed in the so-called Hall of Faith of Hebrews 11 (v. 32).

53 David uses similar language in blessing Ittai the Gittite when he is helping David as he flees from Absalom (2 Samuel 15:20).

54 See also Psalms 69:13; 85:10–11; 86:15; 89:14; 111:8; 117:2.

(Isaiah 16:5; 42:3; 61:8; Jeremiah 32:41; Micah 7:20), reminding His people that they are to live faithfully (Ezekiel 18:9).[55]

Faith and Faithfulness in the New Testament

In Greek, the word often translated as "faithfulness," "reliability," or "faith" is the noun *pistis*. "As 'trust' or 'faith' it occurs only in religious usage."[56] In the Gospels, Jesus commends great faith (Matthew 8:10; 15:28), He sees faith (Matthew 9:2; Mark 2:5), and He affirms that even a little faith produces great results (Matthew 17:20; 21:21).[57] Even though Jesus performs healing miracles, faith is necessary on the part of the recipient (Matthew 9:22; Mark 5:34; 10:52; Luke 7:50). Salvation is possible through faith in Christ (Acts 3:16).

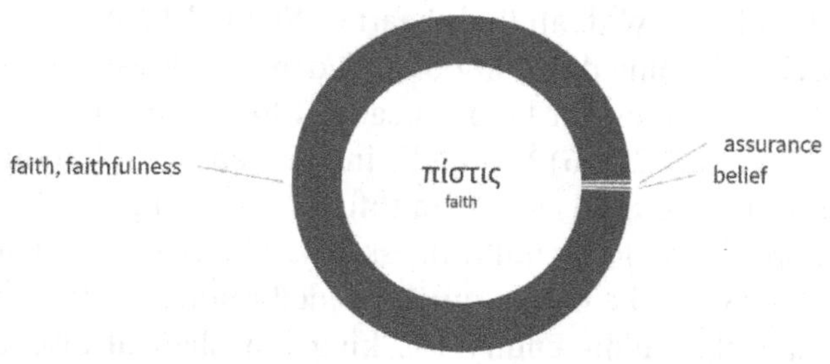

Figure 3.2 The noun "faith" (pistis) in the New Testament

When one accepts the Gospel message, one has faith. Without faith, it is impossible to please God (Hebrews 11:6), and it is faith that turns one from idols to the living God (1 Thessalonians 1:8). Faith points to a personal relationship with Christ when one accepts His message (1 John 5:4). Consequently, the one saved by faith "does not come to judgment, but has passed from death to

55 Through Hosea, God indicts His people because "there is no faithfulness… in the land" (Hosea 4:1).

56 Bultmann, Πιστεύω, W., *Theological Dictionary of the New Testament*, vol. VI, (Grand Rapids, MI: Eerdmans, 2006), 204.

57 Apart from 1 John 5:4, the noun *pistis* does not appear in the Johannine corpus.

life" (John 5:24). In Pauline literature, faith is connected with the blessing of salvation (Romans 1:17; 3:26; Galatians 2:16, 20; 3:11; Ephesians 2:8–10). Faith is a daily function of the believer who walks in faith (2 Corinthians 5:7). James exhorts the believers in need of wisdom to ask in faith (James 1:5–6) and to unite this faith with good works (James 2:14–20).

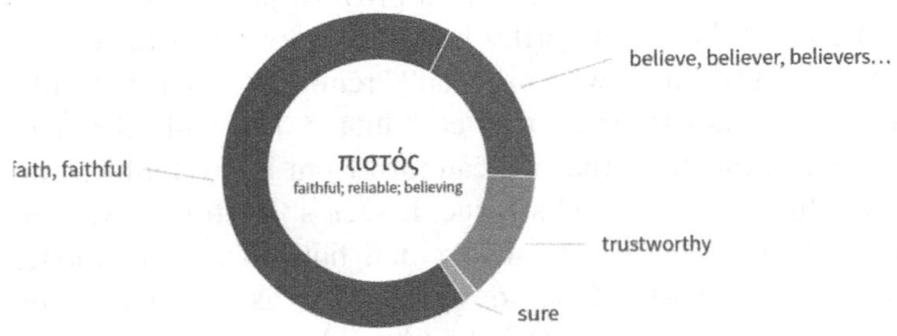

Figure 3.3 The adjective pistós in the New Testament

The adjective *pistós* is generally translated as "faithful," "trustworthy," or "believing." Just like in wisdom literature, faithfulness and wisdom are found together. Jesus commends the faithful and wise servant who waits for Christ's Second Coming (Matthew 24:45–46; Luke 12:42) and the faithful servant who invests his talents well (Matthew 25:21–23; Luke 19:17). After Jesus rises from the dead, He commands Thomas to "not disbelieve but believe" (John 20:27). Consistent with descriptions in the Old Testament, God is described as faithful (1 Corinthians 1:9; 10:13; 2 Corinthians 1:18; 1 Thessalonians 5:24; 2 Thessalonians 3:3; 2 Timothy 2:13; Hebrews 10:23; 1 John 1:9), and He requires His followers to be faithful and trustworthy (1 Corinthians 4:2; 7:25). Paul's ministry partners Tychicus and Epaphras are commended for being faithful (Ephesians 6:21; Colossians 1:7; 4:7). In the book of Hebrews, Jesus is described as the faithful high priest (Hebrew 2:17) who is superior to Moses in that "Christ is faithful over God's house as a son" (Hebrews 3:5–6). In the book of Revelation, Jesus is the faithful witness (1:5), the faithful and true witness (3:14), and the rider on the white horse who is called "Faithful and True" who in "righteousness he judges and makes war" (19:11).

Faithfulness in the Book of Proverbs

The Wise Combine Steadfast Love with Faithfulness

"Many a man proclaims his own steadfast love, but a faithful man who can find (Proverbs 20:6)?" This proverb points to the fact that being faithful or trustworthy is not the norm. The rhetorical question "a faithful man who can find?" reminds us that faithfulness is a rare characteristic in fallen humans. It is only through God's work in our lives that we can turn from being faithless to being faithful. We need God's grace. It seems that this is why in the book of Proverbs, steadfast love and faithfulness are found together several times. Moses describes God as "abounding in steadfast love and faithfulness" (Exodus 34:6), so the one who is supposed to reflect and represent God will also display these two characteristics. Solomon exhorts his son not to let "steadfast love and faithfulness forsake you; bind them around your neck; write them on the tablet of your heart" (Proverbs 3:3). Those who seek to do good "meet steadfast love and faithfulness" (Proverbs 14:22), and it is because of steadfast love and faithfulness that our sins are atoned (Proverbs 16:6). In Proverbs 20:28, we find that "steadfast love and faithfulness preserve the king." Having a good diet of steadfast love and faithfulness benefits the wise both in their personal and professional lives.

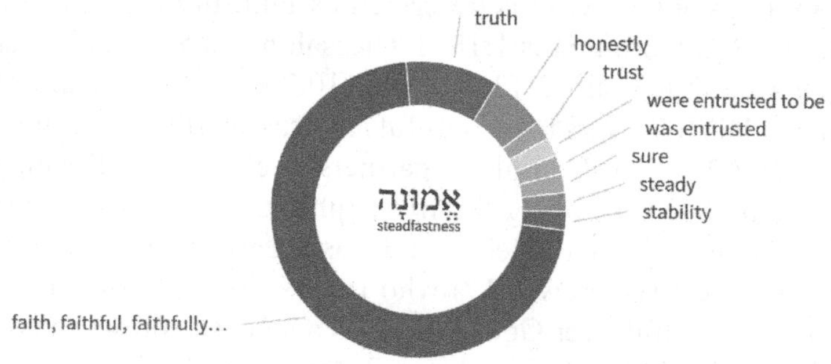

Figure 3.4 The noun "faithful" ('ĕmûnâ) in the Old Testament

The Wise Are Trustworthy

Employers depend on faithful workers. What happens when the worker is wicked? Proverbs 13:17 reminds us that "a wicked messenger falls into trouble, but a faithful envoy brings healing." Garrett notes that "a messenger is an example of a person charged with a serious responsibility. Those who are reliable are appropriately rewarded, but those who are not soon find themselves in serious trouble."[58]

Faithfulness is desirable not just from a business perspective but also from an ethical one. "A faithful witness does not lie, but a false witness breathes out lies" (Proverbs 14:5). The blessings a faithful witness brings can only be understood when one realizes the damage a false witness creates. A false witness creates division (6:19) and hurt (25:18). By speaking the truth, the wise mends and heals. Furthermore, a faithful messenger is refreshing "like the cold of snow in the time of harvest...he refreshes the soul of his masters" (25:13). Those living in an agrarian society understand the analogy better than those living in an urban setting. Nevertheless, just like everyone understands the blessing of being refreshed, everyone understands the blessing of a faithful, ethical worker.

In the realm of relationships, even the wounds of a friend are deemed faithful. "Faithful are the wounds of a friend; profuse are the kisses of an enemy." The word describing the kisses of the enemy can also be translated as "deceitful," which would fit the contrasting "faithful" that describes the wounds of a friend.

Faithfulness and Purity in Proverbs 5

As believers, we are constantly at war, fighting three main battles: the battle for truth, the battle for purity, and the battle for humility. Solomon devotes three chapters to dealing with the battle for purity as he warns against impurity and infidelity, the very opposite of faithfulness and trustworthiness.

In Proverbs 5, Solomon warns young men about the dangers of the forbidden woman: "For the lips of a forbidden woman drip honey, and her speech is smoother than oil, but in the end she is bitter as wormwood, sharp as a two-edged sword" (Proverbs

58 Garrett, *Proverbs, Ecclesiastes, Song of Songs,* 138.

5:3–4).[59] Here, we are reminded of Satan's *modus operandi*, lying. Back in the garden, he lied to Eve, "you shall not surely die" (Genesis 3:4), even though God said, "you will surely die" (Genesis 2:16–17). As with the forbidden woman, what is supposed to be sweet becomes bitter, and what is supposed to be life-giving becomes deadly. "Her feet go down to death; her steps follow the path of Sheol" (Proverbs 5:5). Satan doesn't just want to maim or hurt, he wants to kill and destroy. The apostle Peter wrote to the first-century church to "be sober-minded, be watchful. Your adversary the devil prowls like a roaring lion, seeking someone to devour" (1 Peter 5:8).

Not only is the forbidden woman evil, and not only does she lead others astray, but she is ignorant. "She does not ponder the path of life; her ways wander, and she does not know it" (Proverbs 5:6). The forbidden woman is an adulteress (Proverbs 5:20) who seduces the undisciplined fool (Proverbs 5:23). The consequences of infidelity are both temporal and eternal. The young man is instructed to keep away from the forbidden woman. "Keep your way far from her, and do not go near the door of her house, lest you give your honor to others and your years to the merciless, lest strangers take their fill of your strength, and your labors go to the house of a foreigner, and at the end of your life you groan, when your flesh and body are consumed, and you say, 'How I hated discipline, and my heart despised reproof!'" (Proverbs 5:9–12).

We are reminded of the apostle Paul's instruction to Timothy, "Flee youthful lusts and pursue righteousness, faith, love, and peace, along with those who call on the LORD from a pure heart" (2 Timothy 2:22). After giving in to sin, he realizes that he is "at the brink of utter ruin in the assembled congregation" (Proverbs 5:14), being "held fast in the cords of his sin" (Proverbs 5:22). In the end, "he dies for lack of discipline, and because of his great folly he is led astray" (Proverbs 5:23). We all enjoy the beautiful songs about grace, like "Amazing Grace." But why don't we have

59 Some critical scholars suggest that the Strange Woman in Proverbs 5 symbolizes foreign, dangerous wisdom, "namely Greek philosophy from the Hellenistic period." See Matthew Goff, "Hellish Females: The Strange Woman of Septuagint Proverbs and 4QWiles of the Wicked Woman (4Q184) in *Journal for the Study of Judaism* 39 (2008): 20–45.

songs like "Amazing Discipline"? Believers need to combine grace and discipline in their daily diet. They are both amazing, and they are both life-giving.

The young man is given the tools necessary to overcome the temptations of the forbidden woman. He is to listen to the teacher's wisdom and obey the teacher's instruction (Proverbs 5:1, 7). Then, he is to keep away. We have heard of social distancing, but we are to practice sacred distancing. "Keep your way far from her, and do not go near the door of her house" (Proverbs 5:8). Proactively, the young man is encouraged to stay satisfied by his own wife. "Drink water from your own cistern, flowing water from your own well…let your fountain be blessed, and rejoice in the wife of your youth…let her breasts fill you at all times with delight; be intoxicated always in her love" (Proverbs 5:15–19).

The imagery of gardens and fountains is best understood in light of the Ancient Near Eastern context in general, and the book of Song of Songs, in particular. The garden represents her whole body, while the fountain represents her sexual organ. In the Song of Songs, Solomon describes the Shulammite in these terms. "A garden locked is my sister, my bride, a spring locked, a fountain sealed. Your shoots are an orchard of pomegranates with all choicest fruits" (Song of Songs 4:12–14). And then she invites him into sexual union of the most intimate type when she says, "Awake, O north wind, and come, O south wind! Blow upon my garden, let its spices flow. Let my beloved come to his garden and eat its choicest fruits" (Songs of Songs 4:16). Fredericks and Estes are right, "With the right person at the right time and in the right setting, sexual intimacy is a God-given delight that should be treasured and savored. This theme in the Song is echoed in the New Testament, when Hebrews 13:4 extols the undefiled bed in contrast to fornication and adultery."[60]

Faithfulness and Purity in Proverbs 6

In chapter 6, Solomon emphasizes obedience to parents as a safeguard against impurity and infidelity. "For the commandment is a

60 Daniel C. Fredericks and Daniel J. Estes, *Ecclesiastes & The Song of Songs* (Downers Grove, IL: IVP, 2010), 352.

lamp and the teaching a light, and the reproofs of discipline are the way of life, to preserve you from the evil woman, from the smooth tongue of the adulteress" (Proverbs 6:23–24). Wise parents understand that a woman's beauty is tempting, so they teach him to "not desire her beauty" and not to be captured "with her eyelashes" (Proverbs 6:25).

In his first letter, the apostle John reminds us that "the desire of the eyes…is not from the Father but is from the world" (1 John 2:16). Decisions based solely on outward appearance will always be wrong decisions. Samson fell into that trap when he told his parents to get him a Philistine wife because "she is right in my eyes" (Judges 14:3). Samson didn't care that she was not a Yahweh worshiper. He made a decision based only on what his eyes could see. David fell into the same trap when "he saw from the roof a woman bathing; and the woman was very beautiful" (2 Samuel 11:2). Like a spoiled child who always gets what he wants, "David sent messengers and took her, and she came to him, and he lay with her" (2 Samuel 11:4). David didn't care that he was married. David didn't care that she was married. Like Samson, he made a decision merely based on what his eyes could see.

Both Samson and David suffered the consequences of their sin. Solomon wanted to protect his son from impurity and infidelity because there is a price to pay for disobedience, namely, "a married woman hunts down a precious life" (Proverbs 6:26). Just like one is burned by fire (Proverbs 6:27) and burned by hot coals (Proverbs 6:28), so the one who is who commits adultery will be punished (Proverbs 6:29). Ultimately, the Bible says that "he who commits adultery lacks sense," and in the long run, "he who does it destroys himself" (Proverbs 6:32). In the short run, "he will get wounds and dishonor, and his disgrace will not be wiped away" (Proverbs 6:33).

Faithfulness and Purity in Proverbs 7

Solomon continues with the same theme of warning against immorality in chapter 7. The first step is obedience to wise counsel. "My son, keep my words and treasure up my commandments with you…say to wisdom, 'you are my sister,' and call insight your intimate friend, to keep you from the forbidden woman, from the adulteress with her smooth words" (Proverbs 7:1–5). In Proverbs 2, we learn that "The LORD gives wisdom; from His mouth comes knowledge and understanding" (Proverbs 2:6). A few verses later, Solomon emphasizes the value of following the LORD's wisdom. "So you will be delivered from the forbidden woman, from the adulteress with her smooth words" (Proverbs 2:16).

Living a life of purity, then, is not just good parental advice but godly wisdom. To make his point, Solomon gives an example of a young man who lacked sense (Proverbs 7:7), who first takes the road to the house of the forbidden woman, the smooth-tongued adulteress (Proverbs 7:8). The foolish young man is doing this "in the evening, at the time of night and darkness" (Proverbs 7:9), hoping that the cover of darkness will hide his intentions and actions. The next scene describes the woman as a huntress on a hunt. Outwardly, she is "dressed as a prostitute," and inwardly, she is "crafty at heart" (Proverbs 7:10).[61] She is loud and rebellious, leaving the stability of the home in order to lie in wait in the street and in the market (Proverbs 7:11–12).[62] She is aggressive because before she kisses him, she seizes him (Proverbs 7:13).[63] She has no shame.

Like Jacob of old, she uses religious language while in the process of committing sin.[64] "I had to offer sacrifices,[65] and today I have paid my vows; so now I have come out to meet you, to seek you eagerly, and I have found you" (Proverbs 7:14–15). Not only is she secularizing her religion, she is exchanging what should be

---

61 The ESV translates it "wily;" the NASB translates it "cunning."

62 "For a prostitute is a deep pit; an adulteress is a narrow well. She lies in wait like a robber and increases the traitors among mankind" (Proverbs 23:28). The one who lies in wait is called "wicked" (Proverbs 24:15).

63 The verb root means "to be (come) strong," but in the causative Hiphil stem, it means "to take hold of, seize." (See Genesis 19:16; Exodus 9:2; 1 Samuel 17:35.)

64 When Isaac asks Jacob how he was able to hunt so successfully and so quickly, Jacob uses religious language to lie and deceive, "Because the LORD your God granted me success" (Genesis 27:20).

65 The word is used of peace offerings as described in Leviticus 7:16–18.

a time of celebration for a time of sinning. "The sacred significance of the sacrifice is said to be lost on the woman. For her it has degenerated to a secular feast, much as Christmas has for many in modern Christendom."[66]

Her seduction moves from religious language to the language of opulence. A bed perfumed with myrrh, aloes, and cinnamon covered with Egyptian linens is the place to which she hopes to get the foolish young man (Proverbs 7:16–17). In the absence of her husband, she shamelessly drags him down like a beast preparing to devour its prey. "Come, let us take our fill of love till morning; let us delight ourselves with love. For my husband is not at home; he has gone on a long journey; he took a bag of money with him; at full moon he will come home" (Proverbs 7:18–20). And just as Delilah dragged Samson to an early grave (Judges 16), so the forbidden woman with the adulteress' seductive speech persuades the foolish young man (Proverbs 7:21). The language changes to predator/prey language, "he follows her, as an ox goes to the slaughter, or as a stag is caught fast, till an arrow pierces its liver; as a bird rushes into a snare; he does not know it will cost him his life" (Proverbs 7:22–23).

The message is clear: the wages of sin is death. We need to take God seriously, and sometimes He speaks through parents and/or authority figures. The chapter starts with "My son, keep my words and treasure up my commandments with you" (Proverbs 7:1), and the chapter ends the same way, "And now, O sons, listen to me, and be attentive to the words of my mouth" (Proverbs 7:24). There is a way out. There is no temptation that is too powerful (1 Corinthians 10:13). "Let not your heart turn aside to her ways; do not stray into her paths" (Proverbs 7:25). "But why not?" "But why can't I just…" The answer is simple: "the wages of sin is death" (Romans 6:23). "For many a victim has she laid low, and all her slain are a mighty throng. Her house is the way to Sheol, going down to the chambers of death" (Proverbs 7:26–27).

The Bible offers the way out of temptation and sin through the person and work of Christ. Horton puts it masterfully,

---

66 Garrett, *Proverbs, Ecclesiastes, Song of Songs,* 103.

> If I speak to one who is bound with the cords of his sin, helplessly fettered and manacled, dead as it were in trespasses, I know there is no other name to mention to you, no other hope to hold out to you. Though I knew all science, I could not effectually help you; though I could command all the springs of human feeling, I could not stir you from your apathy, or satisfy the first cries of your awaking conscience. But it is permitted to me to preach unto you—not abstract Wisdom, but—Jesus, who received that name because He should save His people from their sins.[67]

The Faithful Will Be Rewarded

Is it worth being faithful and trustworthy? Are there benefits to living an ethical, moral life? The book of Proverbs answers affirmatively, "A faithful man will abound with blessings, but whoever hastens to be rich will not go unpunished" (Proverbs 28:20).

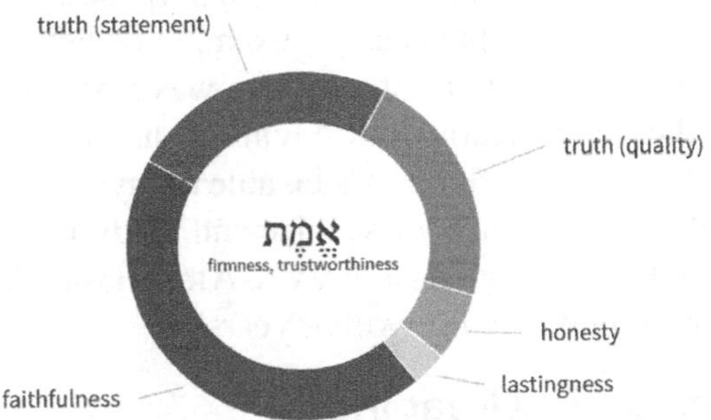

Figure 3.5 "Trustworthiness" in the Old Testament[68]

The book of Proverbs does not give a comprehensive list of how one will be blessed for being faithful, but it does mention that

67 Robert F. Horton, "The Book of Proverbs," in *The Expositor's Bible: Psalms to Isaiah*, ed. W. Robertson Nicoll, vol. 3 (Hartford, CT: S.S. Scranton Co., 1903), 374.

68 The word is translated as follows: sixty-one times as faith, faithful, or faithfully; thirty-two times as truth or truthful; twenty-one times as true; fewer times as security, sure, right, or truly.

these blessings are in abundance.[69] Faithfulness benefits not just individuals but entire groups of people. Proverbs 29:14 mentions faithfulness in leadership, "If a king faithfully judges the poor, his throne will be established forever." If a king is faithful in carrying his responsibilities in a godly and righteous way by protecting the poor, not only will the poor benefit but also "the security of a king's reign depends on equitably dispensing justice."[70]

A Lesson from Church History

Alvin was a British missionary who, in the nineteenth century, wanted to be a missionary to Africa. At that time, though, it was very hard to be a missionary. In fact, the average survival time of a missionary in Africa was six months. So, when Alvin was getting ready for his trip, he had to build a clothes chest or trunk out of wood. Because he was only expected to live six months, he decided to build his clothes trunk in the form of a coffin. This way, his clothes trunk would serve two purposes: for his travel and for his burial. Alvin stands as an example of faithfulness in ministry. He was the kind of witness who was ready to work and die, work or die. Let us learn from Alvin and hammer for ourselves a clothes trunk and a coffin. Let's be able to say: "Lord, I want to be a faithful witness, ready for service and ready for sacrifice." At a time when the average missionary to Africa lasted for six months, Alvin served in Africa for twelve years!

A Christological Reading

Because humanity's greatest problem is sin, humanity's greatest need is forgiveness. Proverbs 16:6 reminds us, "By steadfast love and faithfulness iniquity is atoned for, and by the fear of the Lord one turns away from evil." Our atonement for sin is accomplished through Christ's death and resurrection. The author of Hebrews reminds his Jewish audience that Jesus was the "merciful and faithful high priest in the service of God, to make atonement for

---

69 The word "blessings" is prefixed by the word *rab,* which can be translated "numerous, many, plentiful, much, great, and enough."

70 Garrett, *Proverbs, Ecclesiastes, Song of Songs,* 231.

the sins of the people" (Hebrews 2:17). He is the faithful One even when we are faithless. "Christ is faithful over God's house as a Son" (Hebrews 3:6), and He is the One who becomes the sacrifice "once for all" (Hebrews 9:12; 10:10). At the end of the Bible, Jesus is described as "the faithful and true witness" (Revelation 3:14) and "chosen and faithful" (Revelation 17:14). As John gets a glimpse of heaven, he sees a white horse, and "the one sitting on it is called Faithful and True, and in righteousness He judges and makes war" (Revelation 19:11). Thomas notes that, "in the future Christ will come as a Warrior-Prince instead of as a Lamb, the commander-in-chief of the host of heaven."[71]

71 Robert L. Thomas, *Revelation 8–22: An Exegetical Commentary* (Chicago: Moody Publishers, 1995), 383.

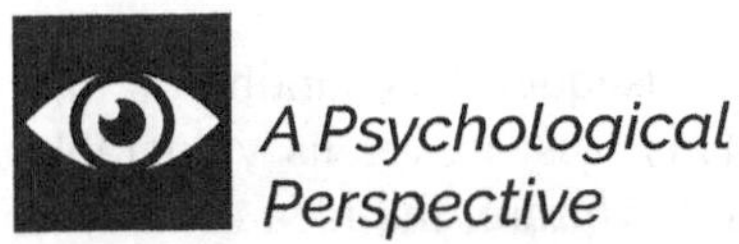

Reflections on Faithfulness

Dr. Kevin Roberts

Trust in the L*ORD with all your heart,*
and do not lean on your own understanding.
In all your ways acknowledge him,
and he will make straight your paths.
—Proverbs 3:5–6

The words trustworthy and faithful have considerable overlap in the Hebrew and in psychological literature. The term faithful is often thought of as belief or trusting in what is not seen. But in many psychological research studies, it is more associated with persistence and diligence. In psychological literature, the concept of being trustworthy is often found to have overlap with terms like authenticity, honesty, and integrity. For the purposes of this chapter, we will examine the importance of trust in building and maintaining relationships, and the nature and benefits of trust in both psychological literature and within Scripture.

The Importance of Trusting in God

The term trust is often misunderstood and is somewhat difficult to define. Scripture makes it abundantly clear that trust is needed for our faith. In fact, we are commanded to trust and believe in God (Psalm 4:5; Proverbs 3:5–6). Trust, in the human sense, is often understood from an interpersonal perspective that requires making some part of us vulnerable to another person and, consequently, counting on that person to act in our best interest.[72] This trust leaves us vulnerable to the discretion of that individual. In Scripture, the idea of trust is commonly associated with leaning or putting all our weight onto the thing that we trust, namely God. For example, each time I place my weight on a chair, I trust that the chair is going to hold me up. How many times each day do you sit on a chair without fear of the chair failing to hold you up? This type of trust involves either a quick assessment of the stability of a chair or a blind trust in chairs.

Similarly, we are instructed in Scripture to trust God by committing our way to Him and acknowledging Him in all we do (Proverbs 3:6). In Scripture, we also learn that we can trust God because of His omnipresence (Psalm 19:1; Proverbs 15:3), omniscience (Proverbs 15:11; 24:11–12), compassion (Proverbs 22:22; 29:13), justice (Proverbs 15:25; 17:3; 21:12; 22:12), love (John 17:23; 1 John 4:8), and the sovereignty of God (Proverbs 16:4; 21:31). These characteristics of God give us the confidence to trust Him with our deepest pain because we believe that God will be faithful and not betray us. We also believe in God's love and mercy. We can trust the God of the universe without fear of our vulnerability leading to pain and suffering, which we sometimes experience with other people. Thinking back to the chair example, this faith in the functionality and dependability of a chair bears some resemblance to the type of faith we need to have in God. We must believe in the inerrancy of Scripture and trust in God's Word so that our faith may be deepened as we lean into and trust Him. It is in this process of trusting God that our faith grows as we gradually deepen our understanding of God. However, you and I live in this world, and we must deal with trust issues from a human perspective, so in what ways does trust impact our development?

Trusting from the Beginning

The concept of trust in psychological literature was first observed in the work of Erik Erickson when he developed the eight stages of psychosocial development.[73] It was Erickson's belief that the

72 Harold H. Kelley et al., "An Atlas of Interpersonal Situations" (2003).

73 Erik H. Erikson, *Childhood and Society* (New York: Norton, 1950).

first stage of human development was termed Trust vs. Mistrust. He explained that the mother-child relationship and the trustworthiness of the mother establish whether the child perceives his or her world as a safe place. He further articulated that the failure to establish a trusting relationship would lead to problems with attachment. Erickson theorized that failure to develop meaningful attachments would lead to a host of other psychological-related problems.[74] It was Erikson's belief that trust provides the opportunity for self-identity to develop.[75]

Trust is built in thousands of small moments over the course of our lives with family, friends, and other loved ones. Trust is built in the safe-keeping of our secrets or holding things in confidence and remaining vulnerable with these individuals while simultaneously trusting that they will act in our best interest. Scripture warns us of the dangers of gossiping (Proverbs 11:13; 16:28; 17:4; 20:19; 21:23; 26:20) because in loosening our lips, we find how being untrustworthy can bring pain to our lives. In Proverbs, we are even warned about having any relationship with people who gossip (Proverbs 16:28). This is why gossiping with another friend is a false intimacy (Proverbs 18:8), because we mistakenly believe mutual disdain for another individual creates meaningful connection when it does not.

In marriage, one might argue that trust is the single most important variable in predicting marital success. Yet the book of Proverbs makes it clear that trusting in man is problematic. As we see in Proverbs 20:6, "Many a man proclaims his own steadfast love, but a faithful man who can find?" Our sin nature and desire to satisfy our own longings often result in us not being trustworthy people. In fact, our sin nature frequently results in the violation of trust in a human relationship, which comes at great personal expense. John Gottman, who is a premier researcher on marriage, has found that trust and commitment to one another are two of the most important variables in predicting long-term success in marriage.[76] This is often seen in how couples handle issues in the day-

74 Erikson, *Childhood and Society.*

75 Erikson, *Childhood and Society.*

76 John Mordechai Gottman, *The Science of Trust: Emotional Attunement for Couples* (New York: W. W. Norton, 2011).

to-day relationship-building moments. Couples must learn how to communicate effectively without overreacting, thereby gaining an opportunity to grow in trust and understanding of one another.[77] The trustworthy spouse focuses on building the relationship by deepening the shared trust through meaningful engagement. Sadly, this pursuit of one another is in direct contrast to our worldwide reality, where we see extramarital affairs on the rise.[78] Although we are commanded to be trustworthy and faithful, we continue to see rises in marital unfaithfulness.[79]

As believers, we are instructed to be both faithful and trustworthy before God. In Ecclesiastes 12:13, Solomon addresses the need for us to faithfully keep our eyes focused on God, "The end of the matter; all has been heard. Fear God and keep His commandments, for this is the whole duty of man. For God will bring every deed into judgment, with every secret thing, whether good or evil." If every deed and action is going to be brought into judgment, then it is our job to pursue God daily so that we may learn how to be faithful and trustworthy before Him.

Dangers of Mistrust and Biological Ramifications

Erickson warned about the potential pitfalls of children who fail to develop trusting relationships.[80] Trust can be violated in many ways, but it is particularly damaging when it comes in the form of experiencing traumatic events or highly stressful home environments.[81] Ward et al. found that many of the young women who experienced trauma in their childhood failed to develop secure

77 Gottman, *The Science of Trust: Emotional Attunement for Couples.*

78 Chrisanna Northrup, Pepper Schwartz, and James Witte, *The Normal Bar: The Surprising Secrets of Happy Couples and What They Reveal about Creating a New Normal in Your Relationship* (New York: Crown Archetype, 2012).

79 Northrup, Schwartz, and Witte, *The Normal Bar: The Surprising Secrets of Happy Couples and What They Reveal about Creating a New Normal in Your Relationship.*

80 Erik H. Erikson, *Childhood and Society.*

81 Mary J. Ward, Shelley S. Lee, and Evelyn G. Lipper, "Failure-to-Thrive Is Associated with Disorganized Infant-Mother Attachment and Unresolved Maternal Attachment," *Infant Mental Health Journal* 21, no. 6 (2000): 428–42.

attachments with their mothers and consequently failed to develop those same attachments with their own children.[82] This pattern of mistrust can therefore become a generational problem. The problem we see is that failing to trust God often has many negative and often missed or even unintentional consequences. For example, when rearing children, we often have considerable fear, worry, or concern as they mature and begin making many of their own choices (see Figure 3.6). Because trusting in God to handle the matter is difficult, we often like to try and get involved by controlling many of the variables. The problem here is that attempting to control another human being's behavior often has the exact opposite reaction to what we desire.[83] Consequently, we realize through Erickson, Ward, and now Glasser that fear plays a powerful role in human relationships. What we find is that less-trusting kids are frequently prone to make decisions based on fear instead of being trust-driven. Could some of this indicate the reason why many churchgoers who were unable to develop trusting relationships in their early formative years might continue to struggle to trust in human relationships and in their heavenly Father? And could it be that not trusting in God is not merely just a learned behavior but might become biological as well?

There is a massive body of psychological literature that shows the impact of high stress and trauma on human brain development. We human beings are acutely aware of our needs and reliance on others for our own existence, and it appears we are biologically built to trust in others.[84] Kosfeld et al. found that oxytocin is released in both humans and animals to create prosocial behavior. In fact, trust can be thought of as a currency of sorts because the brain gets a rush of pleasure when trust is rewarded.[85] The more trust that exists in the relationship, the higher the oxytocin levels,

82 Ward, Lee, and Lipper, "Failure-to-Thrive Is Associated with Disorganized Infant-Mother Attachment and Unresolved Maternal Attachment."

83 William Glasser, *Choice Theory: A New Psychology of Personal Freedom* (New York, NY: Harper Collins, 1998).

84 Michael Kosfeld et al., "Oxytocin Increases Trust in Humans," *Nature* 435, no. 7042 (2005): 673–76.

85 Kosfeld et al., "Oxytocin Increases Trust in Humans."

thus producing more prosocial behaviors such as kindness, cooperation, sharing, and working well with others.

In contrast, children who grow up in traumatic or unsafe environments will see negative changes in their amygdala and hippocampal area.[86] This is important because the amygdala is often associated with fear. In unsafe environments, amygdala activation becomes a learned response, which in turn influences one's behavioral responses.[87] The hippocampal area relates directly to memory, and these two combined may influence the emotional processing of certain parts of our memory.[88] In other words, negative early learning experiences become hard-wired in our brains and can influence our judgments, emotions, and the ability to form and maintain relationships. But is there any hope for someone who has had a series of negative or traumatic events and consequently struggles to trust others or their heavenly Father?

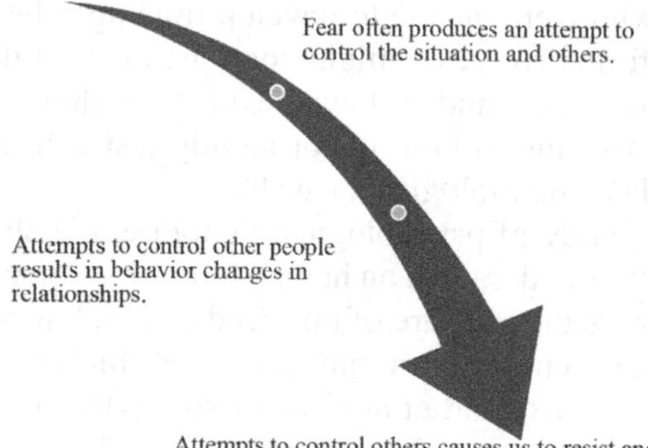

Figure 3.6 Lack of trust often produces fear

86 David C. Knight et al., "Amygdala and Hippocampal Activity during Acquisition and Extinction of Human Fear Conditioning," *Cognitive, Affective, & Behavioral Neuroscience* 4, no. 3 (2004): 317–25.

87 Knight et al., "Amygdala and Hippocampal Activity during Acquisition and Extinction of Human Fear Conditioning."

88 Knight et al., "Amygdala and Hippocampal Activity during Acquisition and Extinction of Human Fear Conditioning."

Benefits of Living Out a Trustworthy and Faithful Existence

The LORD provides a variety of promises and benefits of being trustworthy and faithful (Proverbs 11:28; 12:19; 13:11). We also see His character in His promises in Psalm 25:9–10, which states, "He leads the humble in what is right, and teaches the humble his way. All the paths of the LORD are steadfast love and faithfulness, for those who keep his covenant and his testimonies." God also promises to never forsake us (Deuteronomy 31:6). We see in these verses that Scripture promises to reward those that are faithful and trustworthy, as also noted in the parable of the talents in Matthew 25:14–30.

As we examine the role of trust, we must first realize that a trusting relationship with God and others is foundational for our spiritual and psychosocial development. It is essential that we develop trusting social relationships to avoid experiencing social isolation. The research on social isolation indicates that whether we are talking about adolescent or adult mental health or physical health, the more connected we are to others, the more potential benefits we experience.[89] Waite and Gallagher found that trust and commitment were also positively correlated to better recovery, improved health, increased wealth, and a longer lifespan.[90]

---

89 Timothy Matthews et al., "Social Isolation and Mental Health at Primary and Secondary School Entry: A Longitudinal Cohort Study," *Journal of the American Academy of Child & Adolescent Psychiatry* 54, no. 3 (2015): 225–32; John R. Beard et al., "Predictors of Mental Disorders and Their Outcome in a Community Based Cohort," *Social Psychiatry and Psychiatric Epidemiology* 42, no. 8 (2007): 623–30; Lyndal Bond et al., "Social and School Connectedness in Early Secondary School as Predictors of Late Teenage Substance Use, Mental Health, and Academic Outcomes," *Journal of Adolescent Health* 40, no. 4 (2007); Manami Ejiri et al., "Predictors of Older Adults' Objectively Measured Social Isolation: A Systematic Review of Observational Studies," *Archives of Gerontology and Geriatrics* 94 (2021): 104357.

90 Linda Waite & Maggie Gallagher, *The Case for Marriage: Why Married People are Happier, Healthier and Better off Financially* (New York: Broadway Books, 2002).

Application Exercises and Questions for Faithfulness and Trust

As we look back at this chapter, I believe there are questions about trusting God and others that we must be willing to ask ourselves.

1. Have you considered what impact early experiences in your life have had on your ability to trust people? Have those same experiences had any impact on learning to trust God?
2. We know that having trusting relationships are essential for our mental health and spiritual development. If this is true, how many people really know you? How many people have you been willing to make yourself vulnerable with? Trust is loaded with elements of accountability, but without accountability in relationships, it is difficult to be fully honest with others and ourselves.
3. If you have very few close connected relationships, have you ever asked yourself why you do not move toward safe relationships? Do you avoid having trusting relationships because of the accountability inherent in these relationships? Or do you avoid having trusting relationships because you are avoiding taking personal responsibility?
4. Can you relax and learn to trust or "lean into" God during times of trials? Do you trust that anything is possible with God? If not, what is the barrier? In times of having difficulty trusting, do you also tend to use controlling behaviors as a means of keeping yourself safe? If the answer is yes, then what role does God's sovereignty play in trusting Him?
5. Can you trust in God when you face life's trials? Remember that God does not disappoint, whereas human trust can be violated.

A Pastoral Perspective

Faithfulness at Church

Pastor Knute Larson

Faithful people are the cement of the church, holding it together through the years. Though others around them come and go or get up and go down, the faithful stay true to their commitment to our Lord, His Scriptures, and His mission for the Church. They simply believe, no matter what. It's not just that they are consistent in their attendance and their service at church, though they are, they are also faithful in their single life or marriages, conscious that they bring love and joy and peace to their neighborhood, and they are the kind of people who are dependable at work.

Faithfulness to God, as seen in the life of the church, is not just about consistency on Sundays or in groups or ministries during the week—it is about honesty. The writer of Proverbs says that he knows a lot of people who might boast of their own steadiness, "but a faithful man who can find?" (Proverbs 20:6). As a pastor for over forty-three years, I can find these men and women. I can name them by name. They were always the people you could depend on for prayers, love for others, desire for unity of mission, volunteers for a project or a person, and even feelings about church. One of them was my grandmother, who had a fourth-grade education and taught two to four Bible classes every week in some forsaken spots in Harrisburg, PA, and some classes at church. The church has been built by faithful leaders and nameless ones who simply give their money, time, and love.

Every church that has a strong ministry and a faithful witness has people who pray daily for that church, faithfully trusting God for the projects of the church and doing good around the area, but also helping individual lives and families. Some of them get elected to positions or are selected for oversight, but most of them are somebody sitting in the third row or the tenth, quietly responding to the Word as it is preached and living it out the next day. Some of them sing off-key but mean every word. They greet newcomers in the halls, share food with the family experiencing tragedy, and pray for their pastor and others who lead and shepherd. Many of them never make the church ballot or get their names on a plaque, but the church would have died without them.

Faithfulness also looks like strong and faithful marriages and exemplary singles, for the Proverbs writers, as noted in the commentary section, are very candid about sexual purity and the strong temptations battling it. Solomon himself is very graphic about man-woman drives, probably because of his own promiscuous ways, as well as the obvious inspiration of the Holy Spirit. He speaks of this woman who has crafty intent as she lures a man off the street with, "Come, let's drink deep of love...with persuasive words she led him astray; she seduced him with her smooth talk" (Proverbs 7:10–21).

"Don't do it," Proverbs warns again and again.

Why Faithfulness Is So Important

"The church is no different than the world," is the accusation from countless dropouts. And the statistics about immorality, divorce, gossip, and unkind deeds do not counter the charge. They happen way too often in the church. Many of the descriptions of the faithful in Proverbs are about daily actions and steadfast faithfulness. Most everyone who knows the Scriptures can name Solomon and his father and many of the leaders of the Old Testament, and who can't name Paul as the main writer of the New? But it is all those people described in Proverbs and named at the end of some of

Paul's letters—people we never heard of, like Pudens, Linus, and Eubulus. These are the ones who helped the whole nation turn back to the Lord in the Old and who decided to live faithfully in combination with Christ in the New.

Don't forget to thank their counterparts next Sunday at church or today by email or text.

If I ever heard anyone talk about "Knute Larson's church" when I was pastoring, I smiled and tried to correct them. After dutifully and faithfully saying that this church belonged to Christ, I would also add, "And if you want to use any human being's name with our church, let me give you a list of people who have been so faithful in their praying and giving and worshiping and serving. They make the church. It is theirs." Famous pastors like Andy Stanley, as well as less-publicized pastors, do not have a church. They serve at the church bought and owned by our Lord Christ. "In him the whole building is joined together…And in him you too are being built together to become a dwelling in which God lives by his spirit" (Ephesians 2:21). Every faithful believer should joyfully see himself in that verse and remain faithful. We all choose either the wise way of God's design or the foolish way of human desire, unbridled. If we believe God to be all-wise, as did Solomon after learning the hard lessons of vanity, we will obey Him.

Why Faithfulness Doesn't Always Show Up

Every church has cried because of dropouts. Someone gets a reason in his or her head, some degree of truth, perhaps, but not a good enough reason to betray faith and trust in the Lord Jesus. One man told me when I asked him why he had seemed to quit church, "I tried Jesus, and it did not work." As I recall, I did not know what to say at first. Sometimes churches and individuals emphasize saving faith and think too little about daily growth or sanctification. When that happens, their faith is just on paper and should be in their hearts and lived out in their lives. Proverbs 12:22 says that "lying lips are an abomination to the Lord," and they hurt His church also. "Steadfast love and faithfulness preserve the king," says the king in Proverbs 20:28, and they also strengthen the church. Steadfast love and faithfulness are not natural traits of any human being. None of us ever had to go to kindergarten to learn how to lie—we picked it up naturally, even before we learned our first four-letter word: "mine." Such foolishness and selfishness came with the fall and inhabit all of us, even when we go to church. If we do not grow in our deliberate abiding in Christ and trusting Him for wisdom and spiritual strength, we will play church and help it look foolish to the outsiders who watch us split or deteriorate.

All of us have been embarrassed by the church leaders who made the front page of the big city papers because of their temperament or moral failure, or selfishness. But also by the common members who misrepresent the church with their attitudes of meanness, even on biblical or spiritual matters. If the Holy Spirit does not show up in our hearts, our faithfulness will be flimsy. Solomon gave the immediate theme of seeking wisdom and following the Lord and then followed through with details in all thirty-one chapters. "So you will walk in the ways of the good and keep to the paths of the righteous," and the church will flourish as God defines that (Proverbs 2:20–22). When someone is part of the church and claims to have forgiveness and eternal life through Christ but cares little for his daily walk, he or she should beware of the danger of going "to the slaughter," as Solomon so candidly described the man following the propositioning woman (Proverbs 7:22). Proverbs takes the narrow, God-designed way of marriage very seriously, without a doubt as to what is sin. This book of wisdom calls all of us to be faithful to God in our stance on morality and our faithfulness in common practice. God's clear plan and design were thought through before creation, described in Genesis, taught in Proverbs, and repeated in many other Bible contexts. The only question is if we will obey Him, believing He is wisely calling for our faithfulness.

What We Can Do Personally to Be Faithful

We can be individually consistent in the Word and conscious of how we glorify God and affect others. We must remember the words of one wiser than Solomon: "Let your light shine before others, so that they may see your good works and give glory to your Father who is in heaven" (Matthew 5:16). That is wise indeed. "A faithful envoy brings healing" is the challenge to all of us in Proverbs 13:17. And all of us are envoys of our Savior both in and out of the church. I must not just hope a leader or recognized officer of the church confronts a person with harmful attitudes or encourages a person in need. My voice is strong if I speak the truth in love. By prayer and often a word, we can help the church be faithful; and then we simply do our part with prayer and faithful worship and lives that show the love and truth of Jesus Christ. "Those who devise good meet steadfast love and faithfulness," and they or we make the church more what it should be in Christ our Lord (Proverbs 14:22). There is no such thing as a faithful church. There are simply faithful followers of Christ who seek His wisdom and live by what they believe instead of what they feel. You and I can both do that. These people come to the end of each day knowing they have at least tried to run after wisdom and be faithful rather than doing whatever they felt like doing. Anyone can do that.

And we can all pray—for ourselves and our families, for our leaders, and all who attend, for the ones just daring to try church because somehow they realize they are missing something.

A Personal Prayer for Faithfulness

Praise: Praise God the Son for His faithfulness to the mission to go to the cross for us, for His excellent and enduring faithfulness, and for personal ways He has been faithful to you recently.

Repent: As humans, we are often unfaithful. Take time to confess any ways you have been unfaithful and receive forgiveness as He promised.

Ask: This would be a good time to pray for spiritual courage and strength, to be faithful every day, and to be a strong influence for obedience and for the love of our Lord—at church and wherever you go. Perhaps there is a specific project or a problem to focus on as you seek to be faithful.

Yield: To some of the various commands and descriptions of faithfulness that came up in this chapter.

CHAPTER 4

Wise Parenting

A Theological Perspective

The Wise Are Godly Parents

Dr. Tiberius Rata

The first lesson for a child should be concerning his mother's God. Teach him what you will, if he learns not the fear of the LORD*, he will perish for lack of knowledge.*
—Charles Spurgeon

Parenting in the Old Testament

The book of Proverbs gives us important principles to apply when it comes to parenting, but parenting principles didn't begin there. God designed the first family in the garden of Eden. Adam and Eve, a man and a woman, lived in a covenant relationship with God and each other until they were banished for disobeying God. Nonetheless, God blessed them with two sons, and tragically, we saw the consequences of sin playing out outside of the garden. Cain killed Abel (Genesis 4), Noah got drunk and made a fool of himself in front of his children (Genesis 9), and Abraham didn't wait for God's blessing and had a child with his wife's servant (Genesis 16). The Bible doesn't shy away from showing the mess sin creates. If our churches had a Hall of Fame for Families, few Bible families would make it.

The Identity of Our Children

Scripture tells us that our children are created in the image of God (Genesis 1:26–28), and they are a blessing from the LORD: "Behold, children are a heritage from the LORD, the fruit of the womb a reward" (Psalm 127:3). Since children are a reward, verse 4 compares them to arrows in the hand of a warrior. If life is war, it would be wise to be well prepared. Many times children go astray because they are treated as "accidents" rather than the blessing that they are. Some parents call their children "oops" babies. Certainly, that will not help develop a correct view of the world or themselves. Psalm 127:5 affirms the blessedness of those "whose quiver is full of them." Just like a warrior benefits from a multitude of arrows, a home full of children is a blessing to the parents.

Parents as Teachers and the Word of God as Curriculum

God chose parents to be teachers, and He also wrote the curriculum. God chose Abraham to be the father of the nation of Israel, but he was supposed to teach his children "the way of the LORD." God says, "For I have chosen him, that he may command his children and his household after him to keep the way of the LORD by doing righteousness and justice, so that the LORD may bring to Abraham what he has promised him" (Genesis 18:19). God tasks parents to teach their children about God and who He is.

A lot of post-Exodus rituals are supposed to be didactic in nature, meaning they are meant to teach. Moses taught the elders of Israel that it would be the parents' responsibility to teach their children the meaning of God's mighty acts. "And when your children say to you, 'What do you mean by this service?' you shall say, 'It is the sacrifice of the LORD's Passover, for he passed over the houses of the people of Israel in Egypt, when he struck the Egyptians but spared our houses" (Exodus 12:26–27). Moses taught the new generation that would enter the Promised Land that the parents would need to teach the children how to love the LORD. "Only take care, and keep your soul diligently, lest you forget the things that your eyes have seen, and lest they depart from your heart all the days of your life. Make them known to your children and your children's children—how on the day that you stood before the LORD your God at Horeb, the LORD said to me, 'Gather the people to me, that I may let them hear my words, so that they may learn to fear me all the days that they live on the earth, and that they may teach their children so'" (Deuteronomy 4:9–10).

As parents, one of the first things our children should know from us is our testimony—how God worked His salvation in our lives. We also need to teach our children how God is working in our lives today. We have gained wisdom in our walk with the LORD so that one day when they are confronted with similar situations later in life, they might come and ask for our counsel since we have been on that road before. Eugene Merrill writes, "What is implied is that such an experience with the living God must be rooted and grounded in an historical event, an event that must be recalled and celebrated regularly and faithfully by all who participate in it and benefit from it."[91] Our experiences with God should be recounted to make known the ways of the LORD.

One of the most important passages in the Old Testament for the Israelites was what came to be known as the Shema. "Hear O Israel, the LORD our God, the LORD is one" (Deuteronomy 6:4). The role of the parents is again emphasized in the subsequent verses, "You shall love the LORD your God with all your heart and with all your soul and with all your might. And these words that I command you today shall be on your heart. You shall teach them diligently to your children, and shall talk of them when you sit in your house, and when you walk by the way, and when you lie down, and when you rise" (Deuteronomy 6:5–7). Children learn to love the LORD through their parents.

The word of God must be the foundational piece of any curriculum. If we only teach them math, science, literature, history, and philosophy, we help them major in minors without having the word of God as the foundation. Not only are we to teach about

91 Eugene H. Merrill, *Deuteronomy,* The New American Commentary, vol. 4 (Nashville: Broadman & Holman, 1994), 119.

God's Word, but we need to teach them about God Himself. In his book *This Momentary Marriage*, John Piper writes:

> The most fundamental task of a mother and father is to show God to the children. Children know their parents before they know God. This is a huge responsibility and should cause every parent to be desperate for God-like transformation. The children will have years of exposure to what the universe is like before they know there is a universe. They will experience the kind of authority there is in the universe and the kind of justice there is in the universe and the kind of love there is in the universe before they meet the God of authority and justice and love who created and rules the universe. Children are absorbing from dad his strength and leadership and protection and justice and love; and they are absorbing from mom her care and nurture and warmth and intimacy and justice and love—and, of course, all these overlap.[92]

The Shema gives us not only the curriculum but also the schedule: "When you sit in your house, and when you walk by the way, and when you lie down, and when you rise" (Deuteronomy 6:7). There is no time or place when God's Word should not be shared with our children. Today's technology can help. When our children were younger, and we had to drive them to school or sports events, we would listen to Scripture passages via a Bible app. Technology can become a tool for good when it comes to teaching our children the word of God.

And the job doesn't stop when our children leave the home. Generation after generation must benefit from God's Word: "Make them known to your children and your children's children" (Deuteronomy 4:9). The teaching is both taught and caught. "You shall therefore lay up these words of mine in your heart and in your soul, and you shall bind them as a sign on your hand, and they shall be as frontlets between your eyes. You shall teach

92 John Piper, *This Momentary Marriage: A Parable of Permanence* (Wheaton: Crossway, 2009), 143.

them to your children, talking of them when you are sitting in your house, and when you are walking by the way, and when you lie down, and when you rise" (Deuteronomy 11:18–19). The figures of speech here represent the totality of life. There is not a time and place where the parent does not impart to the children a love for God and His Word. Parenting is a holistic endeavor that leaves no room for compartmentalization.[93]

The historical books continue to emphasize the idea that parents need to teach their children about God. Today's parents might show their children pictures of people or places that remind them of God's faithfulness. In Old Testament times, one commemorated an important event by piling stones. Sometimes these stones looked like an altar, but this altar was not for sacrifices—they were for remembering what God has done. "When your children ask in time to come, 'What do those stones mean to you?' then you shall tell them that the waters of the Jordan were cut off before the ark of the covenant of the LORD. When it passed over the Jordan, the waters of the Jordan were cut off. So these stones shall be to the people of Israel a memorial forever" (Joshua 4:6–7).[94]

In his farewell address, Samuel, Israel's last judge, teaches us that we need to teach our children not just the word of God but also how to pray: "Far be it from me that I should sin against the LORD by ceasing to pray for you, and I will instruct you in the good and right way" (1 Samuel 12:23). The home must be a house of prayer. When I was a child, I would spend most summers at my grandparents' house in a small village in the southwestern part of Romania. Saturday evenings, our grandfather would sit us down

---

93 See also Deuteronomy 31:12–13, "Assemble the people, men, women, and little ones, and the sojourner within your towns, that they may hear and learn to fear the LORD your God, and be careful to do all the words of this law, and that their children, who have not known it, may hear and learn to fear the LORD your God, as long as you live in the land that you are going over the Jordan to possess," and 32:46, [Moses] said to them, "Take to heart all the words by which I am warning you today, that you may command them to your children, that they may be careful to do all the words of this law."

94 Stones as memorials are also present in the Jacob narrative (Genesis 28:18–22; 35:14) and in the post-Exodus wilderness narratives (Deuteronomy 27:2–3).

after dinner to listen to Radio Free Europe since a sermon would be preached via short-wave radio from the West. After that, he taught us to kneel by the bed and pray. I learned about the power of prayer on an uneven, dusty wooden floor. When I became a father, I taught my children how to kneel by their beds and pray. If we are to be disciple-makers, our children should be among our first disciples.

The psalmist affirms that the curriculum is who God is and what He has done, and those things are worth passing on to our children. Because parents are fallible, children must learn not only from their parents' successes but also from their failures. "We will not hide them from their children but tell to the coming generation the glorious deeds of the Lord, and his might, and the wonders that he has done. He established a testimony in Jacob and appointed a law in Israel, which he commanded our fathers to teach to their children, that the next generation might know them, the children yet unborn, and arise and tell them to their children, so that they should set their hope in God and not forget the works of God, but keep his commandments; and that they should not be like their fathers, a stubborn and rebellious generation, a generation whose heart was not steadfast, whose spirit was not faithful to God" (Psalm 78:4–8).

It is all a matter of discipleship. We are to be disciple-makers, disciples of Jesus Christ. Before I invest in my students, I need to invest in my children; they are my first disciples. I have no business telling other people about God and His love if I do not first tell my children about God and His love, grace, and mercy.

Parenting in the New Testament

The New Testament continues the Old Testament teaching about parenting. Paul quotes from the Ten Commandments when he instructs the believers in Ephesus, "Children, obey your parents in the Lord, for this is right. 'Honor your father and mother' (this is the first commandment with a promise), 'that it may go well with you and that you may live long in the land.' Fathers, do not provoke your children to anger, but bring them up in the discipline and instruction of the Lord" (Ephesians 6:1–4). Being a good father is the prerequisite of a church leader: "He must manage his own household well, with all dignity keeping his children submissive... Let deacons each be the husband of one wife, managing their children and their own households well" (1 Timothy 3:4, 12).[95]

One example of great parenting is Timothy's mother. As Paul writes to young Timothy, he reminds him of his godly upbringing. "I am reminded of your sincere faith, a faith that dwelt first in your grandmother Lois and your mother Eunice and now, I am sure, dwells in you as well" (2 Timothy 1:5). Later, Paul gives us a glimpse into how that faith was passed through three generations, and it all had to do with a wise curriculum. "But as for you, continue in what you have learned and have firmly believed, knowing from whom you learned it and how from childhood you have been acquainted with the sacred writings, which are able to make you wise for salvation through faith in Christ Jesus" (2 Timothy 3:14–15). The sacred writings of Scripture led Timothy to salvation through faith in Christ. And things have not changed. As we disciple our children to follow the Lord, we need to instill in them a love and passion for God's Word. It is this Word that is "living and active" that leads to a transformed life (Hebrews 4:12).

Parenting in the Book of Proverbs

The book of Proverbs has some key principles on both how to parent and what parents should teach their children. The household is the primary sphere of blessing. Clements notes that it is no surprise that by elevating the status of the household, "the teachers of wisdom celebrate this household as the sphere where good or evil prevail. The individual household effectively displaces the cult as the sphere of blessing."[96]

Wise Parents Discipline Their Children

Since children are not morally neutral, they need to be disciplined when they go off the straight and narrow path. Paul Tripp writes,

95 See also Titus 1:6.

96 R. E. Clements, *Wisdom in Theology* (Grand Rapids: Eerdmans, 1992), 131.

"Children are not born morally or ethically neutral...The child's problem is not information deficit. His/her problem is that he/she is a sinner. There are things within the heart of the sweetest little baby that, allowed to blossom and grow to fruition, will bring about eventual destruction."[97] While this might not be popular in our secular western culture, the concept of parental discipline is a foundational principle. "Whoever spares the rod hates his son, but he who loves him is diligent to discipline him" (Proverbs 13:24). The context of this verse is key. Verse 22 points to the fact that the parents leave an inheritance to their children, and this inheritance is material in nature. "A good man leaves an inheritance to his children's children, but the sinner's wealth is laid up for the righteous" (Proverbs 13:22). Moreover, parents also leave a moral and spiritual heritage for their children. That's where the rod of discipline comes in. Parents show that they love their children by disciplining them. In the third chapter of Proverbs, Solomon affirms that God's love and His discipline go hand in hand. "My son, do not despise the LORD's discipline or be weary of his reproof, for the LORD reproves him whom he loves, as a father the son in whom he delights" (Proverbs 3:11–12).[98] This rod is not a figure of speech but rather an actual rod used for parental discipline. The Canadian-American pastor H. A. Ironside says it best:

> Family discipline should be patterned after the divine discipline of Hebrews 12. It is not love, but the lack of it, that leaves a child to himself; to develop, unchecked, tendencies and propensities which shall result in future sorrow. Ours is a day of great laxity on this point. The coming generation will reap the bitter fruit of the absence of restraint and the evident aversion to chastening, so manifest in the majority of homes. A sickly sentimentality, supposedly wiser and more compassionate than God Himself, has made it fashionable to decry the use of the rod, as a relic of a barbarous age; but the differ-

97 Paul David Tripp, *Parenting: 14 Gospel Principles That Can Radically Change Your Family* (Wheaton: Crossway, 2016), 105.

98 The author of Hebrews quotes Proverbs 3:11–12 in Hebrews 12:5–6 as he argues that God deals with His people like a father deals with his children.

> ence in the character of children and the home is certainly in the favor of Scripture, as any one may see who will.[99]

The function of the rod is not meant to be punitive. "The rod and reproof give wisdom, but a child left to himself brings shame to his mother" (Proverbs 29:15). In the book of Proverbs, the wise and the fool are contrasted. There is no middle ground. The function of the rod is to bring wisdom. Tedd Tripp, author of *Shepherding a Child's Heart*, writes, "Fearing God and acquiring wisdom comes through the instrumentality of the rod...The child who is not submitting to parental authority is acting foolishly. He is rejecting the jurisdiction of God. He is living his life for the immediate gratification of his wants and desires. Ultimately, to refuse God's rule means to choose his own rule that leads to death. It is the height of foolishness."[100]

In his book, *Shepherding a Child's Heart,* Tedd Tripp outlines the meaning of the rod as it appears in the book of Proverbs.

A parental exercise	The rod of discipline is not meant for the pastor, is not meant for the school teacher; it is mandated by God for the parents.
An act of faith	As parents we obey God, not because we perfectly understand how the rod works, but because God has commanded it. The use of the rod is a profound expression of confidence in God's wisdom and the excellency of His counsel.
An act of faithfulness	The rod is an act of faithfulness towards the child. Recognizing that in discipline there is hope, refusing to be a willing party to his child's death, the parent undertakes the task; it is an expression of love and commitment.
A responsibility	It is not the parent determining to punish. It is the parent determining to obey. It is the parent, as God's representative, undertaking on God's behalf what God has called us to do. We are not on our own errand but fulfilling God's errand.

99 H. A. Ironside, *Notes on the Book of Proverbs* (Neptune, NJ: Loizeaux Brothers, 1908), 154.

100 Tedd Tripp, *Shepherding a Child's Heart* (Wapwallopen, PA: Shepherd Press, 1995), 107.

A physical punishment	The rod is the careful, timely, measured, and controlled use of physical punishment. The rod is never a venting of parental anger... It is not a response to feeling that his child has made things hard for the parent. It is always measured and controlled. The parent knows the proper measure of severity for this particular child at this particular time. The child knows how many swats are to come.
A rescue mission	The issue is never, "you have failed to obey ME." The only reason for a child to obey mom and dad is that God commands it. Failure to obey the parents then, means failure to obey God.

Figure 4.1 Tedd Tripp's Function of the Rod[101]

Wise Parents Affirm Their Children's Abilities

One of the best-known verses on parenting from Proverbs is "Train up a child in the way he should go; even when he is old he will not depart from it" (Proverbs 22:6). Garrett argues that a better interpretation is "Train a child in a manner befitting a child."[102] In his Proverbs commentary, the eighth-century monk Bede the Venerable comments on how the proverb is worded. "The proverb is formulated like this, therefore, to persuade its readers to be zealous for virtue in youth, lest they be unable as adults to learn the practices which they had despised to acquire at a tender age, for 'the odor of what with which a new vessel is imbued will endure for a long time.'"[103]

Waltke affirms that "the proverb promises the educator that his original, and early, moral initiative has a permanent effect on a person for good."[104] Indeed, the wise parent has respect for the individuality and vocation of the child.

---

101 Tedd Tripp, *Shepherding a Child's Heart,* 108–110.

102 Garrett, *Proverbs, Ecclesiastes, Song of Songs,* 188.

103 J. Robert Wright, ed., *Proverbs, Ecclesiastes, Song of Solomon,* Ancient Christian Commentary on Scripture , Old Testament IX (Downers Grove, IL: InterVarsity Press, 2005), 141.

104 Bruce K. Waltke, *The Book of Proverbs: Chapters 15–31,* The New International Commentary on the Old Testament (Grand Rapids: Eerdmans, 2005), 206.

This comes into sharper focus in the story of Benjamin West, the artist who came to be known as the "Raphael of America." Benjamin West was just trying to be a good babysitter for his little sister Sally. While his mother was out, Benjamin found some bottles of colored ink and proceeded to paint Sally's portrait. But by the time Mrs. West returned, ink blots stained the table, chairs, and floor. Benjamin's mother surveyed the mess without a word until she saw the picture. Picking it up, she exclaimed, "Why, it's Sally!" Instead of getting angry, she bent down and kissed her young son. In 1763, when he was twenty-five years old, Benjamin West was selected as a history painter to England's King George III. He became one of the most celebrated artists of his day. Commenting on his start as an artist, he said, "My mother's kiss made me a painter." Her encouragement did far more than a rebuke ever could have done.[105]

Figure 4.2 Benjamin West's "The Artist's Wife Elizabeth and Their Son Raphael"

Steinmann notes that "parents are to help steer a child to take advantage of his God-given abilities and talents. This will give him a good start in life and also serve him well throughout his entire life, both as he works in society and as he serves in the

105 *Our Daily Bread*, May 17, 1996.

church."[106] More importantly, "this proverb teaches that parents are to consecrate, discipline, and educate their children according to the Word of God in the way of wisdom, which is the way of faith and everlasting life."[107]

Wise Parents Teach Their Children to Avoid Evil Conduct

Wise parents teach their children to avoid gossip. "The words of a gossip are like delicious morsels; they go down in the inner parts of the body" (Proverbs 18:8; 26:22 NIV). Wise parents know that words have power. In fact, "death and life are in the power of the tongue" (Proverbs 18:21). The misuse of words when one gossips hurts not just the person gossiped about, but the gossiper self-inflicts hurt on himself. Garrett affirms that this verse "is a direct warning to the reader. Gossip makes its way to the innermost being of the hearer; that is, it corrupts the soul."[108]

Wise parents also teach their children to avoid envy. "A tranquil heart gives life to the flesh, but envy makes the bones rot" (Proverbs 14:30). Parents need to lead by example. If the parents are content, the children will learn to value contentment. As parents, we need to teach our children the context of the verse that is so often taken out of context, "I can do all things through him who strengthens me" (Philippians 4:13). Paul's main point is contentment. Paul writes, "Not that I am speaking of being in need, for I have learned in whatever situation I am to be content. I know how to be brought low, and I know how to abound. In any and every circumstance, I have learned the secret of facing plenty and hunger, abundance and need. I can do all things through him who strengthens me" (Philippians 4:11–13).

Many times, the love of money and envy are the one-two punch that brings one to his knees. Scripture teaches that "the love of money is a root of all kinds of evil" (1 Timothy 6:10). There is nothing wrong with being rich, however. Abraham was rich, and so were Job and Joseph of Arimathea. Money is amoral. But the love of money is both immoral and leads to all kinds of other evil.

---

106 Steinmann, *Proverbs,* 441–42.

107 Steinmann, *Proverbs,* 441–42.

108 Garrett, *Proverbs, Ecclesiastes, Song of Songs,* 214.

Wise Parents Teach Their Children to Embrace Godly Conduct

Wise parents teach their children to speak the truth in love. "Lying lips are an abomination to the LORD, but those who act faithfully are his delight" (Proverbs 12:22). According to the wisdom of God, words and actions go hand in hand. As parents, we need to emphasize truth-telling. "Truthful lips endure forever, but a lying tongue is but for a moment" (Proverbs 12:19). New Testament writers continue the same line of reasoning. To the church at Ephesus, Paul mentioned this idea twice. "Therefore, having put away falsehood, let each one of you speak the truth with his neighbor, for we are members one of another" (Ephesians 4:25). The "belt of truth" is an essential part of the believer's armor (Ephesians 6:14). But the greatest challenge is not just to speak truth, but to do so in love. "Rather, speaking the truth in love, we are to grow up in every way into him who is the head, into Christ" (Ephesians 4:15). Indeed, "speaking the truth without love is brutality, but love without truth is hypocrisy."[109] The concept of speaking the truth is set against those who practice false teaching, but it's also part of growing in Christ.

Wise parents teach their children to be industrious. To live in laziness is the foolish way. God invites us on the path of wisdom, which is the way of being industrious. "Go to the ant, O sluggard; consider her ways, and be wise. Without having any chief, officer, or ruler, she prepares her bread in summer and gathers her food in harvest. How long will you lie there, O sluggard? When will you arise from your sleep? A little sleep, a little slumber, a little folding of the hands to rest, and poverty will come upon you like a robber, and want like an armed man" (Proverbs 6:6–11). Growing up, my dad instilled in us this truth: "It is not a shame to work hard. It's a shame to steal, to lie, and to cheat. But it is not a shame to work hard." And not only did he teach us that, but he also lived it out. His father died when my dad was six years old, so after spending four years in an orphanage, he returned home to his mom and other brothers and sisters. At the age of sixteen, he

---

109 Warren W. Wiersbe, *The Bible Exposition Commentary,* vol. 2 (Wheaton, IL: Victor Books, 1996), 38.

entered the factory where he worked until the age of forty-eight, when he defected to the United States. The wise are industrious, but fools are lazy, and their laziness will make them suffer. Proverbs 19:15 says, "Slothfulness casts into a deep sleep, and an idle person will suffer hunger."

Gospel Principles for Parenting

In his book *Parenting: 14 Gospel Principles That Can Radically Change Your Family,* Paul David Tripp outlines some key principles that he believes are present in the Bible that could help those who want to rear their children in the fear and admonition of the LORD.

CONCEPT	PRINCIPLE
Calling	Nothing is more important in your life than being one of God's tools to form a human soul.
Grace	God never calls you to a task without giving you what you need to do it. He never sends you without going with you.
Law	Your children need God's law, but you cannot ask the law to do what only grace can accomplish.
Inability	Recognizing what you are unable to do is essential in good parenting.
Identity	If you are not resting as a parent in your identity in Christ, you will look for identity in your children.
Process	You must be committed as a parent to long-view parenting because change is a process and not an event.
Lost	As a parent you're not dealing just with bad behavior, but a condition that causes bad behavior.
Authority	One of the foundational heart issues in the life of every child is authority. Teaching and modeling the protective beauty of authority is one of the foundations of good parenting.
Foolishness	The foolishness inside your children is more dangerous to them than the temptation outside of them. Only God's grace has the power to rescue fools.

Character	Not all the wrong your children do is a direct rebellion to authority; much of the wrong is the result of a lack of character.
False gods	You are parenting a worshiper, so it's important to remember that what rules your child's heart will control his behavior.
Control	The goal of parenting is not control of behavior, but rather heart and life change.
Rest	It is only rest in God's presence and grace that will make you a joyful and patient parent.
Mercy	No parent gives mercy better than the one who is convinced that he desperately needs it himself.

Figure 4.3 14 Gospel principles that can radically change your family[110]

A Lesson from Church History[111]

John Wesley was the father of the Methodist movement, but his mother, Susanna, will always be remembered for being an exemplary parent. She raised ten children and published her "principal rules" for parenting. Some of these principles might be useful for today's parents as well.

Prayer. "The children of this family were taught, as soon as they could speak, the Lord's prayer, which they were made to say at rising and bedtime."

Worship through music. The day in the Wesley home began with the reading or singing of a Psalm.

Education. Nine to noon, and two to five were reserved for the children's education. Each child was taught how to read by the age of five.

110 Paul David Tripp, *14 Parenting Gospel Principles That Can Radically Change Your Family.*

111 This material is adapted from Charles Wallace, ed., *Susanna Wesley: The Complete Writings* (Oxford: OUP, 1997).

Discipline. While some infractions should be overlooked, Susanna wrote that "no willful transgression ought ever to be forgiven children without chastisement, less or more, as the nature and circumstances of the offence require."

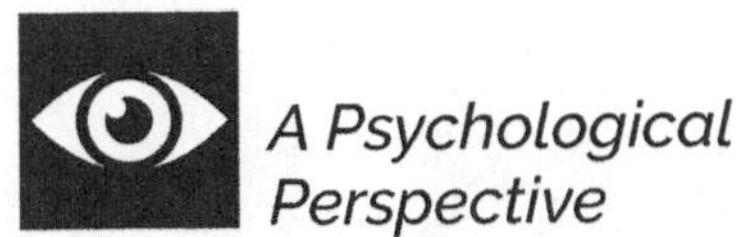

Reflections on Wise Parenting

Dr. Kevin Roberts

My son, keep your father's commandment, and forsake not your mother's teaching. —Proverbs 6:20

Parenting has never been for the faint of heart as it is both the best and worst job in the world, depending on the day! The role of parents is simultaneously loving our children as treasured gifts from God while discipling our children. Proverbs 22:15 teaches us that "Folly is bound up in the heart of a child, but the rod of discipline drives it far from him." To have a biblical view of parenting, we must first and foremost understand that God provided a structure and foundation for the family in the book of Genesis (Genesis 1:27–28; 2:24–25). Our role as parents is to steward the children that God has given us (Ephesians 6:4; Colossians 3:21). As parents of these children, we have responsibilities that Scripture lays out for us, including providing a loving and encouraging foundation for our kids, reducing their foolishness (Proverbs 22:15; 23:13; 29:17; Hebrews 12:7–10), and instilling wisdom (Proverbs 3:1–12, 14–16) into their daily lives. Figure 4.4 shows the three building blocks of biblical parenting. This chapter will seek to show how Proverbs illustrates the role of parents and the importance of following a biblical model.

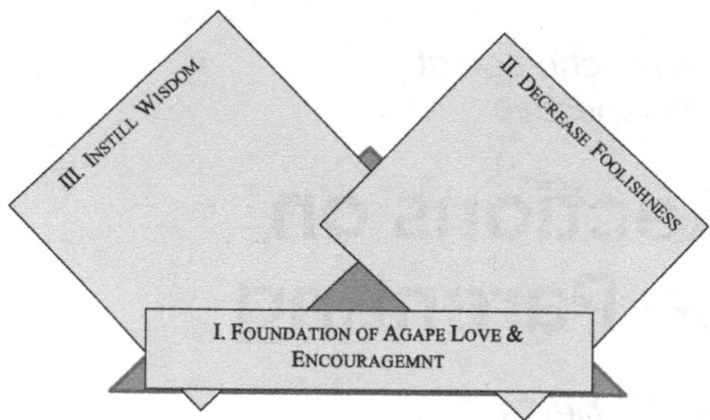

Figure 4.4 Providing a foundation of agape love and encouragement

Building a Foundation

God established the institution of the family in Genesis. Furthermore, in Ephesians 5:21–6:4, we are instructed on how to interact with each other. These verses illustrate that we humans are very social beings. Our role as parents is to help our children develop physically, emotionally, socially, and spiritually. To build a strong foundation, parents must demonstrate both agape love and encouragement.

Agape Love

Developing strong emotional attachments between young children and their parents is imperative.[112] This development of a loving and caring environment helps form secure attachments.[113] Throughout those early years of development, most children must determine if the adults and/or loved ones in their lives are trustworthy.[114] It is also the role of Christian parents to show agape love to their children (Deuteronomy 6:5–7; Romans 15:1), which requires a willingness to offer up sacrificial love for them. In this

112 John Bowlby, "Attachment and Loss; Retrospect and Prospect," *American Journal of Orthopsychiatry* 52, no. 4 (1982): 664–78.

113 M. D. S. Ainsworth et al., *Patterns of Attachment: A Psychological Study of the Strange Situation* (Erlbaum, 1978).

114 John Bowlby, "Attachment and Loss; Retrospect and Prospect."

expression of love, parents provide a base for the child. Children are also developing socially and must determine their own place in the world, but for this to occur, a child must first determine if he or she has developed and sustained trust.[115] Once children have a sense of trust and believe people can be loving and reliable, then it is time for them to explore other relationships.[116] As children receive agape love from their parents, they are free to experience other relationships and develop their own independence and identity apart from their parents.

If our goal is to love our children with agape love, then what are some of the keys to building up that relationship? This is done in very small ways each day. This means looking at them as you talk with them, smiling at them, and communicating their value by giving both quantity and quality time. It means listening to them and remaining silent enough to really hear them and expressing your deep love for them. They know you have good things to say, but you must *really* listen to fully comprehend the nature of their struggles. If you interrupt them and start teaching, then you can accidentally communicate that their opinions do not hold much value. Psalm 33:18 states, "Behold, the eye of the Lord is on those who fear him, on those who hope in his steadfast love." As we see in Scripture, it is in God's steadfast love that we must build this foundation of agape love for each child.

One of the things I appreciate in a good foundation is that I know what to expect as I walk on it. The same is true in child-rearing. Consistency in parenting results in many benefits for children, who need safety and consistency for proper development. When we have consistency in our home, it helps establish that our home is both secure and dependable. Children need to know what to expect, so routines are very important, as well as carrying through on the consequences of their misbehavior. As older children and adolescents age, however, the level of instruction can be altered to age-appropriate ways to provide more freedom and

115 Erik H. Erikson, *Identity and the Life Cycle: Selected Papers* (International Universities Press, 1959).

116 Erikson, *Identity and the Life Cycle: Selected Papers.*

opportunity to take personal responsibility for their decisions. As older children and adolescents are provided with more freedom, we must not forget our role as parents to be ongoing sources of encouragement, to embrace the tasks of life, and most importantly, to seek to honor God.

Providing Encouragement

Many analogies exist to describe the importance of encouraging our children. I have always seen parenting in terms of a bank account. The transactions with a bank involve both deposits and withdrawals. In this analogy, encouraging and affirming statements serve as deposits, and criticisms or corrections serve as withdrawals. You need to keep a reasonable balance of both encouragement and correction. Colossians 3:20–21 states it this way, "Children obey your parents in everything, for this pleases the LORD. Fathers, do not provoke your children, lest they become discouraged." We must be slow to discipline, thus, we do not do so out of anger, provoking discouragement. Our children know when we are disciplining out of anger or revenge versus out of reluctant but needed discipline. Essentially, we must struggle to find the balance between driving out the foolishness of sin in their hearts and providing wise words that bring life. This is stated clearly in Proverbs 12:18, "There is one whose rash words are like sword thrusts, but the tongue of the wise brings healing." It is within our ability to provide both encouragement and consistent discipline to provide a healthy development of a child's identity.

Adlerian therapy, which is better known as Individual Psychology, teaches the idea that human beings fail to complete the tasks of life (love, work, community, self, and spirituality) because they are discouraged. In contrast, people who are properly encouraged to pursue life tasks that contribute to their positive mental health have the courage to take risks and explore their world. In parenting, this encouragement can take many forms, including learning how to have difficult conversations that seek to resolve conflict peaceably. Another example is affirming a child's efforts when he or she displays honesty in the face of an easier path.

Finally, parents should encourage their children when they display humility and honesty with themselves to both acknowledge and take responsibility for their own behavior (Proverbs 6:6–11; 21:25; 28:13). Manaster and Corsini describe the powerful role of providing encouragement for our children's goal pursuits in this way: "Two people may have exactly the same goals, the same amount of energy, everything may appear identical, but one has the courage and pursues goals actively, persistently, intelligently and consistently, while another person will hesitate, fumble and back away."[117] Encouragement has the power to change a child's trajectory throughout his or her life!

Reducing Foolishness

In the first section, we addressed the need for providing a loving base from which our children will draw upon to learn to trust in others, explore their environment, and develop a sense of their own identity. We also explored the importance of encouraging our children. However, the book of Proverbs warns us repeatedly about the dangers of failing to drive out foolishness from the child (Proverbs 13:20). The role of reducing foolishness, according to Proverbs, has several components, including disciplining to increase self-control, providing choices to our children, and teaching them to accept personal responsibility. Figure 4.5 outlines different types of discipline and consequences.

117 Manaster and Corsini, *Individual Psychology,* 11.

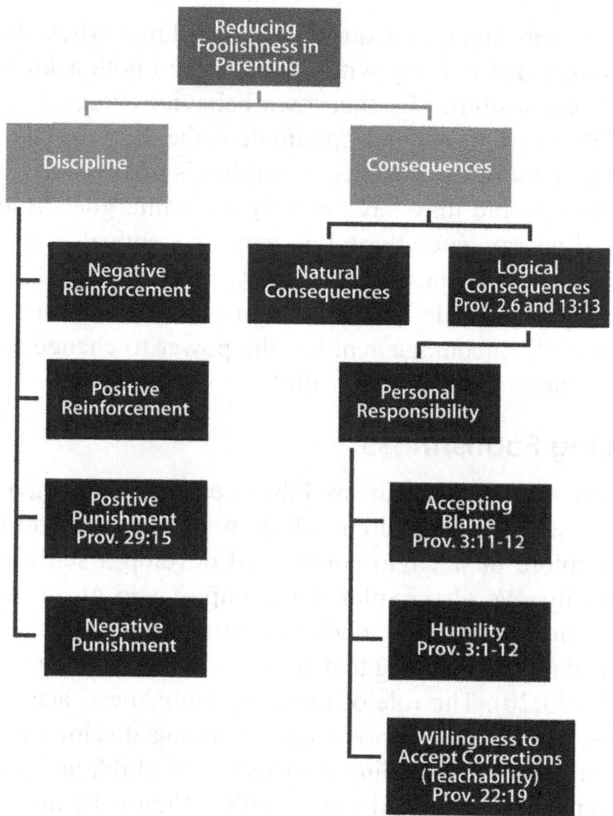

Figure 4.5 How to reduce foolishness through discipline

The Components of Discipline

Parenting requires an ongoing balance of love, giving kids age-appropriate freedoms, providing loving discipline, and holding them accountable for their behavior. Scripture is clear that if we want to build self-control in our children, we must be willing to discipline them. Proverbs 29:17 states, "Discipline your son, and he will give you rest; he will give delight to your heart." As Christian parents, we hope to raise our children to be wise and to fear the LORD. But sometimes that requires discipline just as God disciplines us (Proverbs 3:12). Our children need discipline, and anyone who has raised kids knows that they desire it. For children, discipline shows parental engagement and consistency, thus giving them a sense of stability and safety that they need as they develop. They need to know their limits and the boundaries of appropriate behavior, and the potential consequences of violating those same rules or limitations. Parents need to view discipline as a demonstration of God's love for us and for our kids through consistent, loving discipline with the purpose of teaching. Proverbs warns us that withholding discipline can have severe consequences. "Do not withhold discipline from a child; if you strike him with a rod, he will not die. If you strike him with the rod, you will save his soul from Sheol" (Proverbs 23:13–14). Before disciplining, it is often wise to pause and reflect, asking ourselves what message we are trying to communicate through this discipline. We do not want to demonstrate our own lack of emotional restraint/self-control through disciplining out of anger. The use of appropriate discipline communicates that a child is loved and worth the effort of ongoing correction and time investment.

There are many ways to discipline our children (Proverbs 13:24; 22:6, 15; 29:15). Scripture makes it clear that from a very young age, we need to discipline because failure to do so could have dire consequences. Proverbs 29:15 states, "The rod and reproof give wisdom, but a child left to himself brings shame to his mother." The Bible is clear that discipline may involve both a rod and a reprimand. The psychological literature addresses four specific types of disciplining and learning models for children, which include positive and negative punishment, along with positive and negative reinforcement.[118]

Positive and Negative Reinforcement

If we want our children to learn, we can use reinforcement as a means of cementing ideas into their heads. We often refer to positive reinforcement as a reward. If a child shows compassion or is reading their Bible unprompted, then the child may receive praise for this type of behavior. This recognition serves as a reinforce-

118 Sarah Grison and Michael Gazzaniga, *Psychology in Your Life* (W. W. Norton & Company, Inc., 2022).

ment and encourages similar behavior in the future. There is also negative reinforcement, which is often thought of as receiving some form of relief.[119] An example is a child who is repeatedly reminded or nagged about taking out the garbage. When the child finally complies, the parent stops reminding him, giving the child relief from the nagging parental figure.

Positive and Negative Punishment

There are also two different types of punishment which include positive and negative punishment.[120] In parenting literature, we often utilize the term *positive punishment* because we are working with the child to change his or her behavior. As Grison and Gazzaniga stated, "Positive punishment occurs when the addition of a stimulus decreases the probability of a behavior being repeated."[121] The term *positive punishment* references the need to add something unpleasant for behavior that parents deem undesirable.[122] For example, if a child gets angry and hits another child, then they are likely to receive a severe scolding or a spanking as a means of decreasing the likelihood that this behavior would ever happen again.

In contrast, *negative punishment* is when something is removed as a result of undesirable behavior. For example, if a child starts swearing, then the source of this swearing may be removed, such as his or her ability to watch television or stream a movie. One of the mistakes we make in disciplining is not being clear and consistent with our standards. The punishment should match the sin or crime that was committed. The goal is to lessen foolishness, not to make someone look perfect. If the goal is perfect behavior, then we accidentally send the message that mistakes must be covered up. "For the wrongdoer will be paid back for the wrong he has done, and there is no partiality" (Colossians 3:25).

---

119 Grison and Gazzaniga, *Psychology in Your Life.*

120 Grison and Gazzaniga, *Psychology in Your Life.*

121 Grison and Gazzaniga, *Psychology in Your Life*, 240.

122 Grison and Gazzaniga, *Psychology in Your Life.*

Using Consequences to Build Responsible Choice-makers

As Christian parents, we want our children to grow up to both love and fear God. We also want our children to grow into responsible and wise decision makers. But how do we do this? Do we give them tons of rules? Do we make all their decisions for them? Or do we give them tons of freedom, and trust God to direct them? How do we create wise decision makers who will not stray from the path of following God?

As parents, it is often very difficult to sit back and watch your children make mistakes and learn through them. We do not enjoy the pain and suffering we experience from our own poor decisions, so we try to prevent our kids from making those same mistakes. It's even more difficult to watch them experience the pain and suffering of bad choices. Instead, we often want to rush to their defense and protect them from the difficult realities of making bad decisions to ease our own suffering. However, if we seek to protect our children from the natural or logical consequences of their choices, then we can sometimes be guilty of spoiling the child or unintentionally communicating that they are not capable of making responsible choices. Worse yet, we can send a message that others are responsible instead of our own child.

The idea of *natural consequences* is built on the concept that we must learn from the painful mistakes of our past. In developing logical consequences for children, Bullard explains that the consequences given must be appropriate for the severity of the crime, fair or equal for all, and the consequences must be for violations that are against long-standing rules or socially acceptable behavior.[123] As parents, we should not enjoy giving these consequences. We should feel disappointed and saddened when these consequences are experienced due to the child's poor behavior.[124] Sometimes, it is wise for us to intervene, especially when children are younger, and educate and model the appropriate response.

123 Maurice L. Bullard, "Logical and Natural Consequences," in *Alfred Adler: His Influence on Psychology Today*, ed. Harold H. Mosak (Park Ridge: Noyes Press, 1973).

124 Manaster and Corsini, *Individual Psychology.*

However, we also want our children to learn from their mistakes, and this must sometimes be done by allowing the mistakes and natural consequences to occur. Manaster and Corsini describe it this way: "What the procedure amounts to is doing nothing. The parent, employer, trainer, or supervisor, essentially (a) gives information about the consequences of the behavior or non-behavior to the person to be trained (only if this seems necessary), (b) looks on while the person acts or does not act properly, and (c) permits the person to receive the natural consequences of the behavior."[125] By allowing them to experience natural and logical consequences, we often avoid using criticism or correction since life is providing the lesson. Instead, we can sympathize and work to ensure that proper interpretations of the consequences are occurring.

Building Wisdom

As was stated in the previous two sections, relationship, discipline, and natural or logical consequences are required for a child to continue to learn and grow. In this section, we examine two main models of building wisdom into our children. Both models require that parents have a strong understanding of God's Word, for we are responsible for both teaching and modeling Christ-like behavior.

Teaching God's Truth

Teaching is done with a heart of love and a spirit of patience as opportunities to instruct are presented. Therefore, the best teaching is often done during informal moments and when the time is right. These messages are often lessons that get passed down from generation to generation, as was instructed in Deuteronomy 4:9, "Only take care, and keep your soul diligently, lest you forget the things that your eyes have seen, and lest they depart from your heart all the days of your life. Make them known to your children and your children's children." However, these lessons need not be long sermons. Often young children will only need a few words of instruction. If you are going to teach them, then do it in an age-ap-

125 Manaster and Corsini, *Individual Psychology,* 220–21.

propriate way and make it positive or even fun! Do not teach just to teach; instead, choose to teach in the moment (Deuteronomy 6:7) and especially when they ask questions (Exodus 12:26). The teachings of the mother are illustrated in Proverbs 31:1–31, which starts by stating, "The words of King Lemuel. An oracle that his mother taught him." We see the need for ongoing teaching and memorization of God's Word for our children, and in the New Testament, we see this message reiterated in 1 Timothy 4:10–11, "For to this end we toil and strive, because we have our hope set on the living God, who is the Savior of all people, especially of those who believe. Command and teach these things." We are clearly instructed as parents to pass on God's message to others.

Modeling Our Faith

Teaching wisdom can also come in the form of modeling. Christian parents should seek to model Christ-like behavior to their children in such a way that promotes intrigue (Deuteronomy 6:20) and helps them make sense of the world around them. We do this through teaching God's truth but also in the modeling of our faith, especially in our most intimate relationships and with our children. In this section, we will seek to discuss how observational learning influences the development of our kids. How does this development occur?[126]

Albert Bandura was the first to write about observational learning, which involves watching others, retaining the information observed, and then performing those behaviors.[127] Bandura maintained that observational learning is not just copying someone else's behavior, but instead, it comes in four distinct phases: attention, retention, reproduction, and motivation.[128] This means that all four elements are essential for real learning to take place. For example, if you do not have a good relationship with one of your children, then they are less likely to pay close attention to your

126 Albert Bandura, *Social Learning Theory* (Englewood Cliffs, NJ: Prentice-Hall, 1977).

127 Grison and Gazzaniga, *Psychology in Your Life*.

128 Bandura, *Social Learning Theory*.

behaviors because of their perceptions.[129] The retention and reproduction phases involve how accurate you are at remembering what you've observed and then being able to apply this image to alter behavior. The last of his stages of observational learning involves the level of motivation of the observer and whether there was a potential reward for good behavior or even avoidance of potential harm. We saw an example of this behavior with Abraham and his son, Isaac (Genesis 12:4–18; 26:6–11), when Isaac used the same lie of telling foreign kings that their wives were, in fact, their sisters. Abraham modeled this type of behavior, and Isaac learned to replicate this behavior to protect himself from harm. This example shows that observational learning can significantly influence the next generation as we model behavior for our children.

We often refer to this observational learning as modeling. It is instrumental in the development of young kids, adolescents, and adults learning the socialization process in human interactions.[130] Therefore, the very best teaching method and the most important modeling will be in how we love our spouses, serve one another, and demonstrate the importance of faith at home. We want each of our children to develop a hunger and thirst for the things of God (Proverbs 22:6). This means that our children need to have great role models that play important roles in their lives. We see in Proverbs 22:6 the importance of parental role models, "Train up a child in the way he should go; even when he is old he will not depart from it." These role models provide us an example of how the wise act and thus produce wise followers, as depicted in Proverbs 13:20. However, Bandura illustrated that other things could increase observational learning, including the status or perception of warmth of the individual speaking or if the individual lacks confidence, which is especially true in unfamiliar or novel situations.[131]

---

129 Bandura, *Social Learning Theory.*

130 Grison and Gazzaniga, *Psychology in Your Life.*

131 Bandura, *Social Learning Theory.*

Application Exercises and Questions for Wise Parenting

1. Find and pray about the best environment for teaching your children about foolishness and life's lessons. For each child, the process of learning these scriptural lessons can be played out in sports, music, arts, and through other venues, depending on the child's interest and gifting.
2. Sometimes the best answer is to wait and pray instead of jumping in to help our kids when they make mistakes. Sometimes to wait and pray is to allow the natural and logical consequences to occur.
3. We are to be realistic and know that our kids are going to embarrass us as they learn. In parenting, we must learn to see embarrassment as an opportunity to help them grow closer to God and others.
4. Our children need to develop wise decision-making abilities, and that is difficult to develop without learning through failure. I pulled each of my kids aside before entering high school and told them that I would now start giving them a few more decisions and that we would progressively give them more choices as they learned to make wise decisions. I wanted them to have an opportunity to practice and fail while they were still home, and we could use mistakes as an opportunity to learn and grow.
5. Be open and honest with your children. An important lesson is to remember to keep the doors of communication open with your children. Talk to them honestly about your successes and failures as a parent. They need to know those facts and what issues required significant deliberation and prayer on your part. You communicate their worth when you deliberate and pray over complex or novel situations and simultaneously demonstrate your choice to lean into God and not on your own way. This message, along with discussing failures, demonstrates real humility and our absolute dependence on

God. We are not superheroes, and our children need to see us show humility before God and our willingness to give up our ego. They will see our commitment to being faithful to God even when things appear confusing or messy.

Wise Parenting at Church

Pastor Knute Larson

The church, of course, should be a defender of the family—and it seems strange to write it that way. But many people, including those leading influential and popular media organizations, have downplayed the importance of the spiritually and emotionally strong family. They have dissed it, trying to drown thoughts about its importance. The church knows that family is the vital unit of human beings, with marriage itself being a picture of Christ and the Church, and the parent-child relationship the most important teaching and modeling connection in the church. Certainly, sermons and groups at the church often correct the truth being taught to what it looks like in the home, but the homes then must back that up constantly with teaching, reinforcing, and modeling.

While the church must honor the importance of the single life—think Jesus and Paul, among others—it also seeks to inspire families to live up to the call to godly and others-focused love in the home, neighborhood, workplace, and school.

Church looks like a very safe place to take children. Church reinforces what parents have taught at home when they got it from the Bible. Church calls for family worship at home also.

Sermons and lessons speak highly of marriage, calling adults and children to honor sexual purity and marital faithfulness. They also reinforce what the Proverbs writers say, by God's inspiration, about the discipline of children and teens, affirming the abilities and good desires of the kids and avoiding sinful actions.

Critics and dropouts of the church have often experienced what Proverbs teaches, that "death and life are in the power of the tongue" (Proverbs 18:21). And they have "died" to the church because of what someone said. A strong church teaches its people and its families to be in control, lovingly, of what they say.

Why Wise Parenting Is So Important

Family life was meant to have an important place in God's plan. Families are everything in the sense that almost everyone comes from a family, so it needs to be modeled well by leaders at church and spoken of with high regard from the pulpit and lectern—no more jokes about "the little woman" or stories that promote extravagant or harsh spiritual leadership. And clearly, all church leaders, referenced as elders and deacons in 1 Timothy 3 and Titus 1, are to be exemplary in their love and faithfulness to God and each other.

While churches are not meant to be substitutes for parents, they certainly are called to teach the importance of the home and the pattern God draws for it. We cannot get around the fact that some parents abdicate much of the teaching and modeling of the Scriptures at home, so the church gets excited to teach neighbor children when they do outreach and when church families bring other children. The ideal is for children to be raised in a family. He created males and females and called them to reproduce. So the family is a high priority for God to be honored at church. The honor that King Lemuel gives to "the wife of noble character" in the last chapter of Proverbs and the beautiful picture of family priorities that she models should characterize church families, at least in intent and high motives. (Some of us think this "wonder woman" was extremely extraordinary and should not be held up as the norm every Mother's Day!) One of the things that makes the earth tremble and weakens it is "an unloved woman when she gets a husband," Proverbs 30:21–23 says. It should make the church shake also and try to change this weak situation through the family and care ministry. The sad fact that the divorce rate is almost as high in the organized church as it is in the world of unbelievers should alarm us and call us to Christ and His ways. The church must never crowd out the family in the lives of children and teens, but we can seek to support the family with teaching and ideas and a mood of honor to each home.

Why Wise Parenting Does Not Always Show Up

People—all of us—fail a lot, even when working on the family issues so clear in Proverbs and all throughout the Bible. And because the church should be and often has been forgiving, many stay in the church with broken marriages that either need a lot of work or after divorce. And that is a good thing and wise of them. But the church leans too far when its leaders and teachers change or weaken the Bible's teaching on family so as not to offend those who have failed or been victims of failure in marriage and family. Also, as sinners all, we do fail, but some of us seek forgiveness and want to stay in the church.

So, this place is not completely exemplary in the area of family living and parenting. Of course not. To be a haven for the hurting and a hospital for the ailing, the church will have people who are not doing well in family living but who are learning and watching, just as Jesus, while on earth and even now, invites strugglers into His company. One of our strongest touches with people outside the church, in our church in Akron, was the Thursday evening Divorce Recovery ministry. Sadly, when I was in fourth grade and my parents divorced, the church waved goodbye to us. It did not know what to do. Perfection will always be a goal, with progress being made, but so will help and support for the imperfect, which at times is all of us.

Clearly, church leaders are called to be exemplary in their marriage and family examples. (See 1 Timothy and Titus and their list of qualifications related to the family for church pastors and servants.)

What Each of Us Can Do Personally for Wise Parenting

"A man who loves wisdom brings joy to his father" (Proverbs 29:3) and to his family and church. Each of us can believe that discretion will protect us and understanding will guard us, as we are wise to follow the guidelines of Proverbs and stay within the guardrails of all of God's Word for us. That will make a healthy church that models a good family.

The wise writer asks us all to "let love and faithfulness never leave you…write them on the tablet of your heart," and we will "win favor and a good name in the sight of God and man" and the church and those viewing it (Proverbs 3:3, 4 NIV). We can all do that, and the church will shine.

We can all be strong in our commitment to Christ as a single person or a family member. We can learn that love is "righteous action to meet the needs of another," with fear-of-God wisdom that does life very close to correctly. We can also teach it well, together with help from scholars and experts on the practice of marriage and parenting.

Scary as it may sound to some, people of the Proverbs should help others by lovingly pointing out blind spots to friends who mistreat someone in their marriage or family. The Golden Rule from the New Testament applies here, as do many Proverbs that tell us to share wisdom as a friend. And all who are married and/or are parents can be wise in disciplining their children, as taught in Proverbs. We can all help to affirm the abilities of other children, for they are sometimes neglected by their parents. We can support the goals of Proverbs that children and youth should avoid evil conduct, including laziness, and embrace godly habits, including hard work.

A Personal Prayer for Wise Parenting

Praise: Praise God for ways you have experienced His love and faithfulness as your heavenly Father, and for His holiness in all ways.

Repent: All of us can admit failures as a family—do that, confessing any lack of love or forgiveness toward one another. Give thanks for His kind forgiveness that is promised.

Ask: For members of your family and their needs, and for your church to be a strong friend and support to families. Pray for your loved ones by name.

Yield: Think of any applications of love and care for your family directed or implied in Proverbs. Commit your ways of single life or family life to our LORD.

CHAPTER 5

Patience

A Theological Perspective

The Wise Are Patient

Dr. Tiberius Rata

To lengthen my patience is the best way to shorten my troubles.
—George Swinnock

As children, we are taught that patience is a virtue. The New Testament teaches that love is patient (1 Corinthians 13:4), but patience seems out of place in the Old Testament, where people lie to get out of trouble (Genesis 12 and 20) and seem to get away with murder (2 Samuel 11). Or are we not looking deeply enough?

Patience in the Old Testament

Patience is one of God's character qualities. In the theophany prompted by Moses's request that he would like to see God, Yahweh appears to him and describes Himself as one who is patient. "The LORD passed before him and proclaimed, 'The LORD, the LORD, a God merciful and gracious, slow to anger, and abounding in steadfast love and faithfulness'" (Exodus 34:6). The Hebrew expression translated "slow to anger" is literally "long-nosed" "with its probable origin as an idiomatic expression in the idea of anger being seen in some larger animals by the way that they snort."[132] The expression can also be translated as "long-suffering" or "long forbearing.

132 Stuart, *Exodus,* The New American Commentary, 715.

Moses repeats God's character qualities to the new generation that will enter the Promised Land. "The LORD is slow to anger and abounding in steadfast love, forgiving iniquity and transgression, but he will by no means clear the guilty, visiting the iniquity of the fathers on the children, to the third and the fourth generation" (Numbers 14:18). Isn't the whole history of rebellious Israel a testament to God's patience? As God provided for them manna from heaven, instead of saying "thank you," the Israelites complained that the menu was limited to manna and quail (Exodus 16:13, 31). As God provided for their freedom from Egypt, instead of saying "thank you," the Israelites worshipped a golden calf (Exodus 32). And yet, Yahweh was patient with them.

Looking back at their history after the return from exile, Nehemiah recognized God's patience. In his prayer, Nehemiah contrasts Israel's faithlessness with God's love and patience. "But you are a God ready to forgive, gracious and merciful, slow to anger and abounding in steadfast love, and did not forsake them" (Nehemiah 9:17). God's patience is not restricted to the nation. David is grateful for God's patience toward him and appeals to God's love and patience when in danger from his enemies. "O God, insolent men have risen up against me; a band of ruthless men seeks my life, and they do not set you before them. But you, O LORD, are a God merciful and gracious, slow to anger and abounding in steadfast love and faithfulness" (Psalm 86:14–15).[133]

Patience in the New Testament

In Jesus's teachings, patience is the fruit of the seed planted in good soil. "As for that in the good soil, they are those who, hearing the word, hold it fast in an honest and good heart, and bear fruit with patience" (Luke 8:15). Paul encourages the believers who are going through persecution to be "patient in tribulation" (Romans 12:12). The first characteristic of love in 1 Corinthians 13 is that it is patient (1 Corinthians 13:4). The literal translation is "love waits patiently." Paul continues the idea introduced in

133 See also Psalms 103:8 and 145:8. The prophets remind Israel and the nations of God's patience. See Joel 2:13, Jonah 4:2, and Nahum 1:3a.

the Old Testament that God is patient. "Paul's description of love begins with this twofold description of God, who through Christ has shown himself forbearing and kind toward those who deserve divine judgment."[134]

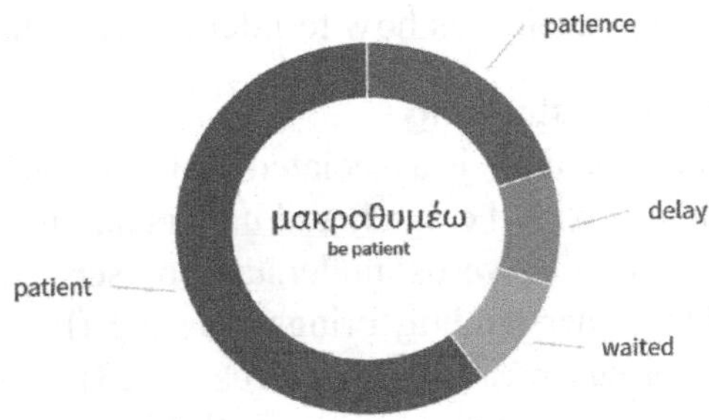

Figure 5.1 The verb "to be patient" in the New Testament

The noun translated as "patience" appears a few times in the New Testament. Paul uses the word to describe how God dealt with people in the past (Romans 9:22), and Peter uses the word to describe God's dealing with us now. "The LORD is not slow to fulfill his promise as some count slowness, but is patient toward you, not wishing that any should perish, but that all should reach repentance" (2 Peter 3:9). Paul uses the same word as he encourages the believers in Colossae to be clothed with "compassionate hearts, kindness, humility, meekness, and patience" (Colossians 3:12). Patience is what Paul armed himself with as he served God in the midst of opposition and danger (2 Corinthians 6:3–10). The same word is used as part of the fruit of the Spirit. "But the fruit of the Spirit is love, joy, peace, patience, kindness, goodness, faithfulness" (Galatians 5:22).

134 Roy E. Ciampa and Brian S. Rosner, *The First Letter to the Corinthians*, The Pillar New Testament Commentary (Grand Rapids, MI; Cambridge, U.K.: William B. Eerdmans Publishing Company, 2010), 642.

Patience in the Book of Proverbs

The expression "slow to anger" is synonymous with the word "patient."[135] The book of Proverbs is very practical and helps us in day-to-day matters. Patience helps us not just in our personal development but it teaches us how to interact with others.

Patience and Understanding

The word "understanding" is associated with wisdom in the book of Job. "Wisdom is with the aged, and understanding in length of days" (Job 12:12). In Proverbs, understanding serves as guardian (Proverbs 2:11), understanding brings blessing (Proverbs 3:13), understanding brings pleasure (Proverbs 10:23), understanding helps walk on the straight and narrow path (Proverbs 15:21), understanding gives one a cool (refreshing) spirit (Proverbs 17:27), understanding pays off dividends in the end (Proverbs 19:8), and understanding helps one dig deep out of the deep water of the soul (Proverbs 20:5). Someone of great understanding is patient. "Whoever is *slow to anger* has great understanding, but he who has a hasty temper exalts folly" (Proverbs 14:29).

Someone's wisdom and understanding can be seen in the way they act and react to life's multi-faceted and complex situations. On the other hand, someone's folly is on full display, and a "hasty temper" can cause danger to one's life and reputation. Anger is never portrayed in a positive light in the book of Proverbs. "A man of wrath stirs up strife, and one given to anger causes much transgression" (Proverbs 29:22). The first-century church leader James exhorts the believers to be "quick to hear, slow to speak, and slow to anger" (James 1:19). Why? James goes on to affirm that "the anger of man does not produce the righteousness of God" (James 1:20). If we do a survey of great men and women throughout his-

135 In Ecclesiastes 7:8, the who is "long in spirit" is contrasted with the one who is proud in spirit. "While the opposite of pride is humility, that humility can be demonstrated through patience. Indeed, wisdom literature always associates the fool with anger and lack of patience, while the wise is patient." See Tiberius Rata and Kevin Roberts, *Fear God and Keep His Commandments: A Practical Exposition of Ecclesiastes* (Winona Lake, IN: BMH, 2016), 86.

tory, we never find one who was known for their anger but I'm sure we can all remember those who were slow to anger.

The first pastor I had in the US. was brother Pitt Popovici, a humble and patient man who I have never seen to be angry (I'm not saying he was never angry, but I've never seen him lose his temper). As the pastor of the Romanian church of Bellflower, Calif., he dealt with a lot of issues as any church would, but he always dealt with issues in a calm demeanor. The wisest of the wise would say that Pastor Pitt was a James 1 man, slow to speak and slow to anger.

Patience and Conflict

One cannot avoid conflict, and the book of Proverbs shows us that one displays wisdom by how they resolve conflict. One cannot avoid conflict, but one can control how conflict is handled. It all depends on the people involved in the conflict. According to the book of Proverbs, "A hot-tempered man stirs up strife, but he who is *slow to anger* quiets contention" (Proverbs 15:18). I am reminded of the words of Jesus in the Sermon on the Mount, "Blessed are the peacemakers for they shall be called the children of God" (Matthew 5:9). There are peace-breakers, peace-fakers, and peace-makers.

Peace-breakers

The peace-breakers are those people who go out of their way to break down relationships to cause trouble and division. They disagree with everything and everybody. For such people, the Bible has these words in Romans 16:17–18 (NIV): "I urge you, brothers and sisters, to watch out for those who cause divisions and put obstacles in your way that are contrary to the teaching you have learned. Keep away from them. For such people are not serving our LORD Christ, but their own appetites." The easiest way to be a peace-breaker is with your tongue. James writes that "the tongue is a small member, yet it boasts of great things. How great a forest is set ablaze by such a small fire! And the tongue is a fire, a world of unrighteousness. The tongue is set among our members, staining the whole body, setting on fire the entire course of life, and set on fire by hell" (James 3:5–6).[136]

Peace-fakers

The peace-fakers are the ones who prefer peace over truth. Peace-fakers see "peace" as simply the absence of any argument or discord. They will go to any length to avoid any conflict or confrontation. A pastor named Bill tells of a time when one of his close friends took a bad turn in life, and he asked him to lunch so they could talk. Over the meal, Bill said to his friend, "I'm not trying to run your life, but I am concerned about the direction it's taking." His friend got so mad that he jumped over the table and punched Bill in the face. So, Bill backed off and said, "Sorry, I'll never mention this again." And he didn't. His friend shipwrecked his life, and when Bill saw his friend again, he had to tell him, "I failed you. I should have said, 'Hit me if you have to, if it makes you feel better, but I'm going to stay on your case because I'm concerned about your future, my friend.'"

Peace-makers

On the other hand, peace-makers care about the peace between someone and God first and foremost. If the peace-maker has a friend or a loved one who is not saved and is at war with God, then the peace-maker will do everything they can to bring that person to a saving knowledge of Christ. Peace-makers tell the truth in love even if it hurts. They want real peace. Jesus is our example of the perfect peacemaker. He came to make peace between humanity and God. Paul writes to the church in Ephesus, "For he himself is our peace, who has made us both one and has broken down in his flesh the dividing wall of hostility by abolishing the law of commandments expressed in ordinances, that he might create in

---

136 James goes on to elaborate on the power of words. "For every kind of beast and bird, of reptile and sea creature, can be tamed and has been tamed by mankind, but no human being can tame the tongue. It is a restless evil, full of deadly poison. With it we bless our Lord and Father, and with it we curse people who are made in the likeness of God. From the same mouth come blessing and cursing. My brothers, these things ought not to be so" (James 3:7–10).

himself one new man in place of the two, so making peace, and might reconcile us both to God in one body through the cross, thereby killing the hostility (Ephesians 2:14–16).

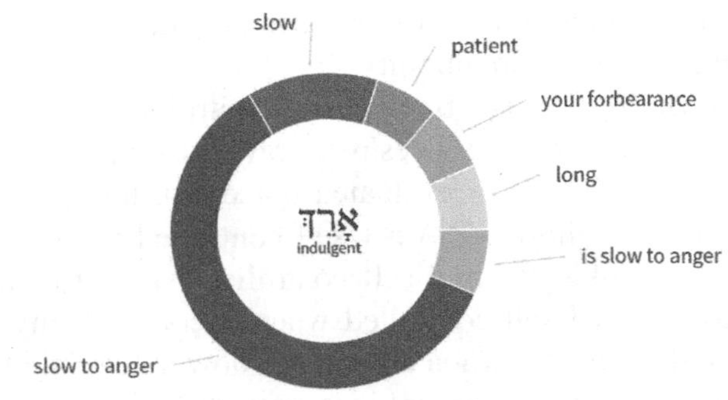

Figure 5.2 The word "patient/slow to anger" in the Old Testament

Patience and Greatness

"Whoever is *slow to anger* is better than the mighty, and he who rules his spirit than he who takes a city" (Proverbs 16:32). The parallelism here compares one who is slow to anger with one who rules his spirit. This is the definition of self-control. Ancient Near Eastern (ANE) people declared "mighty" those who conquered armies or ruled cities. In the Old Testament, Nimrod was characterized as a "mighty hunter" (Genesis 10:9), Goliath was considered by the Philistines to be their great warrior (1 Samuel 17:51), and David's bodyguards were "mighty men" (2 Samuel 20:7). But when it comes to everyday living, greatness is measured by one's self-control.

The greatness of the wise is to be desired more than military warriors or civic leaders. In contrast with the wise is the fool. "A man of quick temper acts foolishly" (Proverbs 14:17), and "he who has a hasty temper exalts folly" (Proverbs 14:29). Indeed, "a man without self-control is like a city broken and left without walls" (Proverbs 25:28). A city without walls is a city without a defense system, a city left at the mercy of its enemies. And so is a man without self-control. He is left at the mercy of his desires and passions. Gregory the Great said, "taking cities is a smaller victory because the places we conquer are outside of ourselves. A great [victory] is won by patience, because a person overcomes himself and subjects himself to himself, when patience brings him low in bearing with others in humility."[137]

Jerry Bridges defines biblical self-control as "a governance or prudent control of one's desires, cravings, impulses, emotions, and passions."[138] If we evaluated ourselves, how would we respond to the following? Am I self-controlled when it comes to eating or drinking? Am I self-controlled when it comes to my emotions? Am I self-controlled when it comes to my finances? Am I self-controlled when it comes to how much time I spend on my phone, TV, computer, or video games? A great man or woman is self-controlled.

Patience and Persuasiveness

"With patience a ruler may be persuaded, and a soft tongue will break a bone" (Proverbs 25:15). Generally speaking, ANE rulers were not known for their benevolence, humility, and flexibility. But when it comes to persuading a ruler, the book of Proverbs affirms that patience is key. "Patience is so great of a virtue that eventually it may persuade a ruler that the longsuffering believer holds the correct position."[139] Patience is important in dealing with children, spouses, and colleagues, but this proverb emphasizes that a wise person is patient in dealing with those in authority.[140]

---

137 J. Robert Wright, *Proverbs, Ecclesiastes, Song of Solomon,* 112.

138 Jerry Bridges, *Respectable Sins* (Colorado Springs: NavPress, 2017), 105–106. Bridges goes on to observe that "unfortunately, Solomon, who wrote those words in Proverbs 25:28, is a sad but striking demonstration of his own words. The Scriptures record that Solomon had seven hundred wives and three hundred concubines...Solomon gave free rein to his passions...instead of exercising self-control, he disregarded his own words of wisdom and let his passions run out of control."

139 Steinmann, *Proverbs,* 513.

140 The LXX translates the word "ruler" as "king," so the verse only applies to a monarch.

A Lesson from Church History[141]

In the late 1700s in Scotland, a young lady gathered a class of poor, rough boys into Sunday school. Among them was a boy named Bob, the most wretched and unpromising of the group. The superintendent of the school told these boys to come to his house during the week and he would give them a new suit of clothes. They came and received the clothes as promised. After a Sunday or two, Bob failed to appear, but the teacher went after him and found the clothes in rags with Bob playing in the dirt with other boys. She begged him to come back and promised him another suit of clothes. This was repeated for a third time, and Bob came to faith in Christ. In a short time, he felt a call to the ministry and was granted a license to preach. Robert Morrison became the first missionary to China, the man who translated the Bible into Chinese.

A Christological Reading

Patience, then, which is an attribute of our God and of our Lord Jesus Christ, ought to also characterize each Christian. Paul's prayer for the Colossians is that they might demonstrate this quality (Colossians 1:11). It is part of the fruit of the Spirit (Galatians 5:22), an attribute of love (1 Corinthians 13:4), and a virtue (Colossians 3:12; see also 2 Timothy 3:10). In addition, Christians are exhorted to be patient (1 Thessalonians 5:14). If we are not, we will be treated as the slave in the parable which Jesus told. This slave pleaded with his lord, to whom he owed a great sum, for patience, promising to pay all. The lord was patient and forgave all the debt until he found out that the slave had refused to show the same patience to a fellow servant who owed him a pittance in comparison (Matthew 18:26–29).

In some contexts, the word "patience" takes on the more general meaning of waiting long and expectantly for something. The farmer waits patiently for the crop to come (James 5:7). Abraham waited patiently for God's promise to give him the land of Ca-

---

141 Taken from Ronald V. Prosise, *Preaching Illustrations from Church History* (The Woodlands, TX: Kress Christian Publications, 2016), 150.

naan to be fulfilled and died without seeing what was promised, although still believing (Hebrews 6:15; 11:39). Finally, all Christians are commanded to be longsuffering until the coming of the LORD (James 5:7).

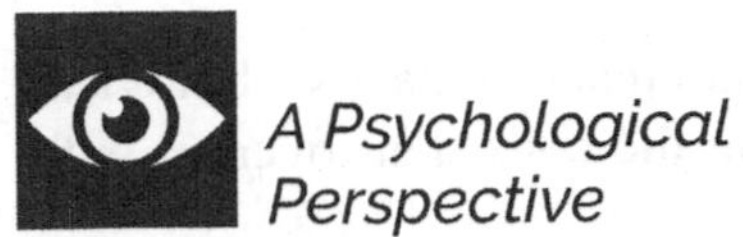

A Psychological Perspective

Reflections on Patience and Self-control

Dr. Kevin Roberts

Whoever is slow to anger has great understanding,
but he who has a hasty temper exalts folly.
—Proverbs 14:29

A man without self-control is like a city
broken into and left without walls.
—Proverbs 25:28

The book of Proverbs repeatedly addresses the need to restrain ourselves from engaging in foolish behaviors and, instead, to demonstrate more patience and, thus, self-control. These foolish behaviors are often seen in both how we use our tongue and in our actions. The use of our tongues includes actions like lying, deceiving, bragging, slandering, and being contentious. Our actions often include things like drunken behavior, anger, wrath, gluttony, and acting out sexually. But what gets in the way of being able to be patient and not acting on our impulses? I would maintain that to self-regulate or demonstrate self-control is instrumental to understanding patience as described in Scripture. It is the lack of patience or self-control that often leads to a list of sinful behaviors. The field of psychology has spent considerable time and attention on researching what makes someone able to have better self-control. We will now look at a summary of that psychological research, recognizing and observing the consistent overlap with the book of Proverbs.

Self-control and Self-regulation

The terms self-control and self-regulation are often used interchangeably in psychological literature. Self-regulation is often defined as a person's ability to apply the brakes and demonstrate control over their responses to others and the environment. Berkman et al. found that self-regulation is seen in the three following domains: cognitive, emotional, and behavioral.[142] On the other hand, the term self-control has historically had more of a moral connotation. Walter Mischel describes the importance of self-control this way, "Self-control is crucial for the successful pursuit of long-term goals. It is equally essential for developing the self-restraint and empathy needed to develop caring and mutually supportive relationships. It can help people avoid becoming impervious to consequences or getting stuck in jobs they hate. It is the master aptitude underlying emotional intelligence which is essential for having a fulfilling life."[143] But how does someone really learn how to practice self-control, and does psychology have a theory for perceiving how these concepts work in everyone's day-to-day life?

In recent years, there has been a shift toward a newer theory known as the Strength Model.[144] It is the belief of the Strength

---

142 Elliot T. Berkman, Alice M. Graham, and Philip A. Fisher, "Training Self-Control: A Domain-General Translational Neuroscience Approach," *Child Development Perspectives* 6, no. 4 (2012). https://doi.org/10.1111/j.1750-8606.2012.00248.x.

143 Walter Mischel. *The Marshmallow Test: Mastering Self-Control*, 1st ed. (Little, Brown, and Company, 2015), 6.

144 Roy F. Baumeister and Todd F. Heatherton, "Self-Regulation Failure: An Overview," *Psychological Inquiry* 7, no. 1 (1996): 1–15. https://doi.org/10.1207/s15327965pli0701_1; Mark Muraven and Roy F. Baumeister, "Self-Regulation and Depletion of Limited Resources: Does Self-Control Resemble a Muscle?" *Psychological Bulletin* 126, no. 2 (2000): 247–259. https://doi.org/10.1037/0033-2909.126.2.247.

Model that self-regulation was largely influenced by three elements.[145] These elements that predicted better self-regulation included: having a clear goal, motivation, and the ability or capacity to thwart or repel temptations or distractions. One such example of a limited capacity to thwart distractions is the diagnosis of Attention Deficit Disorder (ADD) or Attention Deficit Hyperactivity Disorder (ADHD). Over the years, the field of psychology has developed a variety of ways to assess ADD and ADHD. Although often over-diagnosed, these two diagnoses are also often misunderstood. ADD and ADHD have biological causes that make it difficult for people to thwart or repel temptations from their environment. Sadly, this diagnosis interferes with attention and often leads to impulsive decision-making, which can have a long-term impact on their lives. Unfortunately, these patterns of behavior often lead to many problems, including oppositional defiant disorder, conduct disorder, metabolic abnormalities, visual/hearing impairments, and disruptive mood dysregulation, and later in adolescence and adulthood, we often see substance abuse.[146] However, these brain differences observed in ADD and ADHD do not remove people from being personally responsible for their behavior, especially as they mature and they learn more coping skills to successfully manage their diagnosis. In fact, it is not uncommon to also see visual and hearing impairments, sleep disorders, nutritional deficiencies, and other metabolic abnormalities.[147] In this way we see the Strength Model theory appears to describe biologically why someone may demonstrate difficulty in self-regulation or self-control. Although ADD or ADHD may produce a proclivity toward impulsive behavior, it is still the choice of the individual to suppress impulsive tendencies, utilize medication, and develop plans for improving self-control as they age.

---

145 Baumeister and Heatherton, "Self-Regulation Failure: An Overview," 1–15; Muraven and Baumeister, "Self-Regulation and Depletion of Limited Resources: Does Self-Control Resemble a Muscle?" 247–259.

146 *Diagnostic and Statistical Manual of Mental Disorders: DSM-5*, 5th edition (Arlington, VA: American Psychiatric Association, 2013).

147 *Diagnostic and Statistical Manual of Mental Disorders: DSM–5.*

The Strength Model goes further in its explanation of how self-regulation can be hindered. This model maintains that we all have a limited number of resources and that each mental task requires self-regulation resources which further pulls from our limited supply. Therefore, staying in situations that require a great amount of self-control can result in eventually acting out in a way that is not consistent with one's own behavior. In Proverbs 13:20, we see this concept, "Whoever walks with the wise becomes wise, but the companion of fools will suffer harm." This concept is further illustrated in Proverbs 27:17, "Iron sharpens iron, and one man sharpens another." Avoiding bad company and tempting situations is important if you want to maintain self-control and godly behavior. This is in large part because self-regulatory behaviors can be depleted, and the taxing of these resources appears to lead to poor performance in areas like exercise, dieting, academic success, and in other risky behaviors like sexuality.[148]

Throughout Proverbs, we see warnings to avoid the sinners who seek to entice you to sin (1:10) and then further implores us, "My son, do not walk in the way with them; hold back your foot from their paths, for their feet run to evil, and they make haste to shed blood. For in vain is a net spread in the sight of any bird, but these men lie in wait for their own blood; they set an ambush for their own lives" (Proverbs 1:15–18). In essence, this evidence supports the notion that we should avoid tempting situations and bad company because both scenarios are far more likely to end in acting in sinful ways. We see this in the parental warning "Hear, my son" throughout Proverbs as he warns about the results of failing to make wise choices. Is there a reason that he may be illustrating a parental warning for young parents?

---

148 Davina A. Robson, Mark S. Allen, and Steven J. Howard, "Self-Regulation in Childhood as a Predictor of Future Outcomes: A Meta-Analytic Review," *Psychological Bulletin* 146, no. 4 (2020): 324–54. https://doi.org/10.1037/bul0000227.

The Development of Self-Regulatory Behaviors: Anybody Want a Marshmallow?

Walter Mischel, a psychologist well-known for his research in the field of self-control, is most famously known for the marshmallow test. This test involved putting a marshmallow in front of young children beginning around the age of four or five and then asking the child to not consume the marshmallow even when the researcher leaves the room for approximately fifteen minutes. The child is left alone with these tempting marshmallows in front of them, while being instructed that if they can wait and not eat what is in front of them, more marshmallows will await them when the instructor returns. The researchers then measured how many children resisted eating the marshmallows and recorded how long the other children waited before giving in and eating the marshmallows. Obviously, the researchers were measuring self-control and delayed gratification. Interestingly, these children were then followed and tested over the course of their lives. The results from this study were shocking to the psychological community! The young children who were able to delay their initial impulses and refrained from eating the marshmallows later showed increased SAT scores and improved social and cognitive functioning in their adolescence.[149] Also noteworthy, those children who displayed self-control with the marshmallows had a better body mass index and better life satisfaction as adults.[150]

One of the themes in the self-control literature is that our ability to self-regulate improves from childhood to adolescence and further into adulthood.[151] Interestingly, the faith of the child tends to result in faster development of these self-regulatory behaviors

149 Mischel, *The Marshmallow Test.*

150 Mischel, *The Marshmallow Test.*

151 Robson, Allen, and Howard, "Self-Regulation in Childhood as a Predictor of Future Outcomes: A Meta-Analytic Review."

throughout life and into adulthood.[152] So, what we see early on in the literature is that the development of self-regulation behaviors in kids is often connected to the maturing frontal lobe of the adolescent and young childhood environmental factors.[153] One problem faced by parents is that kids often develop at differing paces, and consequently, they need to train these children differently. A variety of biological and environmental factors, like the experience of trauma, can further delay childhood development.[154] However, it would be false to assume that self-control is fixed biologically and is not subject to change. Significant evidence exists that support how consistent parenting efforts and certain activities can help develop self-regulation. For example, when my son was young, I was concerned about his assertiveness, so I enrolled him in martial arts as a constructive means of being more physically active and to help teach discipline during his times of frustration. Activities like the martial arts help develop a child's self-control and thus have been proven to help build self-regulation in kids.[155] This body of research would indicate that self-control is an ongoing process that can be aided by activities and, most importantly, through involvement in their faith, thus lending more supporting evidence to Proverb 22:6, "Train up a child in the way he should go; even when he is old he will not depart from it."

152 Sam A. Hardy et al., "Dynamic Associations between Religiousness and Self-Regulation across Adolescence into Young Adulthood," *Developmental Psychology* 56, no. 1 (2020): 180–97. https://doi.org/10.1037/dev0000841.

153 Sarah-Jayne Blakemore and Kathryn L. Mills, "Is Adolescence a Sensitive Period for Sociocultural Processing?" *Annual Review of Psychology* 65, no. 1 (March 2014): 187–207. https://doi.org/10.1146/annurev-psych-010213-115202.

154 Jean E. Dumas et al., "Home Chaos: Sociodemographic, Parenting, Interactional, and Child Correlates," *Journal of Clinical Child & Adolescent Psychology* 34, no. 1 (2005): 93–104. https://doi.org/10.1207/x15374424.jccp30401_9.

155 Adele Diamond, "Activities and Programs That Improve Children's Executive Functions," *Current Directions in Psychological Science* 21, no. 5 (2012): 335–41. https://doi.org/10.1177/096321412453722.

Throughout the book of Proverbs, we are encouraged to train up our children. Proverbs 29:17 exhorts, "Discipline your son, and he will give you rest; he will give delight to your heart." The principle laid out for us is to love and discipline our children so they make wise choices, and as they age, they will develop self-regulating skills. Evidence in longitudinal studies demonstrates that failure to help our children learn self-regulating behaviors can result in a host of problems. A meta-analysis of more than 150 studies on lower-scoring self-regulatory children found that these kids were more likely to engage in aggressive behavior, cigarette smoking, lower school engagement scores, criminal behavior, and substance abuse throughout their life.[156] Robson et al. also found they were more prone to develop depression, anxiety, and anxiety symptoms throughout their life as compared to high-scoring self-regulation kids.[157] These mental health problems are only further exacerbated by problems related to social competence and the development of social skills.[158] Duckworth and Seligman found that children's self-control, which was assessed through laboratory tests as well as parenting and teacher reports, was a better predictor of final grades than IQ throughout their academic career.[159] This data, as seen in longitudinal work twenty years later, supports the notion that high-scoring self-regulatory kids are more likely to

---

156 Robson, Allen, and Howard, "Self-Regulation in Childhood as a Predictor of Future Outcomes: A Meta-Analytic Review."

157 Robson, Allen, and Howard, "Self-Regulation in Childhood as a Predictor of Future Outcomes: A Meta-Analytic Review."

158 Denise T. de Ridder et al., "Taking Stock of Self-Control," *Personality and Social Psychology Review* 16, no. 1 (2012): 76–99. https://doi.org/10.1177/1088868311418749; Claire L. Fox and Michael J. Boulton, "Friendship as a Moderator of Relationship between Social Skills Problems and Peer Victimization," *Aggressive Behavior* 32, no. 2 (2006): 110–121. https://doi.org/10.1002/ab.20114.

159 A. L. Duckworth and M. E. P. Seligman, "Self-Discipline Outdoes IQ in Predicting Academic Performance of Adolescents," *Psychological Science* 16, no. 12 (January 2005): 939–44. https://doi.org/10.1111/j.1467-9280.2005.01641.x.

build stronger interpersonal relationships, graduate with college degrees, and develop a more physically active lifestyle and thus a lower body mass index than their low-scoring self-regulatory counterparts.[160]

Research continues to demonstrate that a lack of self-regulation leads to a host of problems. But why is that so? Why do these kids often make the impulsive choice, or why do they choose paths that often lead to mental health problems? We know that biology and environment play a role but is there another cause? The one answer appearing in the psychological literature is something called temporal discounting.[161] Temporal discounting refers to an individual's tendency to perceive a desired result in the future as less valuable than in the present.[162] To understand temporal discounting, you need to first realize that as we grow up, we learn there is a direct relationship between our actions and the reinforcement or punishment of that behavior. One such example is in weight loss and the habits we form around eating. In the midst of dieting, we are often exposed to foods that look tempting but do not line up with our weight loss goals. This conflict leads to a choice that we need to make. The choice is between a long delay in the goal of weight loss in the next six months versus the immediate gratification of chocolate cake that I can enjoy right now. Thus, the timing of rewards becomes an important consideration in learning and reinforcement because the longer the gap between behavior and reward, the less likely self-control will be learned.[163]

So how does this apply to Proverbs? Proverbs 4:14–15 speaks clearly of avoiding or fleeing temptations, "Do not enter the path

160 Robson, Allen, and Howard, "Self-Regulation in Childhood as a Predictor of Future Outcomes: A Meta-Analytic Review."

161 Anthony Dickinson, Andrew Watt, and W. J. H. Griffiths, "Free-Operant Acquisition with Delayed Reinforcement," *Quarterly Journal of Experimental Psychology Section B* 45, no. 3b (1992): 241–58, https://doi.org/10/1080/14640749208401019.

162 Dickinson, Watt, Griffiths, "Free-Operant Acquisition with Delayed Reinforcement."

163 Dickinson, Watt, Griffiths, "Free-Operant Acquisition with Delayed Reinforcement."

of the wicked, and do not walk in the way of the evil. Avoid it; do not go on it; turn away from it and pass on." The author warns us to be aware of temporal discounting, telling us the lie that immediate gratification is better than waiting. So, are there consequences for kids who do not learn self-control lessons early on?

Self-control and Mental Health

One of the biggest problems we see with poor self-regulation is the development of mental health problems. The Diagnostic Statistical Manual V (DSM-V) is the guidebook for counselors and psychologists in diagnosing mental health problems, and it includes an entire section of disorders titled "Impulse Control Disorders."[164] Some of the diagnoses in this section include Oppositional Defiant Disorder, Intermittent Explosive Disorder, Pyromania, Conduct Disorder, Antisocial Personality Disorder, Kleptomania, and other types of impulse problems. These disorders tend to be directly related to parenting and failure to develop skills in the areas of self-regulation and self-control. The DSM-V states, "The disruptive, impulse-control, and conduct disorders have been linked to a common externalizing spectrum associated with the personality dimensions labeled as disinhibition and inversely constraint and, to a lesser extent, negative emotionality. These shared personality dimensions have a high level of comorbidity among these disorders and their frequent comorbidity with substance use disorders and antisocial personality disorder."[165] In other words, the inability to develop self-regulation results in angry and defiant outbursts, a lack of concern for the welfare of others, and stiff-necked behavior that is seeking immediate gratification, whereby temporal discounting is able to run amuck.

In Proverbs, we find that individuals who act impulsively are often characterized as naïve. It describes the naïve people as those who see danger and just simply "go on and suffer for it" (Proverbs 22:3). As Proverbs 18:1–7 further states,

164 *Diagnostic and Statistical Manual of Mental Disorders. DSM-5.*

165 *Diagnostic and Statistical Manual of Mental Disorders: DSM-5*, 462.

> Whoever isolates himself seeks his own desire; he breaks out against all sound judgment. A fool takes no pleasure in understanding, but only in expressing his opinion. When wickedness comes, contempt comes also, and with dishonor comes disgrace. The words of a man's mouth are deep waters; the fountain of wisdom is a bubbling brook. It is not good to be partial to the wicked or to deprive the righteous of justice. A fool's lips walk into a fight, and his mouth invites a beating. A fool's mouth is his ruin, and his lips are a snare to his soul.

This warning in Proverbs relates to how a lack of self-control of the naïve and foolish person contributes to all types of mental health problems and the damage they can do to those who associate with them. But what about the person who is not foolish or naïve as Proverbs describes them? What about the person who practices prudence?

Self-control and the Prudent Person

We see in Proverbs (27:12 and 22:3) that a direct contrast between the naïve and the prudent person exists. But what separates the prudent from the naïve? Proverbs 22:3 states, "The prudent sees danger and hides himself, but the simple go on and suffer for it." The prudent person recognizes the danger on the road ahead and then acts to avoid its potential pitfalls. So, what does the psychological literature say about prudence? According to Petersen and Seligman, "Prudent individuals show a farsighted and deliberative concern for the consequences of their actions and decisions, successfully resist impulses and other choices that satisfy short-term goals at the expense of longer-term ones, have a flexible and moderate approach to life, and strive for balance among their goals and ends."[166] The word *prudent* has become more commonly used in our culture as a reference to money, but a prudent man or woman

166 Christopher Peterson and Martin E. P. Seligman, *Character Strengths and Virtues: A Handbook and Classification* (Oxford: Oxford University Press, 2004), 478.

is one who is wise and knowledgeable and examines his or her life goals and plans with faith in mind. However, the prudent person must first seek the wisdom of God because from God alone does knowledge and understanding come (Proverbs 2:1–10). If a person seeks to pursue wisdom, then what types of personality traits seem to be a byproduct of prudence?

In an attempt to define prudence in psychological terms, it most readily correlates with a person who has foresight and is conscientious, organized, practical, thorough, and deliberate.[167] This ability and foresight permit the person to avoid the adulteress described in Proverbs 5:1–6,

> My son, be attentive to my wisdom; incline your ear to my understanding, that you may keep discretion, and your lips may guard knowledge. For the lips of a forbidden woman drip honey, and her speech is smoother than oil, but in the end, she is bitter as wormwood, sharp as a two-edge sword. Her feet go down to death; her steps follow the path to Sheol; she does not ponder the path of life; her ways wander, and she does not know it.

We can see in these passages a very similar theme that the naïve do not consider their path in front of them and fail to prepare for the temptations that will inevitably come. However, the prudent man prepares for these scenarios or finds a way to avoid the temptation altogether. The true battlefield within self-regulatory efforts is in having the ability to overcome our initial responses because it is from these that show sinful hearts and minds. Within the psychological literature, Wegner, Shortt, Blake, and Page found that the two main areas of self-regulatory efforts are around our thoughts and emotions and our ability to learn how to delay gratification.[168] But does anything help in delaying gratification?

---

167 Paul T. Costa, Robert R. McCrae, and David A. Dye, "Facet Scales for Agreeableness and Conscientiousness: A Revision of the NEO Personality Inventory," *Personality and Individual Differences* 12, no. 9 (1991): 887–98.

168 Daniel M. Wegner et al., "The Suppression of Exciting Thoughts," *Journal of Personality and Social Psychology* 58, no. 3 (1990): 409–418. https://doi.org/10/1037/0022-3514.58.3.409.

Research supports that our faith and religious disciplines indeed help improve delayed gratification. For example, Hardy et al. found that faith appears to encourage and improve self-control development.[169] McCullough and Willoughby also found similar results, showing that religiousness is a strong predictor of improved self-regulation.[170] It appears that in the practice of our faith, traditions like prayer, fasting, and Scripture reading develop coping strategies for handling life.[171] For this reason, we have seen adolescents and young adults demonstrating better self-regulatory behavior if they come from a faith tradition. What we see is that in practicing prayer in our day-to-day lives, we turn to God to overcome our temptation. Urry et al. even found that this deeper meditation improves self-regulation all the way down to the neural levels.[172]

Application Exercises and Questions for Patience and Self-control

There are many lessons to gain from the research on self-regulation and biblical teaching, but I will include just a few to deliberate on.

1. We first and foremost need to seek God's wisdom as described in Proverbs 2:1–10. In so doing we must recognize our own limitations and be humble about our ability to demonstrate

---

169 Sam A. Hardy et al., "Dynamic Associations between Religiousness and Self-Regulation across Adolescence into Young Adulthood," *Developmental Psychology* 56, no. 1 (2020): 180–97. https://doi.org/10.1037/dev0000841.

170 Michael E. McCullough and Brian L. Willoughby, "Religion, Self-Regulation, and Self-Control: Associations, Explanations, and Implications," *Psychological Bulletin* 135, no. 1 (2009): 69–93. https://doi.org/10.1037/a0014213.

171 McCullough and Willoughby, "Religion, Self-Regulation, and Self-Control: Associations, Explanations, and Implications."

172 Heather L. Urry et al., "Prefrontal Cortical Activation During Emotion Regulation: Linking Religious/Spiritual Practices with Well-Being," (2012). In Warren, Lerner, and Phelps (Eds.), *Thriving and Spirituality Among Youth: Research Perspectives and Further Possibilities* (2012): 19–29.

self-control. Each of us has certain things that are more tempting for us, and humbly acknowledging our dependence on God and others is crucial.

2. In alcohol and drug treatment, we often warn people to watch for the people, places, things, and even times related to addiction. The same is true in other areas of temptation.
   a. There are certain times of day that can lead to impetuous or ardent decisions. This is a long-researched concept, and we must recognize our most vulnerable times to either send an angry email, give in on dieting, or be tempted to engage in sinful behaviors.
   b. We must also learn to avoid tempting situations because the research shows that with each temptation, we become more likely to give in. Our strength to turn down tempting things is not a limitless resource. Please remember that we become increasingly more prone to wander as we are exposed to more and more tempting situations. So, get the unhealthy food out of the house if you are dieting.
   c. Therefore, we must know the things that tempt us and develop a plan for how to avoid our sinful tendencies and not cave into that which tempts us. We must practice prudence and, in so doing, have the "foresight" to be biblically prepared to deal with temptation, even if that means fleeing or avoiding situations altogether.
3. When you have failures and succumb to those things that are tempting, confess your sin and seek accountability. Even though we are tempted to hide from God in our shame and failures, it is important to confess these sins to God and seek accountability. The worst thing you can do is hide in your shame because it only preserves the temptation and makes each of us more prone to compartmentalize our lives.
4. Be wise in forming your habits and be sure to build wise routines into your life. Do you have routines for being in the word of God or for exercise and other health-producing habits? If

you fail to develop wise and thoughtful routines, then you are more prone to temporal discounting behaviors.

5. Be wise in not succumbing to emotional reactions such as reacting to social media posts or emails. Personally, I have developed a 24 to 72-hour principle for dealing with unpleasant emails. This is not a passive-aggressive avoidance tactic but my attempt to gain another person's perspective and to spend time in prayer before replying out of a place of anger or frustration.
6. Finally, I believe it is essential that we get back to the teaching of patience and self-control, as demonstrated in Proverbs. We are bombarded with opportunities to be distracted every day, and it is necessary that we, our children, and future generations learn and develop self-regulating behaviors. I believe the church could serve as a powerful and integral part of this training, and as the research indicates, our faith is instrumental in the development of self-control and coping.

Patience at Church

Pastor Knute Larson

The only way to learn patience is to stand in line. It just plain has to come by waiting,

... for a new Christian to do better at obeying the LORD and serving others with a humble spirit.

... for more growth to come to the church.

... for the church veteran to accept these new younger ones who never dress up like he or she does.

... for the pastor or another leader to see more people want to have a part in a true discipleship group.

... for the missions giving to finally reach that goal of 25 percent of the church budget.

... for Mr. or Mrs. Whatstheirname to stop being rather grouchy on Sundays and silent toward new guests at church.

... for the pastor to pay a little attention to your grandmother the shut-in who has given so much of her healthy time to the church.

... for the worship leader to pick two songs in a row that you like!

Patience is needed at church almost as much as anywhere—even, at times, in the worship services and with the people, including all of us.

We even need patience about the work of God and people combining to help the church grow to be more effective in the community and global missions—we all can pray and do our part, and then wait. Way too many people have dropped out or moved on because their suggestions were not adopted rapidly.

Patience is, of course, one of the evidences or fruit of God's Holy Spirit. And the church is made up of people who say they are linked to that Spirit through Christ our Savior. So, it should be expected that we are getting better all the time at waiting.

One Sunday in the first of the two churches I pastored for forty-one years in Ashland, Ohio, six or seven "Jesus people" of the day came for their first time into our old building, walked to the front, and sat on the floor in front of the first pew. I, the pastor, then twenty-eight years old, was very new to the church and hoping the church veterans (and almost everyone was a veteran of many years at Grace) would respond with patient love. Indeed, they did, and they greeted these college students afterward, as I did, and nobody mentioned the purpose of the pews!

All these young people became active in that church and were the first of many young adults. Of those I kept track of, there were two pioneer missionaries with Wycliffe, two active lay leaders in a church, one pastor, and one wife and co-leader of a worldwide mission agency.

The only thing any one of us could have done better to show patience and love would have been to go sit on the floor with them.

Why Patience Is So Important

We have each other at church, so we absolutely need patience with each other, and with some more than others! Patience is important because Jesus is patient with us, and we profess that we are linked closely with Him and His wisdom. And, as He knows, people change slowly, and churches maneuver carefully.

Even the almost-super woman of Proverbs 31 did not get that way overnight—even though "her lamp does not go out at night" (31:18) and "she can laugh at the time to come" (31:25).

Most good things, like a strong and effective church fellowship, take time, love, commitment, and patience. There are setbacks. People drop out. Leaders make mistakes. But we pray and see and wait.

Patience, please.

The wisdom called for in Proverbs is more than normal—it involves God's teaching and strength in our lives. It is mighty important for followers of God and His wisdom—since Bethlehem, so clearly displayed in the ways of Jesus Christ—to show evidence of His presence and strength in our behavior and our unity. May it be so at your church.

Neighbors to the church building itself, but also all who attend, have heard that we say we are linked with and committed to the LORD God, Creator, and Savior! They have every reason to see that it is so and that patience is practiced.

We are willing to stand in line.

Why Patience Does Not Always Show Up

Most of us are fallen, below perfect in our natures. Or would that be all of us? And one of the characteristics of a sinner is impatience. It is natural—a descriptive word indeed, to wish that others would grow faster, accomplish more, and be more like us! Instead, Proverbs calls to be godly—to talk about patience and go to God for the best example in the way we treat others.

A church that cares significantly about God's wisdom is a church that welcomes sinners and is very patient toward newcomers who do not know Christian attitudes and traits at first. Patiently we try to encourage and help them, wisely recalling how the adoption of the wise way of God takes time and strength. We even try to think through our answers before saying them out loud so as not to display folly or shame (18:13). That calls for an unhurried response, for wisdom with our words. "A person's wisdom yields patience, and his virtue is to overlook an offense" (Proverbs 19:11 NIV).

Regretfully, we do not always fear the LORD or seek His wisdom, given how easy it is to want our own way or look better than someone else or to hold something over another's head. This whole collection of Proverbs instructs us to do life God's way, how to be obeying Him. Easily, far too easily, church people, even strong believers, "stir up conflict," the Proverbs writer explains. "But the one who is patient calms a quarrel" (Proverbs 15:18 NIV).

Patience does not always show up because we do not always live for the glory of God rather than for our own preeminence.

A person showing patience is better than a strong athlete or a warrior, and "one with self-control [better] than one who takes a city" (Proverbs 16:32 NIV).

Patience shows up when our hearts re-up to obey our LORD.

What Each of Us Can Do Personally to Practice Patience

Be deliberately patient with each other at home first, as most virtues, when real, show up with family. And then, because a Christian, by definition, lives his or her life combined with Christ and in union with the Spirit, we must allow this new life to show up in the family of worship, the church. There we can be patient with each other too.

All of us know how disappointing it is when people connected to Christ by true faith do not show His graces, including patience, in the way they treat others. And there are many opportunities to do that at church and in its many ministries. Even to think through our answers before saying them rather than to display folly or shame (Proverbs 18:13) calls for a thoughtful response.

This whole book is a call to wisdom, to fear the LORD, and honor what He wishes. And high on His list is patience. Our understanding of what God wills for us, seen so clearly in Proverbs, guards our thoughts and actions (Proverbs 2:11) and helps us to be slow to anger and patient at church and everywhere (Proverbs 14:29).

The new pastor is not going to be Tim Keller or Jeff Bogue overnight, so patience with the pastor has to be important.

The board of oversight deserves our prayers and cooperation, not our impatience for them to make the policy we think most important.

And in our groups! Of course, we all mature in our spiritual commitment at various rates—that's just the way it is. And so we are patient with each other, willing to forgive, careful to confront, and good at forgiving. We live out Proverbs in our place of worship.

As noted, probably the only way to learn patience is to stand in line. And since it is also a fruit or evidence of the Holy Spirit, we can determine to walk or live in that Spirit, obeying His Word. (He guided the human writers, so what we read or study there is from our God.)

When we do that, we can count on our LORD's support and strength in our spirit and actions. And we do need to "let love and faithfulness never leave you" (Proverbs 3:3), and that certainly calls for patient endurance. We are challenged by "a friend loves at all times" (Proverbs 17:17) and know that calls for patience, for we all fail each other. As noted in our commentary section, the "man without self-control…is left to the mercy of his desires and passions" (comments on Proverbs 14:17, 29; 25:28). By God's grace and Spirit, we practice patience and self-control in combination with our Savior. We wait.

A Personal Prayer for Patience

Praise: We all know that if our holy and righteous God were not patient with us, we would be in great trouble! Why not reflect on and praise God for His merciful patience in your life.

Repent: For recent ways you have been impatient. They usually are not hard to recall.

Ask: For help to wait longer, for loving patience with those you love and live with, as well as for neighbors and church leaders and friends. We need God's Spirit to show kindness and patience.

Yield: With gratitude for God's patience with you all your life; yield to His wisdom and call to patience in Proverbs. We need His strength!

CHAPTER 6

Generosity

A Theological Perspective

The Wise Are Generous

Dr. Tiberius Rata

The truly generous is the truly wise,
and he who loves not others, lives unblessed.
—Henry Home

Generosity in the Old Testament

From the beginning of history, our God has always been a generous, benevolent, and giving God. The psalmist affirms, "[when] you open your hand, you satisfy the desire of every living thing" (Psalm 145:16). And because we are His representatives on earth, we are to be generous. In the Law, God makes provision for the poor, and those who have must help those who have not. Not only are God's people to help, but they are to do so generously. Moses instructs the new generation that will enter the Promised Land to be generous toward the poor and the needy.

> If among you, one of your brothers should become poor, in any of your towns within your land that the LORD your God is giving you, you shall not harden your heart or shut your hand against your poor brother, but you shall open your hand to him and lend him sufficient for his need, whatever it may be. Take care lest there be an unworthy thought in your heart and you say, "The seventh year, the

> year of release is near," and your eye look grudgingly on your poor brother, and you give him nothing, and he cry to the LORD against you, and you be guilty of sin. You shall give to him freely, and your heart shall not be grudging when you give to him, because for this the LORD your God will bless you in all your work and in all that you undertake. For there will never cease to be poor in the land. Therefore I command you, "You shall open wide your hand to your brother, to the needy and to the poor, in your land." (Deuteronomy 15:7–11)

Those who are stingy close their hands, but the generous are instructed to "open wide your hand to your brother, to the needy and to the poor." King David contrasts the righteous and the wicked and observes "the wicked borrows but does not pay back, but the righteous is generous and gives" (Psalm 37:21). Kidner notes that "a righteous man is no longer righteous when he grows selfish."[173] Not only is the righteous a blessing to the community, but "his children become a blessing" (Psalm 37:26). The one who is generous will reap the benefits of his freely distributing his wealth in that "his righteousness endures forever; his horn is exalted in honor" (Psalm 112:9). The word "horn" depicts an image of power and dignity (Psalm 75:5; 89:17, 24; 92:10; 132:17). Spurgeon notes that "God shall honour him, the universe of holy beings shall honour him, and even the wicked shall feel an unconscious reverence of him."[174]

After the children of Israel return from exile, they submit themselves to God and His Law, making a number of reforms. There is a reform through submission to God and His Law (Nehemiah 10:28–29), a reform to separate from interfaith marriages (Nehemiah 10:30), a reform to observe the Sabbath (Nehemiah 10:31), and lastly, they commit to support the rebuilding of the temple

---

173 Derek Kidner, *Psalms 1–72: An Introduction and Commentary*, vol. 15, Tyndale Old Testament Commentaries (Downers Grove, IL: InterVarsity Press, 1973), 169.

174 C. H. Spurgeon, *The Treasury of David: Psalms 111–119*, vol. 5 (London; Edinburgh; New York: Marshall Brothers, n.d.), 18.

(Nehemiah 10:39). Once they submit to God's Law, it is easy to be generous. The Law required half of a shekel (Exodus 30:13), but they commit to give a third of a shekel every year "for the service of the house of our God" (Nehemiah 10:32). Lastly, the post-exilic Israel committed to bring the 10 percent of the blessings of God, remembering that the tithes were declared to be holy to the LORD (Leviticus 27:30). Generosity and holiness go hand in hand just as wisdom and generosity do.

Generosity in the New Testament

The New Testament continues the idea that God is a generous Father. James writes to the first-century church that "every good and perfect gift is from above, coming down from the Father of lights, with whom there is no variation or shadow due to change" (James 1:17). From its inception, the first-century church understood that they needed to be generous and meet one another's needs. "And all who believed were together and had all things in common. And they were selling their possessions and belongings and distributing the proceeds to all, as any had need. And day by day, attending the temple together and breaking bread in their homes, they received their food with glad and generous hearts, praising God and having favor with all the people. And the LORD added to their number day by day those who were being saved" (Acts 2:44–47).

When writing to the church at Corinth, Paul lauded the Macedonian church for their generosity in helping those in need. "We want you to know, brothers, about the grace of God that has been given among the churches of Macedonia, for in a severe test of affliction, their abundance of joy and their extreme poverty have overflowed in a wealth of generosity on their part. For they gave according to their means, as I can testify, and beyond their means, of their own accord, begging us earnestly for the favor of taking part in the relief of the saints—and this, not as we expected, but they gave themselves first to the LORD and then by the will of God to us" (2 Corinthians 8:1–5).

Because God loves a cheerful giver (2 Corinthians 9:7), Paul encourages the church to be generous (2 Corinthians 9:11ff). The author of Hebrews encourages believers to "do good and to share what you have" (Hebrews 13:16).

When Jesus teaches on generosity, He uses a widow as an example because it is not about the size of the check but the greatness of one's commitment. Jesus warned His disciples to "beware of the scribes who…like greetings in the marketplaces" but "devour widows' houses" (Mark 12:38–40). And as they watched rich people drop their offerings in the offering box, Jesus commended the widow who "put in two copper coins, which make a penny. And He called His disciples to Him and said to them, 'Truly, I say to you, this poor widow has put in more than all those who are contributing to the offering box. For they all contributed out of their abundance, but she out of her poverty has put in everything she had, all she had to live on'" (Mark 12:42–44). In his book *Until He Comes*, Calvin Miller writes,

> There are at least three levels in church giving: the shame level, the game level, and the fame level. At the fame level, a strange bout with pride begins. It is easy at the level to be proud and ostentatious. This was the level at which the Pharisees gave and made a great show of their devotion. When they gave, they held the coins high and dropped them with a brazen ring into the temple coffers. At the game level, the giver tries to figure out what is the most blessing he can buy with the least down payment. Such givers try to figure out how to give a little bit in such flamboyant ways that they purchase a generous reputation with their well-publicized pittances. Game givers try to figure out what would 'be reasonable' in comparison to what others are giving. They compare their offerings with the average and then give just a little bit more. The shame level is the level of those who can never give enough. These givers always look at the price Jesus paid at Calvary. Even when they give all, they wish it were more. They even feel a little ashamed it is so little.[175]

175 Calvin Miller, *Until He Comes* (Nashville: Broadman & Holman, 1998), Day 244.

God blesses us so we can be a blessing to others. John asks, "if anyone has the world's goods and sees his brother in need, yet closes his heart against him, how does God's love abide in him?" (1 John 3:17). What we do with what we have is a reflection of our love and of what's in our hearts. Jesus says, "No one can serve two masters, for either he will hate the one and love the other, or he will be devoted to one and despise the other. You cannot serve God and money" (Matthew 6:24). Why is it a matter of the heart? Because "where your treasure is, there your heart will be also" (Matthew 6:21).

Generosity in the Book of Proverbs

God Cares for the Poor

Wise living means living wisely in relationship with those around us. "Whoever despises his neighbor is a sinner, but blessed is he who is generous to the poor" (Proverbs 14:21). The word translated "generous" comes from the verb root that has a wide semantic range and can mean "to be gracious to, to have pity, and to plead for grace."[176] The word employed here is "descriptive of beneficent actions that are freely offered or received and contributed to the well-being of another...it is active kindness or generosity exhibited toward those in need."[177] The opposite of being generous, according to Proverbs 14:21, is not stinginess but hatred of neighbor. In Hebrew, the idea of hatred has a nuance of rejection. If we are not being a blessing by being generous, we are rejecting those who need us. This verse "states God's disapproval of the person who ignores the temporal needs of others. It also encourages kindness by declaring God's eschatological pronouncement of 'blessed' upon those who believe and do his will."[178]

---

176 Terence E. Fretheim, "חנן," in *The New International Dictionary of Old Testament Theology and Exegesis,* vol. 2, ed. Willem A. VanGemeren (Grand Rapids: Zondervan, 1997), 203–206.

177 Fretheim, 204.

178 Steinmann, *Proverbs,* 336. See "blessed" also in Matthew 5:1–12; 25:34.

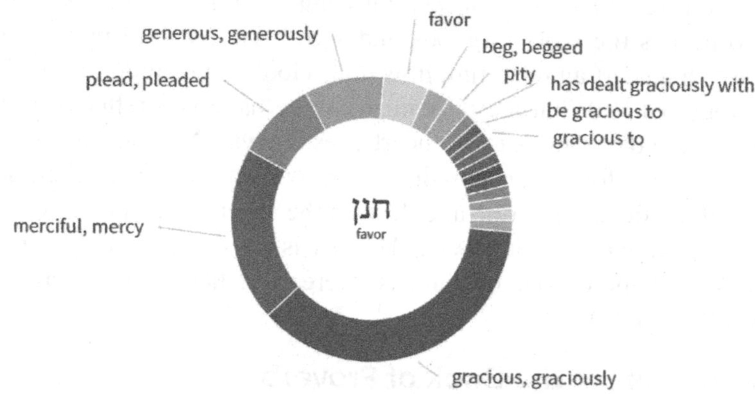

Figure 6.1 The word "favor/gracious" in the Old Testament

The Wise Care for the Poor

"Whoever oppresses a poor man insults his Maker, but he who is generous to the needy honors him" (Proverbs 14:31). The opposite of being generous, according to Proverbs 14:31, is not being stingy but oppressing the poor. This is not a concept that is unique to wisdom literature. Through the prophet Amos, God rebukes the women of Samaria as oppressing the poor and the needy. "Hear this word, you cows of Bashan, who are on the mountain of Samaria, who oppress the poor, and crush the needy" (Amos 4:1). The men are just as guilty. Instead of taking care of the poor and needy, they "trample on the poor" and "exact taxes of grain" from them (Amos 5:11). God responds with "woe" language. "Woe to those who are at ease in Zion, and to those who feel secure on the mountain of Samaria...who lie on beds of ivory and stretch themselves out on their couches, and eat lambs from the flock and calves from the midst of the stall...who drink wine in bowls, and anoint themselves with the finest oils, but are not grieved over the ruin of Joseph!" (Amos 6:1–6). Steinmann notes that "this proverb has special relevance for rulers and leaders, since they wield power that they could abuse by oppressing the weak...Rulers are reminded that despite their exalted position, they come from the same Maker as their lowliest subordinates. When rulers' policies are kind toward the poor, they bring honor to God, who places them in their position of authority."[179]

God Rewards the Generous

The motivation of the wise in taking care of the poor is not to be rewarded, but God rewards the generous. "Whoever is generous to the poor lends to the LORD, and he will repay him for his deed" (Proverbs 19:17). We are not told how, but the one who is generous to the poor will benefit at the expense of the one who "multiples his wealth by interest and profit" (Proverbs 28:8). H. A. Ironside expounds on the relationship between God and the poor.

> It is truly precious to contemplate Jehovah as the patron of the poor. He has left such in the world to test the hearts of those who are better provided for, and He accepts what is done with compassion, to relieve the needy, as so much done for Himself. Money and goods bestowed with loving pity on those in distress are not gone forever. He takes note of every mite, and makes Himself responsible to see that all shall be repaid...Genuine philanthropy is the result of true love of God."[180]

The Antithesis of Generosity

Lack of care and love for others are some of the reasons why some are not generous. Not sharing one's wealth and possessions does not lead to plenty but to scarcity. "One gives freely, yet grows all the richer; another withholds what he should give, and only suffers want." This is indeed a paradox, and only divine wisdom allows us to see that being generous leads to blessings. "A stingy man hastens after wealth and does not know that poverty will come upon him" (Proverbs 28:22). The word translated "stingy" is literally "a man with an evil eye," stressing the fact that one who desires to get wealthy ends up in poverty due to lack of generosity. An evil eye reflects an evil heart, while a generous person has a loving heart and is ready to help those in need. There is nothing wrong

---

179 Steinmann, *Proverbs*, 338.

180 Ironside, *Notes on the Book of Proverbs*, 249–50.

with being rich; after all, Abraham and Job were rich. But Murphy is correct when he points out that greed not only destroys life, but it is the fertile ground on which bribery grows.[181] The apostle Paul warns us about the last days when people will be lovers of self and lovers of money (2 Timothy 3:2). The lover of money cannot be the lover of people because he is first the lover of self.

A Lesson from Church History

In his sermon, "The More Excellent Way," John Wesley speaks of the generosity of a young man studying at Oxford. "One of them had 30 pounds a year. He lived on twenty-eight and gave away forty shillings. The next year receiving sixty pounds, he still lived on twenty-eight, and gave away two-and-thirty. The third year he received ninety pounds, and gave away sixty-two. The fourth year he received a hundred and twenty pounds. Still he lived as before on twenty-eight, and gave to the poor ninety-two." And then Wesley challenges us with the question, "Was not this a more excellent way?"[182]

A Christological Reading

When speaking of Jesus's generosity, we cannot conjecture about His giving or tithing practices since the Bible is silent about the time before He enters public ministry. Luke writes that Jesus was "about thirty years of age" when He began His ministry (Luke 3:23). The New Testament writers talk about Jesus giving Himself. While He did not have worldly possessions to give away, He gave His life. The apostle Paul repeatedly uses the expression "gave Himself" to affirm what Jesus has done. In Galatians, Paul writes that Jesus "gave Himself for our sins to deliver us from the present evil age" (Galatians 1:4), while later in the letter, he makes it more personal, affirming that Jesus "loved me and gave Himself for me" (Galatians 2:20). Paul reminds the church in Ephesus that

---

181 Roland E. Murphy, *Proverbs,* Word Biblical Commentary, vol. 22 (Nashville: Thomas Nelson, 1998), 114–15.

182 Kenneth J. Collins, *A Real Christian: The Life of John Wesley* (Nashville: Abingdon, 1999), 31.

"Christ loved us and gave Himself up for us, a fragrant offering and sacrifice to God" (Ephesians 5:2). Jesus serves as an example to the husbands who are to love their wives "as Christ loved the church and gave Himself up for her" (Ephesians 5:25). To young Timothy, Paul writes that Jesus "gave Himself as a ransom for all" (1 Timothy 2:6), and to young Titus, he writes that Jesus "gave Himself for us to redeem us from all lawlessness and to purify for Himself a people for His own possession who are zealous for good works" (Titus 2:14).

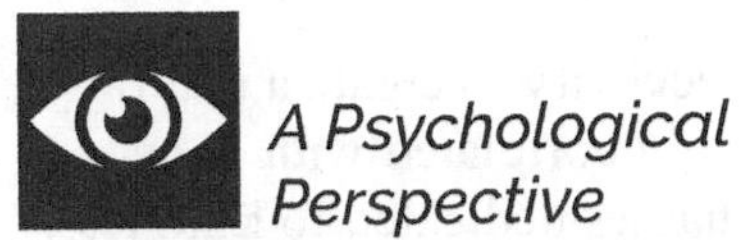

Reflections on Generosity

Dr. Kevin Roberts

Whoever is generous to the poor lends to the LORD, and he will repay him for his deed.
—Proverbs 19:17

Is everyone born with the same generosity trait? Or are some people just born more generous? If we all have the same amount of generosity, then what motivates our generosity? Have you ever seen generosity that instead feels like subtle manipulation? So many questions hover around the term *generosity*. At first glance, the psychological literature does not appear to help in gaining a better understanding because generosity has several other terms that are strongly correlated with it. So, what do we know? Generosity appears to be strongly connected to kindness, empathy, our sense of connection with others, a deep sense of compassion, and altruistic love for others. This chapter will examine the factors commonly linked to generosity and how these factors lead to increased motivation to act generously, along with how the biology of generosity impacts us.

Kindness + Empathy = Generosity?

Many seek the favor of a generous man, and everyone is a friend to a man who gives gifts. (Proverbs 19:6)

There are several traits that appear necessary to create a naturally generous person. The first trait strongly correlated with generosity is kindness. We have an entire chapter dedicated to kindness, but kindness is generally seen in individuals who display a considerate and friendly demeanor. Generosity is commonly linked with improved social connections and relationships. This would indicate that kindness can be a wonderful way of moving closer to others. Could it be that kindness opens the door to relationships? If kindness does open the door, then perhaps empathy helps us move into a deeper relationship with each other.

The role of empathy is essential in discussing the development of a generous heart. The term empathy is often correlated with softness and an ability to see with the eyes of another. This quality is often linked to both generosity and to higher forms of concern for others, termed *altruism.*[183] In fact, Batson found that empathy is a reliable predictor of altruistic motivation, which is a precursor to acts of generosity.[184]

This series could lead us toward several conclusions: (1) kindness may open the door to the opportunity for more social relationships, (2) empathy can serve as a means of connecting people at a deeper level, and (3) our kindness and empathy appear to coincide with developing a deeper compassion for others that results in more altruistic behavior.[185]

Alfred Adler associated this altruistic behavior with mental health. Adler termed this behavior social interest, or in German, Gemeinschaftsgefühl. Social interest is commonly associated with a social feeling and concern for others.[186] In the Adlerian view of

---

183 Bonnie L. McNeely and Bruce M. Meglino, "The Role of Dispositional and Situational Antecedents in Prosocial Organizational Behavior: An Experimentation of the Intended Beneficiaries of Prosocial Behavior," *Journal of Applied Psychology* 79, no. 6 (1994): 836–44.

184 C. Daniel Batson, "How Social an Animal? The Human Capacity for Caring," *American Psychologist* 45, no. 3 (1990): 336–46. https://doi.org/10/1037/0003-066x.45.3.336.

185 Peterson and Seligman, *Character Strengths and Virtues: A Handbook and Classification.*

186 Manaster and Corsini, *Individual Psychology.*

human nature, the individual who gives socially out of kindness and empathy for his fellow man and not from a selfish position is more likely to be healthy.[187] Therefore, individuals who have high amounts of altruism or compassion, including both empathy and kindness, are considered to be more emotionally healthy. If Adlerian theorists are right, then it only stands to reason that emotionally healthy people will also demonstrate higher amounts of emotional intelligence. In fact, in measuring emotional intelligence, we see four main branches evident that include: (1) perceiving emotions (empathy) in oneself and others, (2) using emotions to integrate with our thinking to improve cognitive processes, (3) being able to understand emotions, and lastly, (4) the ability to manage or regulate emotional responses.[188]

Altruism and Acting from a Heart of Deep Compassion

The term altruism has been given many definitions throughout the years of psychological research. Yet it is best known for the expansion of our personal universe, in that we learn to see beyond our own self-interest.[189] The altruistic person will tend to act in selfless ways without a desire to get recognition from peers. Furthermore, it is this selfless act that is at the heart of most religions and embodied in the life of Christ. In Christ, we find the highest form of altruistic love that extends to all tribes and all nations. Jesus was willing to cross the cultural, economic, and religious boundaries because of His deep compassion for *all* of mankind. In Christ, we see His willingness to humble Himself to the point of death on a cross for all of mankind (Philippians 2:8).

The psychological research on altruism points toward the development of a sense of social responsibility and ethical responsibili-

---

187 Manaster and Corsini, *Individual Psychology.*

188 J. D. Mayer and P. Salovey, "What is emotional intelligence?" (1997). In P. Salovey and D. Sluyter (eds.) *Emotional Development and Emotional Intelligence: Implications for Educators* (New York: Basic Books, 1997), 3–31; Daniel Goleman, *Emotional Intelligence* (New York: Bantam Books, 1995).

189 Peterson and Seligman, *Character Strengths and Virtues: A Handbook and Classification.*

ty.[190] It is this sense of responsibility that compels the person high in moral, ethical, or social responsibility to act. Adlerian psychologist Rudolph Dreikurs described social interest as, "the ability to play the game of life with existing demands for cooperation and to help the group to which one belongs in its evolution closer toward a perfect form of social living."[191] Rushton et al. developed a scale for measuring altruism and found that it predicted helping behavior across several cultures.[192] In repeated studies, altruism appears to be a major predictor in volunteering as an active form of expressing a heart of deep compassion for our fellow man.[193] Adlerians would add that "working together harmoniously, is the final answer because fundamentally we are social creatures and only in a truly cooperative society can we find peace and commitment."[194] In the development of true altruistic love for mankind, we can begin to see changes in our moral reasoning and in our spiritual life.[195]

In Christianity, we see this in Christ, who demonstrated deep compassion and sacrifice (Matthew 9:36; Luke 7:13). Christ was willing to sacrifice His time, resources, and personal comfort in

---

190 Leonard Berkowitz and Kenneth G. Lutterman, "The Traditional Socially Responsible Personality," *Public Opinion Quarterly* 32, no. 2 (1968): 169.

191 Rudolf Dreikurs, *Fundamentals of Adlerian Psychology* (Chicago: Alfred Adler Institute, 1953), 8.

192 J. Philippe Rushton, G. Cynthia Fekken, and Roland D. Chrisjohn, "The Altruistic Personality and the Self-Report Altruism Scale," *Personality and Individual Differences* 4, no. 3 (1981): 293–302; Kee-Lee Chou, "The Rushton, Chrisjohn, and Fekken Self-Report Altruism Scale: A Chinese Translation," *Personality and Individual Differences* 21, no. 2 (1996): 297–98; Rajesh Khanna, Poonam Singh, and J. Philippe Rushton, "Development of the Hindi Version of a Self-Report Altruism Scale," *Personality and Individual Differences* 14, no. 1 (1993): 267–70.

193 Allen M. Omoto and Mark Snyder, "Sustained Helping without Obligation: Motivation, Longevity of Service, and Perceived Attitude Change among AIDS Volunteers," *Journal of Personality and Social Psychology* 68, no. 4 (1995): 674–86.

194 Manaster and Corsini, *Individual Psychology,* 52–53.

195 C. Daniel Batson, *The Altruism Question: Toward a Social-Psychological Answer* (Hilldale, 1991).

order to serve others. Not surprisingly, research has shown that people of faith are actually more than 25 percent more likely to give generously.[196] Furthermore, it is in Christ that we find the ultimate altruistic sacrifice, namely His willingness to die for the sins of man.

Self-interest (Selfishness) vs. Altruism

Many studies suggest that people often act generously out of an expectation that their generosity will be reciprocated or because they feel it will help their reputation, often because of their own self-interest. Seeking to get something in return for one's generosity can be a subtle form of manipulation. Can we, in fact, freely give to others without expecting anything in return?

When people focus on their own self-interest, they are selfishly acting to serve their own needs. There is no question in the literature that studies repeatedly show that human beings tend to act in a selfish way. However, it has also been found that individuals who have higher amounts of altruism are much more likely to act because they feel socially responsible for the welfare of others.[197] For example, those who have high scores in altruism are more likely to aid others if they are bystanders to an automobile accident.[198] As Proverbs articulates, "Whoever is generous to the poor lends to the LORD, and he will repay him for his deed" (Proverbs 19:17).

Inside the church, we use terms like "the body" because Scripture indicates and supports the value of each individual as a part of the body. Paul states in Romans,

---

196 Arthur C. Brooks, "Religious Faith and Charitable Giving," *Policy Review* 121 (2003): 39–50.

197 Elizabeth Midlarsky et al., "Altruistic Moral Judgment among Older Adults," *The International Journal of Aging and Human Development* 49, no. 1 (1999): 27–41.

198 Hans Werner Bierhoff, Renate Klein, and Peter Kramp, "Evidence for the Altruistic Personality from Data on Accident Research," *Journal of Personality* 59, no. 2 (1919): 263–80; C. Daniel Batson et al., "Where Is the Altruism in the Altruistic Personality?" *Journal of Personality and Social Psychology* 50, no. 1 (1986): 212–20.

> For by the grace given to me I say to everyone among you not to think of himself more highly than he ought to think, but to think with sober judgment, each according to the measure of faith that God has assigned. For as in one body we have many members, and the members do not all have the same function, so we, though many, are one body in Christ, and individually members of one another. (Romans 12:3–5)

We can see the highest forms of altruistic love embodied in the encouragement to view everyone as members of one another and to not think highly of ourselves but instead live with cooperation and the needs of others in mind. In this spirit, we must continually seek to give more than we receive from others (2 Corinthians 8:3–4). It is from this heart of service that we can embrace the concept of giving to others generously without any hope of getting anything back in return.

The heart of generous giving is rewarded with great joy and sets the stage for change in our communities as well (Psalm 41:1; Proverbs 11:24–25). Furthermore, a free gift without strings brings us great joy, as articulated in 2 Corinthians 9:7, "Each one must give as he has decided in his heart, not reluctantly or under compulsion, for God loves a cheerful giver." A cheerful giver does not give reluctantly or out of duty but gladly gives to others as God puts it upon his or her heart. The bottom line is that kindness and empathy appear to develop a deep sense of altruism or compassion for others. It is from this compassion and altruistic perspective that a person can become a truly cheerful giver.

The Biology of Generosity

Are our bodies naturally "wired" for generous acts? Researchers have consistently found a connection between generosity and the release of the hormone oxytocin in the body.[199] Oxytocin is best known for being released in women after the birth of a child and is directly related to attachment and trust in human relationships. In-

199 Paul J. Zak, "Trust: A Temporary Human Attachment Facilitated by Oxytocin," *Behavior and Brain Sciences* 28, no. 3 (2005).

terestingly, oxytocin is also activated with acts of generosity and is directly related to building trust, emotional processing, and reciprocal relationships, even amongst strangers.[200] This connection between brain science and generosity has been confirmed in brain scans while looking at reward areas in the brain.[201]

The research points toward differences in brain scans, but may even further relate to differences in health outcomes data. In one such research study, they examined a large group of ethnically diverse students and found that generous people tended to have lower medical costs, lower blood pressure, and better sleep quality.[202] If being generous with others has all kinds of potential benefits, how do we start to practice generosity more faithfully?

Application Exercises and Questions for Practical Generosity

So how can one become more generous? For some, being gracious and generous comes naturally, but for others, this takes a significant amount of prayer and commitment. For those in the latter group, I encourage you to remember that we were all made in the image of God, and thus, we have a level of generosity inside of each of us.

1. First, I would recommend going before the Lord in prayer and asking to have the eyes of Jesus, who freely gave of His time and resources to graciously provide for the needs of others. Seeing others the way Jesus sees them is a crucial step to developing empathy and generosity.
2. Take time to look back on your journey and consider all the ways God has blessed you. How have you historically re-

---

200 Michael Kosfeld et al., "Oxytocin Increases Trust in Humans."

201 William T. Harbaugh, Ulrich Mayr, and Daniel R. Burghart, "Neural Responses to Taxation and Voluntary Giving Reveal Motives for Charitable Donations," *Science* 316, no. 5831 (2007): 1622–25; Dharol Tankersley, C. Jill Stowe, and Scott A. Huettel, "Altruism is Associated with an Increased Neural Response to Agency," *Natural Neuroscience* 10, no. 2 (2007): 150–51.

202 W. M. Brown, N. S. Consedine, and C. Magai, "Altruism Relates to Health in an Ethically Diverse Sample of Older Adults," *The Journals of Gerontology Series B: Psychological Sciences and Social Sciences* 60, no. 3 (January 2005).

sponded when others showed you generosity, seeking to first serve you? Now ask yourself, "Am I generous with both my time and God's resources?"

3. We must ask ourselves before each generous act if we are giving and serving with the right motives. Are you motivated to give if no one would ever find out that it was you? We can subtly (and sometimes not so subtly) use our resources to manipulate the people in our lives, especially if they hope to receive our generosity. Where is your heart in each act of generosity? Are you acting out of a deep compassion led by the Holy Spirit or because you wish to be seen as generous?

Generosity at Church

Pastor Knute Larson

There is strong evidence of generosity in Proverbs as it pertains to caring for the poor, not just general giving, even for spreading the gospel (which indeed is also involved). If generosity to the poor is, according to Proverbs 19:17, "lending" to the Lord (a neglected thought indeed), the leaders of the church budget-making process must keep this in mind. Generosity also looks like a church that makes its budget and does generous missions projects locally and globally. It looks like a church that takes care of people in need who attend there and others outside the community of the church. It looks like people giving hours of their time every week to serve others at the church and outside the church and cheerfully giving more of their income to glorify Christ through the ministries of the church.

As a coach for pastors, I have often urged them to be strong in their appeal for giving and to put aside fear and have a special building or missions campaign where they ask for more money than usual. People are very generous in the church, and many can do even more than their past habits. Churches have done much for the poor, for the hurting in their community, and to spread the name of Christ around the world. It is good to see.

Generosity in the church also looks like the people of the church giving to their community to fix up houses, to help the widows, to visit the sick and the shut-ins, to be generous in their study time so they can teach children and others on the weekends and in groups in homes. Our LORD was clear: "It is more blessed to give than to receive" (Acts 20:35), and His body, the Church, is to be convinced of that. Of course, the church worships and follows the most generous person who ever lived, the LORD Jesus Christ. We have to show attributes that look like him. Generosity is a move the church and its individual people make rather than just a feeling. I should have kept better notes, but I can clearly remember the following:

... someone buying a car for the son of a single mom struggling with finances;

... a family arranging the oral surgery for a woman who never could have afforded it;

... numerous anonymous payments for Christian school tuition for other families;

... a whole house repair and painting by a crew for a recent widow;

... hours and hours every week, as in every church, of people preparing to teach or help;

... the very regular tithes and offerings that met the budget and more every year;

... a very generous building and mission expansion with three or four-year pledges, one via a widow who pledged $100 extra a year for three years, and another by a family foundation that offered one million dollars each year, and everything in between!

Talk about generosity! All these people believed the Proverbs!

And the church itself might best model careful and unselfish use of funds, which come from the kind of woman described in Proverbs 31 and many others who follow the directions toward wisdom in Chapter 3. That in itself should motivate very wise and unselfish use of offerings for the spread of the Gospel and the action of love toward people in need.

Why Generosity Is So Important

Generosity should be the middle name of the church. A big part of what we are called to do is to give money and possessions, but also action love, good deeds for the benefit of others, time to sit with someone's baby so that person can be in the worship service, and hours to cook food for the poor in the church kitchen. That and much more are significant because we claim the name of Christ in our church. Even non-church people know enough about Jesus of Nazareth to know He was kind and generous, even to the giving of His life. A church that borrows His name and says that it worships and follows Him will be generous and loving. When the Proverbs writer says we insult our Maker when we oppress a poor person, he is telling us how much God loves and even has a purpose for all people, the very poor and needy also! We would never say a deliberate and unkind insulting remark to our Creator, so we must decide to share with the poor in a deliberate way. We will always have them with us, so we will always have opportunities to honor our LORD and theirs by giving to them.

Why Generosity Does Not Always Show Up

The first four-letter word we all said when growing up was probably "mine." None of us had to go to kindergarten to learn how to lie or be selfish. It comes with the territory of being human in a fallen way, which of course, is no excuse for not being a caring and generous person, especially if we understand how new life in combination with Christ works! The active kindness to help with someone's well-being, as Proverbs teaches, is the way generosity is displayed. This comes best when we seek the Spirit of Christ and act in His strength. When Jesus said, "For you always have the poor with you" (Matthew 26:11), He certainly did not mean to be quoted in defense of negligence. And Proverbs has clear applause for helping the poor rather than insulting them with criticism or neglect (Proverbs 14:31). Nevertheless, true to their fallen human nature, many church people blame poverty on the laziness of the poor and do little to help. Even some churches have officially allocated funds by using the "salt water test"—if the poor are overseas, that church will give, but not for those down the street. While we applaud the desire to "get the Gospel out because the poor need Jesus, not money," as one churchman told me, we know some will hear the Good News better when not starving or freezing. Even when we cannot predict how the poor will think about our Savior after being helped, we should see charity as Proverbs advises, that we are giving to the LORD Himself (Proverbs 19:17).

What Each of Us Can Do Personally to Be More Generous

We can give. We can share time and energy, money and things, with hearts that worship our risen Christ. Generous people do not value privacy over mixing with others, volunteering, and meeting needs—at least at appropriate times. Proverbs has many descriptions of how wise people reach to show love to others. We can enjoy privacy too, of course, but not all the time, and, thankfully, not just to stay to ourselves. A generous person embraces the idea that a believer is a helper, a contributor, and one who pushes himself to help others. And though it is hard, we can urge our good friends to expand their love and be generous. Think through any personal ways you can honor the needy just by being generous to them, as described in Proverbs 14:31. Or maybe think of one needy person or family you know so the search is not a big one. Plan something rather specific to give to them. And think about time and effort, not just money, as you ask God to help you share love and grace in a wise way. Maybe there is a child with a special need you can support. Find out!

A Personal Prayer for Generosity

Praise: This is a good time to be specific about the gracious generosity of God to you through the years, starting with salvation and the strength to obey Him, and including specific provisions in your life and family.

Repent: For lack of generosity, if you say that, as a true need. Receive His forgiveness by faith.

Ask: For help to see your possessions and money as gifts from God, and to be generous with others, including time, love, and money. Ask for the needs you have and those of the people you love.

Yield: To the clear calls in Proverbs about giving to others and the ministries of our LORD in your community and around the world.

CHAPTER 7

Humility

The Wise Are Humble

Dr. Tiberius Rata

If you plan to build a tall house of virtues,
you must first lay deep foundations of humility.
—Augustine of Hippo

Humility in the Old Testament

From the beginning of history, God has been opposed to those who refuse to humble themselves before Him. God punished Egypt and its Pharaoh because he refused to humble himself before the LORD (Exodus 10:3).[203] After Israel left Egypt, God allowed His people to experience forty years of wilderness in order to humble His own people (Deuteronomy 8:2, 16).[204]

Humility is a prerequisite to repentance. In giving the Law, God instructs His children that if they repent after rebelling against Him, and "if then their uncircumcised heart is humbled…then I will remember my covenant…and I will remember the land" (Leviticus 26:41–42). King Saul was lauded for being humble (1

203 Exodus 10:3, "So Moses and Aaron went to Pharaoh and said to him, 'Thus says the LORD, the God of the Hebrews, "How long will you refuse to humble yourself before me? Let my people go, that they may serve me."'"

204 Deuteronomy 8:2, "And you shall remember the whole way that the LORD your God has led you these forty years in the wilderness, that he might humble you, testing you to know what was in your heart, whether you would keep his commandments or not."

Samuel 9:21; 15:17). King Josiah received commendation from the LORD because he humbled himself before the LORD after hearing the words of the Law (2 Kings 22:19). When Ahab humbled himself before God, God postponed the disaster He was going to bring on his dynasty (1 Kings 21:29).[205]

Humility is tied to salvation. As David addresses God in his song of deliverance, he sings that God saves "a humble people, but Your eyes are on the haughty to bring them down" (2 Samuel 22:28; Psalm 18:27). The psalmist envisions salvation as a crown on the head of the humble. "For the LORD takes pleasure in His people; He adorns the humble with salvation" (Psalm 149:4). Humility is a characteristic that God desires in His people, and this humility can lead to blessings. God reminds Solomon as He appears to him a second time that "if my people who are called by my name humble themselves, and pray and seek my face and turn from their wicked ways, then I will hear from heaven and will forgive their sin and heal their land" (2 Chronicles 7:14).

The humble also benefit from God's leading. God "leads the humble in what is right, and teaches the humble His way" (Psalm 25:9). The humble also benefit from God's exaltation. "The LORD lifts up the humble; He casts the wicked to the ground" (Psalm 147:6). When God's people do not humble themselves before Him, He finds a way to humble them. As the Chronicler writes Israel's history, he reminds his readers how God "humbled Judah" because she was unfaithful to the LORD" (2 Chronicles 28:19). The people of God humbled themselves as they returned from exile under the leadership of Ezra. "Then I proclaimed a fast there, at the river Ahava, that we might humble ourselves before our God, to seek from him a safe journey for ourselves, our children, and our goods" (Ezra 8:21).

205 Hezekiah and Manasseh experienced God's grace because they humbled themselves before the LORD (2 Chronicles 33).

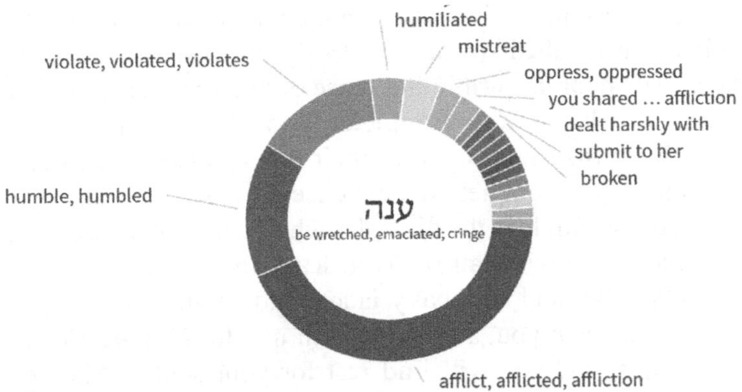

Figure 7.1 The use of the verb "to humble" in the Old Testament[206]

The prophetic message was always critical against the proud. Through the prophet Isaiah, God promises to punish while blessing the humble. "The haughty looks of man shall be brought low, and the lofty pride of men shall be humbled" (Isaiah 2:11; see also Isaiah 2:17 and 26:5). The LORD looks favorably on the one "who is humble and contrite in spirit," and trembles at His Word (Isaiah 66:2). Obedience to the word of God and a humble spirit go hand in hand. In contrast with the humble one stands a person who is proud and thus rejects the word of God. Isaiah's contemporary, the prophet Micah, affirmed that God is looking for one who walks humbly with Him (Micah 6:8). Daniel is commended for humbling himself before God in prayer (Daniel 10:12), and it is the humble who will "seek refuge in the name of the LORD" (Zephaniah 3:12).

Humility in the New Testament

In Jesus's teaching, it is clear that God opposes the proud but looks favorably upon the humble. Jesus affirms the poor in spirit,

206 The verb appears seventy-eight times in the Old Testament with twelve times meaning "humble" or "humbled" (Exodus 10:3; Deuteronomy 8:2, 3, 16; Judges 16:5; Ezra 8:21; Job 30:11; Psalm 55:19, 89:22; Isaiah 58:3, 5; Daniel 10:12).

"Whoever exalts himself will be humbled, and whoever humbles himself will be exalted" (Matthew 23:12; cf. Luke 4:11). Morris explains that "poor in spirit in the sense of this beatitude are those who recognize that they are completely and utterly destitute in the realm of the spirit. They recognize their lack of spiritual resources and therefore their complete dependence on God."[207] Jesus gives Himself as an example to the disciples who seemed to always seek preeminence. He invites all of us to learn from Him, "Come to me, all who labor and are heavy laden, and I will give you rest. Take my yoke upon you, and learn from me, for I am gentle and lowly in heart, and you will find rest for your souls" (Matthew 11:28–29). Right before He humbles Himself to a painful death on the cross, Jesus reminds His disciples that humility is the way of Christ. Because the disciples were wondering who will be the greatest, Jesus reminds them that "the Son of Man did not come to be served, but to serve, and to give His life as a ransom for many" (Mark 10:45).

The apostles continued to exalt the virtue of humility as part of the daily Christian life. Paul urges the first-century believers to "walk in a manner worthy of the calling to which you have been called, with all humility and gentleness, with patience, bearing with one another in love (Ephesians 4:1–2). It is counterculture to walk with humility and gentleness. Society bullies us into being proud, pushy, and presumptuous. Jesus invites us to be humble and gentle. And Jesus leads by example. He humbled Himself, giving us a lesson in humility. Not a theoretical lesson, but a painful lesson in reality when He gave His back to the wood of the cross, His spirit to the Father, and His mother to John (Luke 23:46; John 19:27). In the message to the church at Philippi, Paul contrasts humility with selfish ambition and conceit, "Do nothing from selfish ambition or conceit, but in humility count others more significant than yourselves" (Philippians 2:3). Self-centeredness is contrary to humility. One cannot be both self-centered and humble. Paul is telling the church that if unity is to be achieved, humility needs to

---

207 Leon Morris, *The Gospel according to Matthew*, Pillar New Testament Commentary (Grand Rapids: Eerdmans, 1992), 95.

be attained. When we experience Christ's salvation, we move from being self-centered to being Christ-centered and others-centered. We move from "What's in it for *me*?" to "What's in it for them?"

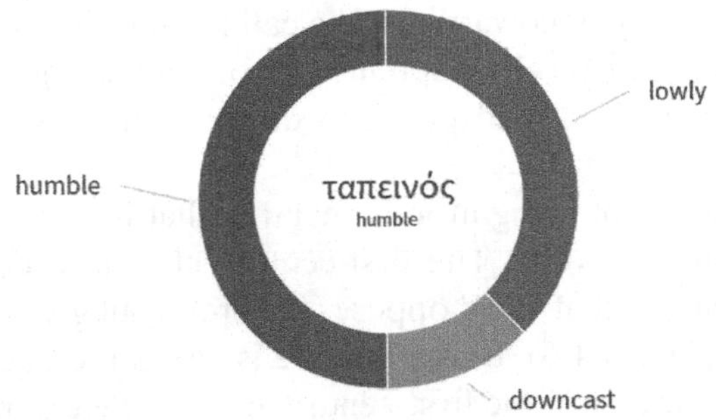

Figure 7.2 The word "humility/humble" in the LXX and the New Testament[208]

Dietrich Bonhoeffer put it well,

> Every personality cult that is concerned with important qualities, outstanding abilities, strengths, and the talents of someone else—even though these may be thoroughly spiritual in nature—is worldly and has no place in the Christian community. Indeed, it poisons that community. The demand one hears so often today for "people of episcopal stature," for "priestly men," and for "powerful personalities," springs too often from the spiritually sick need for the admiration of people, for the erection of visible structures of human authority, because the genuine authority of service seems too unimportant.[209]

Having put off earthly things like sexual immorality, impurity, and covetousness, the believer who is in the life-long process of sanctification has to put on heavenly things. "Put on then, as God's

208 Christians served the LORD with all humility (Acts 20:19), and they are to imitate the humility of Christ (Philippians 2:3).

209 Frank Thielman, *Philippians,* New International Version Application Commentary (Grand Rapids: Zondervan, 1995), 108.

chosen ones, holy and beloved, compassionate hearts, kindness, humility, meekness, and patience" (Colossians 3:12). Moo notes that "humility is a typically Christian virtue, which was often viewed negatively in the ancient world, where it was understood in terms of servility or cowardice. The call to humility in the New Testament is based on the supreme act of 'humbling,' Christ's taking on human form and going to death on the cross on our behalf."[210]

Being proud is not being morally neutral, that is clear in God's attitude toward the proud. The first-century church leader James reminds the church that "God opposes the proud but gives grace to the humble" (James 4:6). Being humble is also a prerequisite for unity. Another leader of the first-century church, Peter, encourages the church to "have unity of mind, sympathy, brotherly love, a tender heart, and a humble mind" (1 Peter 3:8). Peter and James are probably taking "God opposes the proud but gives grace to the humble" from Proverbs 3:34. "Clothe yourselves, all of you, with humility toward one another, for 'God opposes the proud but gives grace to the humble.' Humble yourselves, therefore, under the mighty hand of God so that at the proper time he may exalt you" (1 Peter 5:5–6). Moo notes that "God's gift of sustaining grace is enjoyed only by those willing to admit their need and accept the gift. The *proud*, on the other hand, meet only resistance from God."[211]

Humility in the Book of Proverbs

In his classic work *Humility*, Andrew Murray defines humility as "the place of entire dependence on God." Humility is "from the very nature of things, the first duty and the highest virtue of the creature, and the root of every virtue."[212] Dumbrell defines humility as "the personal quality that makes integration into the world

210 Douglas J. Moo, *The Letters to the Colossians and to Philemon*, Pillar New Testament Commentary (Grand Rapids: Eerdmans, 2008), 277.

211 Moo, *The Letter of James*, 191.

212 Murray, *Humility and Absolute Surrender* (Peabody, MA: Hendrickson, 2005), 6.

order possible and enables the possessor to know his place in the total system."[213]

God looks favorably upon the humble who is contrasted with the scornful, also known as a scoffer, one who expresses contempt toward others. "Toward the scorners he is scornful, but to the humble he gives favor" (Proverbs 3:34). In their pride and arrogance, the scornful mock the way of peace and make mockery of goodness. Thus, the humble embraces goodness and is a peacemaker. Scorners identify with the fools who hate knowledge (Proverbs 1:22), while the humble love to learn. Fools make fun of sin (Proverbs 14:9) while the humble avoid it. The proud are identified as scoffers (Proverbs 21:24) who are incorrigible (Proverbs 9:7). The humble, on the other hand, welcome correction.

The Hebrew word translated "humble" is a derivative from the verb whose root means "bent over (under pressure of circumstances). As affliction does its proper work, humility is the end result."[214] Dumbrell defines humility in wisdom literature as "the human recognition of one's inadequacy when faced with the evidence for creation and providence. Humility is finally defined not in terms of lowliness but in terms of selflessness and is an essential root of all wisdom."[215] There are blessings associated with being humble. "When pride comes, then comes disgrace, but with the humble is wisdom" (Proverbs 11:2). The word translated "pride" here is used of Pharaoh (Nehemiah 9:10), Israel (Nehemiah 9:16, 29), and of false prophets (Deuteronomy 18:20). In contrast, the humble choose the way of wisdom. The same word is used of those who walk humbly with God (Micah 6:8), "where it suggests the biddable spirit that is the opposite of the insubordination just considered."[216] This humility does not come from the depth of one's heart. Rather, it is the fear of the Lord that teaches one humility. "The fear of the Lord is instruction in wisdom, and

213 W. J. Dumbrell, ענו, *NIDOTTE*, ed. Willem VanGemeren, vol. 3 (Grand Rapids: Zondervan, 1998), 462.

214 Dumbrell, ענו, in *NIDOTTE,* 455.

215 Dumbrell, ענו, in *NIDOTTE,* 462.

216 Kidner, *Proverbs,* 86.

humility comes before honor" (Proverbs 15:33). The language is clear that one doesn't just land on wisdom as a bee lands on a flower. Rather, humility is at the end of the path of wisdom that comes through "instruction in wisdom." Acquiring humility, then, is not a passive attitude but an active endeavor. Dumbrell states that "wisdom has a religious foundation, a positive devotion to God, which means the renunciation of pride and the expression of humility."[217]

Proverbs 22:4 is another verse where the fear of the LORD and humility are coupled as appositional parallels. "The reward for humility and fear of the LORD is riches and honor and life." One would expect riches to be the reward of wise business practices, but here it is associated with humility. One would expect honor to be associated with a man's social status, but in God's economy, honor is associated with humility. H. A. Ironside puts it bluntly,

> How different are the paths and the ultimate rewards of the godly and the perverse! Heaven and hell are not more diverse than the roads leading thereto. The godly man is marked out from his fellows by a meek and contrite spirit, and the fear of the LORD. The ungodly is insubordinate and self-willed. The way of the former leads to true riches, the honor that cometh from God, and life everlasting.[218]

One of the best verses on the subject is Proverbs 18:12, "Before destruction a man's heart is haughty, but humility comes before honor." Waltke notes that "this antithetical proverb contrasts the destinies of the arrogant, who lifts himself up against God and by so much against his community, and the humble, who renouncing human pride, is a devout worshiper and by so much serves his community."[219]

---

217 Dumbrell, ענו, in *NIDOTTE*, 462.

218 Ironside, *Notes on the Book of Proverbs*, 302.

219 Waltke, *The Book of Proverbs 15–31,* 77. The word translated humility here appears five times in the Old Testament. Once in the Psalms (18:36), three times in Proverbs (15:33; 18:12; 22:4), and one time in Zephaniah (2:3).

Figure 7.3 The word "humility" in the Old Testament

The Proud Are Foolish and Sinful

If the wise are humble, it follows then that the proud are foolish. Pride is never portrayed in a positive light. Pride is not a neutral characteristic of one who simply isn't paying attention to the way they live. Strong words are used to avoid any confusion. "The fear of the LORD is hatred of evil. Pride and arrogance and the way of evil and perverted speech I hate" (Proverbs 8:13). Lady Wisdom doesn't just tolerate pride; she hates it. The parallelism employed points to the fact that pride is evil. We're reminded of Job, who "feared God and turned away from evil" (Job 1:1). Pride brings upon itself not just the hatred of the LORD but shame and dishonor. "When pride comes, then comes disgrace, but with the humble is wisdom" (Proverbs 11:2). Pride is what leads the scoffer to be arrogant (Proverbs 21:24), and it is the same pride that will deceive one into feeling safe until the LORD will bring them down (Jeremiah 49:16; Obadiah 1:3).[220] The God who is loving and merciful is also holy, righteous, and just and therefore will tear down "the house of the proud" (Proverbs 15:25).[221]

We need to be reminded often that "Pride goes before destruction and a haughty spirit before a fall" (Proverbs 16:18). The Ar-

220 Through Jeremiah, God communicates clearly that He is against the proud and will bring down the arrogant (Jeremiah 50:31–32).

221 Proverbs 29:23, "One's pride will bring him low, but he who is lowly in spirit will obtain honor."

abic proverb seems to agree: "the nose is in the heavens, the seat in the mire."[222] Even though the proud will experience material abundance, "it is better to be of a lowly spirit with the poor than to divide the spoil with the proud" (Proverbs 16:19). In his love for the house of the LORD and the fellowship of believers, David affirms, "I would rather be a doorkeeper in the house of my God than to dwell in the tents of wickedness" (Psalm 84:10). "The Germans express the connection between abundance and folly by the terse apothegm, "Voll, toll;" "Full, fool."[223] But pride is not just an insignificant moral flaw; it is sin. "Haughty eyes and a proud heart, the lamp of the wicked, are sin" (Proverbs 21:4).

In his book *Respectable Sins: Confronting the Sins We Tolerate*, Jerry Bridges notes that "of all the characters in the Bible who seem so repugnant to us, probably no one is more so than the self-righteous Pharisee in the parable of Jesus, who prayed, 'God, I thank you that I am not like other men, extortioners, unjust, adulterers, or even like this tax collector' (Luke 18:11). But the irony is that even as we condemn him, we can easily fall into the same self-righteous attitude."[224] Moral self-righteousness "expresses itself in a feeling of moral superiority with respect to other people."[225] Bridges identifies three types of pride that we battle daily. First, there is the pride of correct doctrine. Doctrinal pride is "the assumption that whatever my doctrinal beliefs are, they are correct, and anyone who holds another belief is theologically inferior."[226] While is important to have convictions, it is also important to learn how to hold these convictions with humility.

The second type of pride is the pride of achievement. While we are tempted to be proud about our successes in academia, sports, or business, the Bible teaches us that "success in any endeavor is

---

222 John Peter Lange et al., *A Commentary on the Holy Scriptures: Proverbs* (Bellingham, WA: Logos Bible Software, 2008), 156.

223 H. D. M. Spence-Jones, ed., *Proverbs*, The Pulpit Commentary (London; New York: Funk & Wagnalls Company, 1909), 313.

224 Bridges, *Respectable Sins,* 89.

225 Bridges, *Respectable Sins,* 90.

226 Bridges, *Respectable Sins,* 92.

under the sovereign control of God."[227] As the children of Israel are about to enter the Promised Land, Moses reminds them that it was God who gave them success.

> And you shall remember the whole way that the LORD your God has led you these forty years in the wilderness, that he might humble you, testing you to know what was in your heart, whether you would keep his commandments or not. And he humbled you and let you hunger and fed you with manna, which you did not know, nor did your fathers know, that he might make you know that man does not live by bread alone, but man lives by every word that comes from the mouth of the LORD. Your clothing did not wear out on you and your foot did not swell these forty years. (Deuteronomy 8:2–4)

And because we tend to be forgetful, He reminds to "take care lest you forget the LORD your God" (Deuteronomy 8:11).

Lastly, pride can also be seen in an independent spirit. Bridges affirms that "this spirit expresses itself primarily in two areas: a resistance to authority, especially spiritual authority, and an unteachable attitude."[228] The Bible is clear that as believers we are to submit to authority. The author of Hebrews writes, "Obey your leaders and submit to them, for they are keeping watch over your souls, as those who will have to give an account" (Hebrews 13:17). Furthermore, as believers, we are to be lifelong learners. The book of Proverbs portrays the wise as ready and willing to learn. "The wise of heart will receive commandments" (Proverbs 10:8). Even the Greek philosopher Socrates said, "to gain knowledge, one must first admit one's ignorance." Knowledge is not poured into the wise through some miraculous means. "An intelligent heart acquires knowledge, and the ear of the wise seeks knowledge" (Proverbs 18:15). Verbs of action are employed with the desire to learn. Knowledge must be pursued by going and listening to someone wiser. The fools, on the other hand, "despise wisdom

---

227 Bridges, *Respectable Sins,* 94.

228 Bridges, *Respectable Sins*, 97.

and instruction" (Proverbs 1:7). Waltke comments, "These conceited fools, in contrast with the teachable wise, are fixed in the correctness of their own opinions…that they despise God's revelation."[229] Bridges urges the believer to ask God to bring to mind "any tendencies of pride" and then to confess them. "As you do so, remember God's promise in Isaiah 66:2: 'This is the one to whom I will look: he who is humble and contrite in spirit and trembles at my word.'"[230]

A Lesson from Church History

When William Carey, the great missionary pioneer to India, was on his deathbed, he was visited by a missionary named Alexander Duff. He spent some time talking primarily about Carey's missionary life until finally, the dying man whispered, "Pray." Duff knelt down and prayed and then said goodbye. As he passed from the room, he heard a feeble voice calling him back. Carey said to him, "Mr. Duff, you have been speaking about Dr. Carey. When I am gone, say nothing about Dr. Carey—speak about Dr. Carey's Savior."[231]

A Christological Reading

Jesus is our example of humility. The prophets foretold that the Messiah would be humble. He would have a humble beginning by being born in the little village of Bethlehem, not in an Ancient Near Eastern metropolis (Micah 5:2). Even as the prophets foresaw Jesus's entrance into Jerusalem, He would not make a kingly entrance on a stallion, but a humble one on a donkey (Zechariah 9:9; Matthew 21:4–5). The Gospel writers portrayed Jesus as One who is humble (Matthew 11:29) and as One who serves (Mark 10:45; Luke 22:27). Jesus's words, as preserved in the Gospel of John, point to the fact that Jesus always humbled himself. Jesus said, "The Son can do nothing of His own accord" (John 5:19), "I can do nothing on my own" (John 5:30; 8:28), "I do not receive

229 Waltke, *The Book of Proverbs*, 181.

230 Bridges, *Respectable Sins*, 99–100.

231 Prosise, *Preaching Illustrations from Church History*, 113.

glory from people" (John 5:41), and "I do not seek my own glory" (John 8:50). Murray elaborates, "These words open to us the deepest roots of Christ's life and work. They tell us how it was that the Almighty God was able to work His redemptive work through Him…this life of entire self-abnegation, of absolute submission and dependence upon the Father's will, Christ found to be one of perfect peace and joy. He lost nothing by giving all to God…His humility was simply the surrender of Himself to God, to allow Him to do in Him what He pleased, whatever men around might say of Him, or do to Him."[232]

The Christ hymn in Philippians 2 is "a beautiful example of a very early hymn of the Christian church"[233] that points to the humility of Christ. Since we are His followers, we need to follow His example. Jesus's humility comes into sharper focus when we understand that He gave up His pre-incarnate glory when "the Word became flesh" (John 1:14), "who, though he was in the form of God, did not count equality with God a thing to be grasped" (Philippians 2:6). The old hymn reminds us that "He left the splendor of heaven, knowing His destiny was the lonely hill of Golgotha there to lay down His life for me." When we humble ourselves like Christ, we need to give up power, position, and prestige. In His incarnation, Jesus shows us humility in that he "emptied himself by taking the form of a servant, being born in the likeness of men" (Philippians 2:7). Thielman asserts that "The incarnation of Jesus Christ represents the antithesis of this human drive to dominate. Although he had access to all the privilege and power to which his identity with God entitled him, and although he could have exploited that privilege and power to dominate his creatures, Jesus considered his deity an opportunity for service and obedience. His deity became a matter not of getting but of giving, not of being served but of serving, not of dominance but of obedience…This means that the church and the believer must adopt an 'incarnational' demeanor."[234]

---

232 Murray, *Humility and Absolute Surrender,* 14–15.

233 Walter Hansen, *The Letter to the Philippians*, Pillar New Testament Commentary (Grand Rapids: Eerdmans, 2009), 122.

234 Thielman, *Philippians,* 129.

A few days before His crucifixion, Jesus further humbled Himself by lowering Himself to the ground to wash His disciples' feet (John 13). Christ continued to humble Himself "by becoming obedient to the point of death, even death on a cross" (Philippians 2:8). "The One who could have rightfully claimed the highest position in human history and justly received supreme honors, deliberately sought the lowest position and submitted himself to extreme humiliation."[235] Let us imitate Christ by humbling ourselves by serving others and by accepting and proclaiming His Lordship because "God has highly exalted Him and bestowed on Him the name that is above every name, so that at the name of Jesus every knee should bow, in heaven and on earth and under the earth, and every tongue confess that Jesus Christ is Lord, to the glory of God the Father" (Philippians 2:9–11).

235 Hansen, *The Letter to the Philippians,* 154.

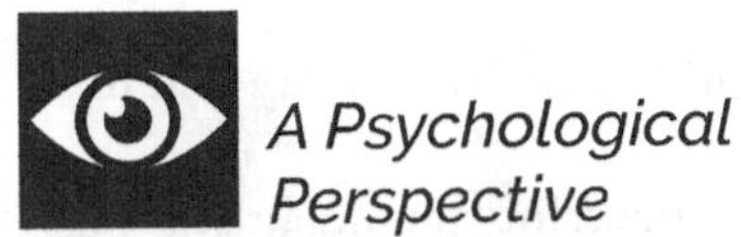

Reflections on Humility

Dr. Kevin Roberts

When pride comes, then comes disgrace,
but with the humble is wisdom.
—Proverbs 11:2

Scripture makes it abundantly clear throughout Proverbs that there are few qualities more important than the development of humility. We can find few things that produce in man the right relationship more clearly than humility before our LORD. Throughout the book of Proverbs, we are compelled to keep learning, but learning comes with the prerequisite of humility. Scripture makes it clear that we can only grow if we are willing participants in the learning process and demonstrate an openness of heart to receive the lessons that are being delivered. How can we as people continue to grow and change if we are not teachable? This is where humility comes in to save us from our pride and our own self-delusions. It is only in humility that we can demonstrate the necessary vulnerability and openness to embrace God's message and to be an empty vessel to be used by Him. However, it is equally important to realize that humility is not about giving in to others and being highly self-critical. In this chapter, we will look at how and why humility is absolutely necessary to live out the Christian life. We will examine the research and the traits that humility develops, as well as what often gets in our way and how insidious our pride can be.

The Scriptures have a frequently recurring theme in the passage in which God opposes the proud but whoever submits and demonstrates humility will be honored (Matthew 18:4). If God opposes the proud, then the only way to learn and grow is through the humbling experiences that this life brings. Despite the many opportunities and painful experiences, many of us fail to embrace our absolute dependence on God. Instead, we choose pride and a stiff-necked response in an attempt to protect our fragile self-image. The term humility has often stood in contrast to pride. In fact, there appears to be a negative relationship between narcissism and humility.[236] But as a believer, our self-image is not in what we do or who we are but in resting in our position as a child of God. But a child needs to demonstrate a teachable and humble spirit before his or her parents and not a self-righteous or narcissistic view. This is why Jesus states it this way, "Truly, I say to you, unless you turn and become like children, you will never enter the kingdom of heaven" (Matthew 18:3). It is with a child's humility that we need to approach our lives through humbly seeking God's guidance and correction.

The psychological literature on humility indicates that humble people are more likely to view themselves and others with a broader perspective.[237] One key aspect of humility, therefore, is modesty, whereby we make a decision to make things less about us and more about others. Interestingly, many individuals have argued from a secular perspective that humility cannot even be understood apart from a faith perspective because the characteristic is uniquely grounded in faith. Exline, Bushman, Faber, and Phillips indicated in their work that people often report feeling

---

236 Kibeom Lee and Michael C. Ashton, "Psychopathy, Machiavellianism, and Narcissism in the Five-Factor Model and the HEXACO Model of Personality Structure," *Personality and Individual Differences* 38, no. 7 (2005): 1571–582. https://doi.org/10.1016/j.paid.2004.09.016.

237 June Price Tangney, "Humility: Theoretical Perspectives, Empirical Findings and Directions for Future Research," *Journal of Social and Clinical Psychology* 19, no. 1 (2000): 70–82.

most humble in light of natural wonders.[238] It may be that in the presence of an omnipotent God, human beings are simply designed to be humble in their responses. There is something extraordinary in the vastness of nature and coming to terms with our own human frailty that seemingly puts us in this humble state. But others would argue that humility is the byproduct of the human experience of awe. Gordon et al. found that the feeling of awe is a positive emotion that is most commonly experienced through experiencing great works of art, architecture, beautiful scenery, and religious experiences.[239] It is in this state of awe that humility appears to be a byproduct, in other words, when the created comes into close contact with the Creator. It is in this sense of awe that we see humility increase and, as a result, the demonstration of prosocial behaviors.[240] Could it be that the fear of the LORD was built into us to easily move us from awe into humility and our true position before the God of the universe?

The concept of humility has found its way into the psychological literature in a variety of ways. Initially, the term was commonly associated with the 12 Steps of Alcoholics Anonymous where the first three steps emphasize trust in God. To establish trust in God, one must be willing to accept his or her own inability to manage life and accept that a "Power" greater than ourselves can restore us to sanity if we turn our will over to Him.[241] The 12 Steps, which were rooted in biblical principles, can possibly be seen as a process for increasing our humility and decreasing our prideful and

---

238 J. J. Exline, B. Bushman, J. Faber, and C. Phillips, "Pride Gets in the Way: Self-Protection Works Against Forgiveness." In *Ouch! Who Said Forgiveness Was Easy? Symposium Presented at the Annual Meeting of the Society for Personality and Social Psychology,* ed. J. J. Exline (Nashville, TN, 200).

239 Amie M. Gordon et al., "The Dark Side of the Sublime: Distinguishing a Threat-Based Variant of Awe," *Journal of Personality and Social Psychology* 113, no. 2 (2017): 310–28.

240 Jennifer E. Stellar et al., "Awe and Humility," *Journal of Personality and Social Psychology* 114, no. 2 (2018): 258–69. https://doi.org/10/1037/pspi0000109.

241 *Alcoholics Anonymous: The Big Book–4th Ed.* (New York City, NY: Alcoholics Anonymous World Services, Inc., 2001).

selfish hearts. Interestingly, as humility is encouraged in the 12 Steps, what we find in the psychological literature is that humility increases self-control, perseverance, and kindness toward others.

There may be several types of humility but one such example is when someone demonstrates intellectual humility.[242] Intellectual humility takes on several positive characteristics including the development of a realistic perspective of your own limitations.[243] The intellectually humble individual is better able to handle dissonant ideas and still be able to freely interact with opposing ideas and views.[244] These individuals are better prepared to engage in challenging and difficult discussions and yet maintain a stable sense of self while promoting social cohesion.[245]

So how does a humble person accomplish this without saying hurtful things to others?

Well, it appears that the development of humility goes one step further by improving our ability to self-regulate emotions.[246] So as humility increases, we see improved self-regulation because humility produces a balance between negative coping strategies that produce an inflated sense of self and allows the person to instead develop a more grounded view of themselves.[247] As a result, the humble person is better able to make realistic appraisals about themselves while being emotionally stable, open, and teachable.

---

242 Joshua N. Hook et al., "Intellectual Humility and Forgiveness of Religious Leaders," *The Journal of Positive Psychology* 10, no. 6 (February 2015): 499–506.

243 Hook et al., "Intellectual Humility and Forgiveness of Religious Leaders," 499–506.

244 Hook et al., "Intellectual Humility and Forgiveness of Religious Leaders," 499–506.

245 Annette Susanne Peters, Wade Clinton Rowat, and Megan Kathleen Johnson, "Associations between Dispositional Humility and Social Relationship Quality," *Psychology* 2, no. 03 (2011): 155–61.

246 Elissa Woodruff et al., "Humility and Religion: Benefits, Difficulties, and a Model of Religious Tolerance." In *Cross-Cultural Advancements in Positive Psychology,* ed. C. Kim Prieto (Dordrecht, Springer Netherlands, 2014), 271–85.

247 Woodruff et al., "Humility and Religion: Benefits, Difficulties, and a Model of Religious Tolerance," 271–85.

We see this humility demonstrated in Proverbs 6:3, "Do this then, my son, and deliver yourself; Since you have come into the hand of our neighbor, Go, humble yourself, and importune your neighbor." In humility, we find no need to protect our own identity, which allows us to be more responsive, cohesive, and emotionally stable.

So, in humility we find improved ability to develop a socially cohesive environment, better relationships, while increasing how much we value and appreciate others.[248] Those who have read the Scriptures are very aware that Jesus was not afraid to disrupt the social order yet He was very well known for His humility (Philippians 2). Is it possible that humility was emphasized in both the words of Solomon and Jesus because in humility we find the precursor to a deeper relationship with God? The psychological literature indicates that humble people tend to feel less threatened by others, tend to be more helpful, agreeable, generous, and more freely willing to forgive others.[249] Is it that in humility before God we His created beings find meaning, purpose, and a deeper, more realistic view of our value? We see in Proverbs how important it is to develop wisdom and understanding to avoid taking the foolish paths. But it is equally important that we have significant a measure of humility for when we wander down the wrong paths so that in the midst of our personal failures, we may demonstrate a teachable spirit and use God's wisdom to correct our path. Or did God, in His infinite wisdom, know that humility in His cre-

248 Annette Susanne Peters, Wade Clinton Rowat, and Megan Kathleen Johnson, "Associations between Dispositional Humility and Social Relationship Quality," *Psychology* 2, no. 03 (2011): 155–61. https://dx.doi.org/10.4236/psych.2011.23025; Kibeom Lee and Michael C. Ashton, "Psychopathy, Machiavellianism, and Narcissism in the Five-Factor Model and the HEXACO Model of Personality Structure," *Personality and Individual Differences* 38, no. 7 (2005), 1571–82. https://doi.org/10.1016/j.paid.2004.09.016; Elissa Woodruff et al., "Humility and Religion: Benefits, Difficulties, and a Model of Religious Tolerance." In *Cross-Cultural Advancements in Positive Psychology*, ed. C. Kim Prieto (Dordrecht, Springer Netherlands, 2014), 271–85.

249 Ryan M. Niemiec and Robert E. McGrath, *The Power of Character Strengths: Appreciate and Ignite Your Positive Personality* (VIA Institute on Character, 2019).

ated beings produces deeper relationships, increased social cohesion, and, thus, improves our ability to live out the purposes of the body?

Application Exercises and Questions for Being Humble

In Alcoholics Anonymous, the recovering community is asked to take a fearless moral inventory of their past and mistakes committed associated with their substance abuse. Have you ever really sat down and completed a moral inventory of your own behavior? These are truly terrifying things to do, because we must come face to face with our own depravity, and more importantly, our absolute dependence on a Savior. It takes a great deal of courage to truly look in the mirror at our own selfishness and be willing to admit them, then humbly fall before God and others. However, this process promises a more realistic self-view—a stronger self-identity and awareness of where we stand before the God of the universe. It is in these difficult moments that we begin to feel simultaneously humbled and blessed by the saving grace of Christ's sacrifice on the cross.

As we reflect on the relationship between humility and the development of our faith, I challenge each of us to spend time reflecting, answering the following questions.

1. If humility is needed to establish a more stable self-identity, and it is in humility that we develop more cohesive relationships, then why do we pretend to be something we are not in our relationships? What are we protecting, and what do we hope to accomplish through not being honest with ourselves?

2. Have you ever asked yourself where your pride has interfered in your relationships? Do you tend to cover up when you make mistakes in relationships, or can you be honest with yourself and humble enough to acknowledge your mistakes and shortcomings?

3. Have you ever considered what really gets in the way of being humble with the people in your lives? Do you honestly be-

lieve that both God and others cannot see your shortcomings? If you know that others and God see, then why choose to hide your guilt and shame and instead restore your relationship with God and others by first becoming humble?

A Pastoral Perspective

Humility at Church

Pastor Knute Larson

Humility looks like God, by His Word and His Spirit, is in charge; that is, His teachings and ways of living are pursued and honored. It looks like people giving deference to one another, and when the pastor gives deference to the word of God rather than his own thoughts alone. It looks like a really good place to worship and connect with people to sharpen each other for trust and obedience. It is not like everyone at church is so humble that no one wants to be up front, or to be chair of the board or soloist. Humility does not negate leadership or nerve, but it does prescribe an attitude of wanting to lead for the good of others rather than the glory of self.

Sometimes only God and the person in question know the major motive behind what we do, but clearly, any church action or attitude should somehow have a commitment to be for the glory of God and the good of others, not the applause of the one doing it. That is profanity. So true humility, as prescribed in Proverbs, looks like we are doing the best we can but not drawing attention to ourselves or checking the amount of feedback we are receiving. To this kind of church work, God "gives favor" (Proverbs 3:34), which is not synonymous with growth or "church of the year" awards, but with fear of the LORD. When we honor Him as a church, we help each other, care for outsiders, and enjoy honest and unselfish relationships. This Proverbs-kind-of humility looks like people seeking to understand each other in a strong discussion about a controversial doctrine in an ABF group. Humility shows up in a board meeting when there are two sides to the story—not that one side gives in, but that both are courteous and careful. "When pride comes," the results are very unhealthy, unbecoming to the church of our LORD—"there is disgrace, but with the humble is wisdom" (Proverbs 11:2).

Humility fashions public manners also. You don't feel like the pastor is talking down to you or pummeling you with truth; rather, he stands as a fellow struggler seeking God's strength and grace. You do not greet only close friends or those who are most popular or successful. You stop to greet and hear the ones in wheelchairs, stooping, so there is an eye-to-eye connection.

My heart sank to a new low once when I watched four men from the local rescue mission come into our hallway, and a few of our regulars looked the other way—probably because they didn't know what to say rather than because they were feeling proud. Perhaps you say the same things you would say to the governor if he or she were visiting: "Good to have you!"

We have the advantage of seeing humility demonstrated in the Gospels by the Savior, who is both God and man, and the most humble person who ever lived. In His description of Himself, He was clear: "I am gentle and humble in heart, and you will find rest for your souls. For My yoke is comfortable, and My burden is light" (Matthew 11: 29–30 NASB). He washes feet.

Why Humility Is So Important

While it is clear that God honors the humble, we are a church of the Savior who washes feet but who also "humbled himself by becoming obedient to the point of death, even death on a cross" (Philippians 2:8). We are under scriptural obligation to keep growing to be more like Him. Otherwise, we are just another organization.

In forty-one years of pastoring two churches and now fourteen years of coaching over 120 churches, I must be candid about myself and about slight and severe problems and skirmishes of churches of all sizes—often, the problem is so much worse because of ego. We could wish all selfish desires and fruits of the old nature were eradicated at conversion, but we all know the tensions of Romans 7:15 at times: "I do not understand my own actions. For I do not do what I want, but I do the very thing that I hate" (ESV emphasis mine). That selfishness often shows up in church life as a lack of humility.

Indeed there are times to stand strong—many of us relish the courage of church fathers who stood strong for the truths of the Bible, and sometimes at the cost of their lives or their friends. But many church-board arguments and even splits have a root cause in personality conflicts, which often is a nicer way to say "lack of humility."

If anyone could have fought for His own way, it was Jesus of Nazareth. If anyone could have walked with pride about His position, it was our Lord. But instead, He humbled himself. He washed feet. He cared for the outcasts.

Children would run to sit on His lap. The lepers had a saying among themselves, "He is one of us," not because He healed all of them but because He touched them and loved them. He befriended people that the religious ones of His day avoided. He went to the house of Zacchaeus, the tax cheat, and ended up at mine and yours.

He is the model of the unselfish and humble lifestyle, as defined in Proverbs. And He still calls us to follow Him.

Why Humility Does Not Always Show Up

"Life is hard" is a common expression. Leading well in the church is hard also, as is being up front or serving behind the scenes in a ministry. One excellent writer on volunteerism at church noted that people usually resign for one of two reasons, one of which is that they did not get thanked. And while we all understand that appreciation is appreciated, we also know that if acclaim or applause for service in the name of Christ is even an unspoken goal, we are not being humble or wise. Kindness and speaking the truth in love are also wisdom principles for believers. I remember sitting in on an oversight board meeting and hearing their rather unkind arguments, and then leaning into them with the question, "What are you trying to do to each other and to this church?" And we should all ask that of ourselves.

Humility is certainly an upside-down virtue, one that is not very honored by the world. And because a person walks in the doors of a church building does not mean he becomes something that is opposite of his heart. True conversion to our loving and humble Savior is mandatory for the Spirit of our God to couple with our spirits so that we can grow in obedient humility. In a sense, choosing Christ as Savior and LORD is choosing what is best for us, including humility.

It is choosing to trust and obey the One who can rescue us not only from eternal separation from our Creator, the all-wise God, but from an empty life of pride and ego. So, this looks like everyone at church, of course, at least everyone who truly believes in and follows Jesus Christ. Our LORD calls for that, and sometimes church people model that in such excellent ways. They put others; first, they honor each other; they submit to their leadership, singing and living in harmony and love. This all works by the wisdom and strength of the Spirit of Christ within us. Otherwise, humility is left in the text and does not show up at church or anywhere. Some church people apparently missed the class on grace and act as if God was rather pleased with them before He saved them. Maybe the LORD needed them on the team, and they act and argue as if they are indispensable! This is the opposite of humility.

What We Can Do Personally to Be More Humble

We can recognize the great privilege of being servants of Jesus Christ in His body, the Church. "So neither he who plants nor he who waters is anything, but only God, who makes things grow," was Paul's explanation when he scolded the Corinthians for their lack of humility and their breaking into sides and favorites instead of maintaining unity (1 Corinthians 3:7 NIV). It is true today, and that honor to God squelches pride and partisanship in the church. "What, after all, is Apollos? And what is Paul? Only servants . . . as the LORD has assigned to each his task" (1 Corinthians 3:5 NIV).

And that attitude will show in a class at church, or in the hallways, or pulpit, and for sure at home. Even on Facebook and the like.

Only we can humble ourselves. Others can make us look bad or get us angry, but only we can deal with our own heart attitudes. "Humble yourselves before the LORD, and he will lift you up," writes the half-brother of Jesus (James 4:10 NIV). "Humble yourselves, therefore, under God's mighty hand, that he may lift you up in due time," wrote the once loud-mouthed Peter, who had done just what he wrote, becoming a gentle shepherd of people (1 Peter 5:6 NIV).

True servanthood and care for others can only be self-imposed, deliberately, and in obedience to God. We must do this if we are to know and live with wisdom. We can choose to fear the LORD more than ourselves or others, and that brings wisdom and humility (Proverbs 15:33). This is especially called for as we go through pain and trouble, personally or as a church, which can help to make us humbly react with wisdom (Proverbs 18:12).

A Personal Prayer for Humility

Praise: For the privilege of being made in His image, to be spirit beings, and to serve others a little bit like Jesus serves us.

Repent: For any areas where you lack humility or just in general. (If you cannot think of any at first, guess at it!)

Ask: For spiritual wisdom and strength to have an attitude of humility and grace to serve others. For family or friends—you know who needs to have their pride adjusted by our LORD.

Yield: To desire to wash the feet of others, whatever specifics that may mean right now.

CHAPTER 8

Speaking Truth

A Theological Perspective

The Wise Speak Truth

Dr. Tiberius Rata

If I speak what is false, I must answer for it; if truth, it will answer for me.
—*Thomas Fuller*

Truth and Truth-telling in the Old Testament

Truth-telling, and the lack of it, comes into focus very early in the Bible. Satan does not tell the truth when he impugns God's character as he tells Eve, "You will not surely die" (Genesis 3:4), even though God said, "in the day that you eat of it you shall surely die" (Genesis 2:17). After Cain kills Abel, he lies to God about Abel's whereabouts with a brazen, "I do not know; am I my brother's keeper?" (Genesis 4:9). Abraham tells his wife Sarai to "say you are my sister, that it may go well with me" (Genesis 12:13). He lies again, "she is my sister," but thankfully God intervenes, and Abimelech does not sin against God (Genesis 20:1–7). Isaac does not learn from his father's mistakes, and the "she is my sister" lie resounds again (Genesis 26:7). Rachel continues what seems to be a generational sin and lies to her father after stealing his household gods (Genesis 31:17–35). Joseph's brothers lie to their father about what happened to Joseph (Genesis 37:31–34), they lie when they tell Joseph that "we are honest men" (Genesis 42:11), and they even lie after their brother forgives them (Genesis 50:15–21).

Truth-telling is so important to God that He put it as the ninth commandment, "You shall not bear false witness against your neighbor" (Exodus 20:16). God wants us to tell the truth because truth is consistent with His character. Even the pagan prophet Balaam affirms that "God is not man, that He should lie, or a son of man, that He should change His mind. Has He said, and will He not do it? Or has He spoken, and will He not fulfill it?" (Numbers 23:19). After entering the Promised Land, Achan steals and lies about stealing, costing the Israelites a great defeat (Joshua 7). Job accuses his friends of being worthless physicians that are guilty of lying (Job 13:4). The Psalms portray God as the Destroyer of those who lie and as One who hates those who are deceitful (Psalm 5:6).[250]

On the other hand, the one who speaks truth will be rewarded with dwelling with God on His holy hill (Psalm 15:1–2). The one who "gives birth to lies" is characterized as evil (Psalm 7:14; 58:3), while the one who tells the truth is "blessed" (Psalm 40:4). Psalm 59:12 gives us the insight that sometimes not telling the truth is rooted in pride, and the one who lies will suffer the consequence of their sin. "For the sin of their mouths, the words of their lips, let them be trapped in their pride. For the cursing and lies that they utter consume them in wrath" (Psalm 59:12–13). We need to desire truth like the psalmist who implores God to "not take the word of truth out of my mouth, for my hope is in Your rule" (Psalm 119:43). After all, God's Law is an unchanging truth. "The sum of your word is truth, and every one of your righteous rules endures forever" (Psalm 119:160). The wise and righteous want to be delivered from the prison of lying and deceit. "Deliver me, O Lord, from lying lips, from a deceitful tongue" (Psalm 120:2).

Through the prophets, God reminds His people that truth-telling is part of His character. "I the Lord speak the truth; I declare what is right" (Isaiah 45:19). God is the God of truth (Isaiah 65:16). Therefore, God condemns those who reject truth and resort to ly-

---

250 The Bible says that God hates those who lie, He hates "the wicked and the one who loves violence" (Psalm 11:5). See also Proverbs 6:16–19 about what God hates.

ing. Isaiah condemns the prophets who teach lies (Isaiah 9:15; 28:15) and the nation who lied and turned to idolatry (Isaiah 57:11; 59:3–4). Injustice, oppression, and dishonesty will be judged and punished (Isaiah 59:14–15). Jeremiah continues the indictment on the scribes who use a "lying pen" to distort the truth of God's Law (Jeremiah 8:8). Even the prophets are prophesying lies in the name of the LORD (Jeremiah 14:14; 23:25–26, 32; 27:10, 14, 16), "they commit adultery and walk in lies" (Jeremiah 23:14). The sin of lying trickles down from the leaders to the common people. "Everyone deceives his neighbor, and no one speaks the truth; they have taught their tongue to speak lies; they weary themselves committing iniquity" (Jeremiah 9:4). Not only are the people lying but also they trust in lies that will lead to their exile (Jeremiah 13:25). Hananiah speaks against Jeremiah and lies about the length of the exile (Jeremiah 28:1–4). Hananiah receives the death penalty from God Himself. "Therefore thus says the LORD: 'Behold, I will remove you from the face of the earth. This year you shall die, because you have uttered rebellion against the LORD.' In the same year, in the seventh month, the prophet Hananiah died" (Jeremiah 28:16–17).

God condemns the false prophets through Ezekiel as well.[251] "You have profaned me among my people…by your lying to my people, who listen to lies (Ezekiel 13:19; 22:28). Through Hosea, God promises to punish those who have spoken lies against Him (Hosea 7:13), and because they "have eaten the fruit of lies" (Hosea 10:13). Through Amos, God reminds His people that "their lies have led them astray" (Amos 2:4) even though they reject those who speak it (Amos 5:10). Using irony, Micah muses that the requirement for being a prophet is going about uttering "wind and lies" (Micah 2:11). Lastly, through the prophet Zechariah, God instructs His people to "speak the truth to one another; render in your gates judgments that are true and make for peace" (Zechariah 8:16). More than that, "love truth and peace" (Zechariah 8:19).

251 The first time false prophets are addressed is in Deuteronomy 18:18–22.

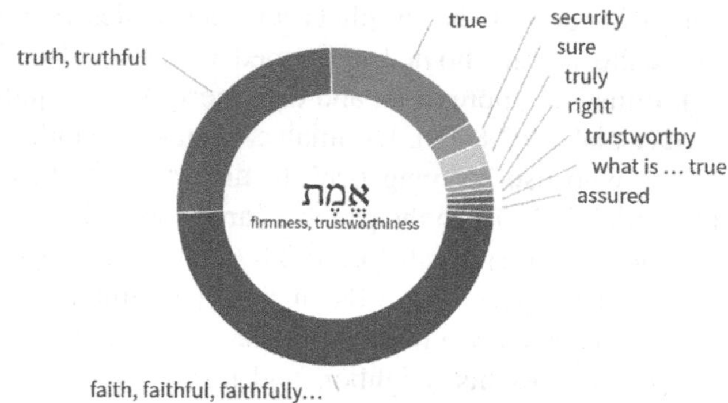

Figure 8.1 Faithful/truth (ĕmet) in the Old Testament

Truth and Truth-telling in the New Testament

The God of the Old Testament is also the God of the New Testament, so the concept of truth or God's desire for His children to speak truth has not changed. The disciples recognized that Jesus is true and that He teaches the way of God truthfully (Matthew 22:16; Mark 12:14). John is the disciple who uses the word most often. For John, Jesus came "full of grace and truth" (John 1:14), and "grace and truth came through Jesus Christ" (John 1:17). Jesus affirms that the Father who sent Him is true (John 8:26). In a world of false gods, in His priestly prayer, Jesus points to the Father, "And this is eternal life, that they know you, the only true God, and Jesus Christ whom you have sent" (John 17:3). True worshippers worship God "in spirit and in truth" (John 4:23–24). In one of the most contentious episodes between Jesus and the religious of the day, Jesus associates lying with the devil. "You are of your father the devil, and your will is to do your father's desires. He was a murderer from the beginning, and does not stand in the truth, because there is no truth in him. When he lies, he speaks out of his own character, for he is a liar and the father of lies" (John 8:44). Unfortunately, many choose to follow the devil and his schemes, and subsequently, truth is abandoned. Jesus states, "But because I tell the truth, you do not believe me" (John 8:45). Jesus affirms that He is "the way, the truth, and the life" and the only way to God. "No one comes to the Father except through Me" are the words of Jesus to His disciples (John 14:6).

The fifteenth-century monk Thomas á Kempis said, "Without the Way there is no going, without the truth there is no knowing, and without the life there is no living."[252] It is through truth that the believer is sanctified, and Jesus affirms that "Your word is truth" (John 17:17). The apostle Paul considers it as ungodliness when people exchange the truth for a lie (Romans 1:18–32). God will judge with wrath and fury those who "do not obey the truth, but obey unrighteousness" (Romans 2:6–8). To the church in Ephesus, Paul writes that in order to achieve unity, the church body has to speak the truth in love (Ephesians 4:15). In the same chapter, he continues the thought, "Therefore, having put away falsehood, let each one of you speak the truth with his neighbor, for we are members one of another" (Ephesians 4:25). To the church in Colossae, he puts it in the imperative form, "Do not lie to one another, seeing that you have put off the old self with its practices" (Colossians 3:9). Paul writes to the church in Philippi that the believer needs to pursue thinking about things that are true (Philippians 4:8).

Figure 8.2 The noun "truth" in the New Testament[253]

252 Thomas á Kempis, *The Imitation of Christ* (New York: Vintage Books, 1998), 167.

253 Ninety-six of 109 times the noun is translated truth, truthful, or truthfully. Six times it is translated as true. Five times it is translated truly. One time it is translated "certainly" (Luke 22:59). One time it is translated as "rightly false" (Romans 2:2).

Focusing on the truth will not happen organically or automatically. We are reminded of what the apostle Paul wrote to the church in Ephesus, "Speaking the truth in love, we are to grow up in every way into him who is the head, into Christ" (Ephesians 4:15). Peter writes to the first-century church that is scattered throughout the Roman empire to "put away all malice and all deceit and hypocrisy and envy and all slander" (1 Peter 2:1).

Truth and Truth-telling in the Book of Proverbs

The first time the word *'ĕmet* appears in Proverbs is in conjunction with Hése*d* where the pair can be translated as "steadfast love and truth," or "steadfast love and faithfulness" (Proverbs 3:3).[254] In context, the word can be translated either "truth" or "faithfulness" since the young man is exhorted to live faithfully in light of commandments and parental instruction given. "Let not steadfast love and [truth] faithfulness forsake you; bind them around your neck; write them on the tablet of your heart" (Proverbs 3:3). This language is also used in conjunction with the Torah, the Law of God (Deuteronomy 6:8–9), telling us that these words are not just good advice, but these words are the very words of God for His people.

In chapter 8, Lady Wisdom affirms that truth-telling is "not so much a matter of intellect as it is faith and obedience."[255] "Hear, for I will speak noble things, and from my lips will come what is right, for my mouth will utter truth; wickedness is an abomination to my lips" (Proverbs 8:6–7). Speaking truth is connected with being noble, while speaking abominations is connected with being wicked. Telling lies is not morally neutral, and thus speaking truth is morally superior. Speaking truth is sometimes rewarded.[256] In Proverbs 11:18, we read, "The wicked earns deceptive wages,

---

254 The pair appears also in Genesis 24:49; 47:29; Exodus 34:6; Joshua 2:14; 2 Samuel 2:6; 15:20; Psalm 25:10; 61:7; 85:10; 86:15; 89:14; Proverbs 3:3 and 20:28.

255 Garrett, *Proverbs, Ecclesiastes, Song of Songs,* 107.

256 Proverbs are principles not promises. We should not think that every time we speak truth, we will be blessed. In many instances, we live by the edict, "Tell the truth and prepare to die."

but one who sows righteousness gets a sure reward." The expression translated "a sure reward" is literally "reward of truth."[257] Speaking truth is sometimes couched in legal language. "Whoever speaks the truth gives honest evidence, but a false witness utters deceit" (Proverbs 12:17). The parallelism connects speaking truth with honest evidence and a false witness with deceit. The Torah prohibits and punishes lying.[258] The way of wisdom is the way of the truth, and the way of truth pays dividends in the long run. "Truthful lips endure forever, but a lying tongue is but for a moment" (Proverbs 12:19).

Growing up in Romania, I learned a traditional proverb that can be translated as "the lies has short legs," meaning that truth will triumph in the long run (pun intended). Lying is not morally neutral. "Lying lips are an abomination to the LORD, but those who act faithfully are his delight" (Proverbs 12:22). "A lying tongue" is one of the things that the LORD hates and considers an abomination (Proverbs 6:16–19). Longman notes that the Israelite religion contained ritual, but it was never "a matter of pure ritual."[259] In a court of law "a truthful witness saves lives," while "one who breathes out lies is deceitful" (Proverbs 14:25). Earlier in the chapter, Solomon affirms that those who go astray do so because they devise evil. In contrast, those who devise good "meet steadfast love and truth" (Proverbs 14:22). The verbs employed suggest that we have to pursue truth, and we have to intentionally combine truth with love. Because lying is not morally neutral, "a false witness will not go unpunished, and he who breathes out lies will not escape" (Proverbs 19:5).

Truth is crucial in leadership. "Steadfast love and truth preserve the king, and by steadfast love his throne is upheld" (Proverbs 20:28). The lies we tell become the seismic faults that produce the big earthquakes that destroy relationships and kingdoms. On the other hand, steadfast love and truth are the mortar that hold

257 This expression occurs only here in the Old Testament.

258 Exodus 20:16; 23:1, 7; Deuteronomy 19:18–20.

259 Tremper Longman III, *Proverbs,* Baker Commentary on the Old Testament Wisdom and Psalms (Grand Rapids: Baker, 2006), 330.

relationships and kingdoms together. The wise pass on "counsel and knowledge" to others to make them "know what is right and true," so that they "may give a true answer" (Proverbs 22:21). Furthermore, giving an honest answer is compared to a kiss on the lips (Proverbs 24:26). Sins usually come in bunches. Proverbs 26:28 confirms that lying is rooted in hate. "A lying tongue hates its victims." Just as steadfast love and truth are paired to build up, hatred and lying join to destroy their victims.

And lastly, the word "true" is associated with God revealing Himself through words. "Every word of God proves true; he is a shield to those who take refuge in him" (Proverbs 30:5). Agur's dying wish is a life absent of falsehood. "Two things I ask of you; deny them not to me before I die; remove far from me falsehood and lying" (Proverbs 30:7–8).

A Lesson from Church History

John Huss was a Czech priest who died as a martyr for speaking truth. He fought particularly against the ecclesiology and sacramentalism of the Catholic church. Like John the Baptist, Huss spoke truth to power and for that he paid with his life. Refusing to recant for speaking truth, he was martyred on July 6, 1415. Before being martyred, he said,

> I, John Hus, in hope a priest of Jesus Christ, fearing to offend God and to fall into perjury, am not willing to recant all or any of the articles produced against me in the testimonies of false witnesses. For God is my witness that I neither preached, asserted, nor defended them, as they said that I had defended, preached, and asserted them… Furthermore, concerning the articles drawn from my books, at least those drawn correctly, I declare, that if any of them contain a false sense, that sense I repudiate. But fearing to offend against the truth and to speak against the opinions of the saints, I am not willing to recant any of them. If it were possible that my voice could now be heard in the whole world, as at the Day of Judgment every lie and all my sins shall be revealed, I would most gladly

> recant before all the world every falsehood and every error I ever have thought of saying or have said.[260]

As the fire was lit, he sang, "Christ, Thou Son of the living God, have mercy on us," he prayed silently for a while and died reciting the LORD's Prayer.[261]

A Christological Reading

Truth is that which corresponds to reality. Truth is not something we construct on our own unless we first reject the correspondence model for truth. The Bible begins with "In the beginning, God created the heavens and the earth" (Genesis 1:1). John begins his gospel with "In the beginning was the Word, and the Word was with God, and the Word was God" (John 1:1). By pointing back to the beginning, John makes a statement about Jesus's divinity and the fact that He was present at creation. "All things were made through him, and without him was not any thing made that was made" (John 1:3).[262] We would not know these things if they were not revealed to us in Scripture. The Bible reveals truth, and we have the freedom to choose to accept or reject truth. But when we reject God's truth, we have to replace it with something else, namely a lie. Jesus affirms, "I am the way, the truth, and the life, no one comes to the Father except through me" (John 14:6). We either accept or reject this truth claim. If we reject Jesus as Truth and the only way to salvation, we'll have to replace it with the lie that there is another way to have eternal life. But what we believe about Jesus has eternal consequences. In His dispute with His opponents, Jesus said, "You search the Scriptures because you think that in them you have eternal life; and it is they that bear witness about me, yet you refuse to come to me that you may have life" (John 5:39–40). At the end of history, Jesus is called "Faithful and True," One who "in righteousness he judges and makes war"

---

260 Matthew Spinka, *John Hus: A Biography* (Princeton, NJ: Princeton University Press, 2017), 284.

261 Spinka, 289.

262 See also 1 Corinthians 8:6; Colossians 1:16; Hebrews 1:2.

(Revelation 19:11). Thomas notes that Jesus "is trustworthy in fulfilling His promises and is the true Messiah announced from ancient times (Revelation 3:7, 14)."[263]

263 Thomas, *Revelation 8–22: An Exegetical Commentary*, 383.

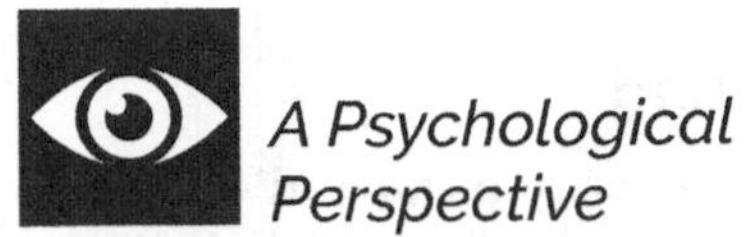

A Psychological Perspective

Reflections on Speaking Truth

Dr. Kevin Roberts

Lying lips are an abomination to the Lord, but those who act faithfully are his delight.
—Proverbs 12:22

From the time we were young, no matter the background, we were all taught to tell the truth. Everyone seems to understand at a basic moral level that lying or dishonesty is wrong and that there are potential consequences for these actions. We grasp the importance of telling the truth because we intrinsically sense when we violate this moral law established by God. Proverbs 6:16–19 instructs, "There are six things that the Lord hates, seven that are an abomination to him: haughty eyes, a lying tongue, and hands that shed innocent blood, a heart that devises wicked plans, feet that make haste to run to evil, a false witness who breathes out lies, and one who sows discord among brothers." However, we continue to violate this law frequently as human beings, freely relegating "white lies" as one of those "lesser sins." In psychological literature, a growing body of research is looking at how deceit, lying, or dishonesty has long-term impacts on the lives of others. In this chapter, we will examine the importance of truth-telling, along with the potential problems of lying both to others and to ourselves.

The Importance of Truth-telling

As parents, we often determine the severity of a child's punishment on whether he or she told us the truth or not. This is likely because we use truth-telling as a means of determining someone's character. We all encourage honesty in our children…or at least we intend to do so. However, we often indirectly communicate that "white lies" are okay when we tell our children, for example, to express gratitude for an awful sweater from Great Aunt Gertrude. The subtle or indirect messages about lying communicate societal norms as children age into adolescence, and this appears to be something that remains relatively stable as they move into adulthood.[264] The research behind moral development would indicate that the accuracy of understanding honesty increases up till high school, as measured by the Moral Integrity Survey, and then remains stable as the individual moves from adolescence into adulthood.[265] This would support the notion that it is instrumental in teaching the value of truth-telling when children are very young and allowing them to continue to develop until honesty is set in their hearts. Interestingly, Setoh et al. found that parents actually discouraged lying or deceptive behaviors in their children by having a great sense of religiosity themselves.[266] This point was again made clear in Mark 7:20–23, "And he [Jesus] said, 'What comes out of a person is what defiles him. For from within, out of the heart of man, come evil thoughts, sexual immorality, theft, murder, adultery, coveting, wickedness, deceit, sensuality, envy, slander, pride, foolishness. All these evil things come from within, and they defile a person.'"

Lying to Others

If we are all taught at a young age the importance of telling the truth, why is there an incredible amount of dishonesty in the

264 L. Olson, "The Assessment of Moral Integrity Among Adolescents and Adults." *Dissertation Abstracts International* 60, no. 6 (1998), 257–64.

265 L. Olson, "The Assessment of Moral Integrity Among Adolescents and Adults."

266 Peipei Setoh et al., "Parents with Greater Religiosity Lie Less to Their Children," *Psychology of Religion and Spirituality* 14, no. 1 (2022): 108–18.

world? At what age do we start to conceptualize our understanding of lying? Why do we lie to others, and what do we tend to lie about? Research on lying, measured by self-report supports the notion that we often lie one to two times each day.[267] Wellman et al. found that preschool children are already able to understand how different people have unique mental facilities and that lying is a sign of advancing development in young kids.[268] These preschool age children develop what is known as a Theory of Mind by which they form a more complete picture of reality and the impact of their own environment on them.[269] Meanwhile, other researchers have been studying what motivates a person to lie and also when they choose to lie. Spidel et al. identified nine areas of lying and further identified categories as either other-centered or self-serving motivations for lying.[270]

Spidel et al. supports the idea that the motivation to lie to others is commonly about our self-preservation, avoidance of consequences, and self-serving in nature.[271] Other researchers have found that those demonstrating high amounts of humility and honesty were less likely to lie for personal gain or self-centered motivations and typically had more genuine relationships with peers.[272] Furthermore, an inverse relationship was found with those who tended to score low on honesty-humility, as they were more prone to attempt to manipulate others.

267 Bella M. DePaulo et al., "Lying in Everyday Life," *Journal of Personality and Social Psychology* 70, no. 5 (1996): 979–95.

268 Henry M. Wellman, David Cross, and Julanne Watson, "Meta-Analysis of Theory-of-Mind Development: The Truth about False Belief," *Child Development* 72, no. 3 (2001): 655–84.

269 Jia Ying Lee and Kana Imuta, "Lying and Theory of Mind: A Meta-Analysis," *Child Development* 92, no. 2 (2021): 536–53.

270 Alicia Spidel et al., "'Wasn't me!' A field study of the relationship between deceptive motivations and psychopathic traits in young offenders," *Legal and Criminological Psychology* 14, no. 2 (2011): 335–47.

271 Spidel et al., "'Wasn't me!' A field study of the relationship between deceptive motivations and psychopathic traits in young offenders."

272 Michael C. Ashton, Kibeom Lee, and Reinout E. de Vries, "The Hexaco Honesty-Humility, Agreeableness, and Emotionality Factors," *Personality and Social Psychology Review* 18, no. 2 (2014): 139–52.

MOTIVATION	OPERATIONAL DEFINITION
Self-serving Motivations	
Avoid negative evaluation	Telling a lie to avoid feelings of shame or judgment; to create a positive self-image to fit in with others.
Avoid punishment	Telling a lie to avoid getting into trouble by denying or claiming behaviors they have or have not performed.
Heighten self-presentation	Telling a lie to impress others; to present one's self in a positive light, denying the negative aspects of self.
Obtain a reward	Telling a lie to manipulate people to gain something you do not deserve and would not have been obtained in other circumstances.
Compulsive lies	Telling lies spontaneously and for no obvious purpose.
Carelessness	May be due to impulse control issues where individuals lie because they do not care about providing correct answers; consequences of being caught in a lie do not matter.
Duping delight	Telling a lie for the pleasure of deceiving someone else; find enjoyment in outwitting or conning another person.
Secretive lies	Telling a lie to keep personal information concealed.
Protective lies	Telling a lie to protect one's self from physical retaliation from another person.
Other-oriented Motivations	
Prosocial	Telling a lie to bring pleasure to yourself and others, such as telling a child that Santa Claus is real.
Altruistic	Telling a lie to protect others from harm; to make others feel better.

Figure 8.3 Motivations for lying and their operational definitions[273]

273 Spidel et al., "'Wasn't me!' A field study of the relationship between deceptive motivations and psychopathic traits in young offenders."

When we lie, we do not have to deal with reality, at least temporarily. For example, a man flees a crime scene and is later apprehended by the police. When questioned as to why he ran, he lies and says he was afraid rather than admit he is guilty. He is attempting to avoid reality and preserve his sin. While many of us have never committed a crime that involved lying to the police, perhaps a different example might ring true. A wife brings up a sensitive subject to her husband, and in an effort to avoid conflict, the husband makes up an excuse, and the subject is dropped. What the husband fails to grasp, though, is that by honestly dealing with the conflict, he has the opportunity to deepen his relationship with his wife. As we can see from the above examples, it is better to live truthfully rather than live in deceit and avoid difficult conversations or avoid the consequences of our behavior. This requires us to live honestly and courageously with others and requires humility to become vulnerable and take personal responsibility for our actions.

God gives us the courage to face these burdens and troubles that life brings each day. As we become more honest with others and take responsibility for our actions, we are presented with an incredible opportunity for real growth as we attempt to walk the path toward righteousness.

Lying to Ourselves

If lying is sometimes motivated by a desire to create a positive self-image, then are we lying not only to others, but also to ourselves? Do we sometimes lie to others because admitting who we are and what we truly represent is too painful of a reality? Lying to others is often an attempt to avoid reality, conflict, or consequences. The psalmist states it this way, "Deliver me, O LORD, from lying lips, from a deceitful tongue" (Psalm 120:2). Embracing honesty by telling the truth often forces us to come face to face with our sin. In the book *Falling Upward*, author Richard Rohr makes the point that we must all face our "necessary suffering" in our lives, and failure to do so impedes our development.[274] We can use a host of distractions to avoid looking in the mirror at

274 Richard Rohr, *Falling Upward: A Spirituality of the Two Halves of Life* (San Francisco: Jossey-Bass, 2013).

our own depravity, including a variety of compulsive and addictive behaviors, but eventually, we must look past our excuses and see the root problem of our sin. Solomon is communicating as a father to a son in Proverbs 4, encouraging him to watch his own feet and to not veer off the path to the left or right. In many cases, addiction, lying, and other sinful behaviors are beckoning us toward a path that looks easier. But we must diligently pursue righteousness. As Proverbs 4:25 states, "Let your eyes look directly forward, and your gaze be straight before you." There is always a path that looks right in the eyes of man, but in truth leads to death and destruction (Proverbs 14:12).

Rather than lying to ourselves, we must accept our own depravity and embrace truth which will lead us back to the cross of Christ. The apostle Peter confronts Ananias about why he had allowed Satan to fill his heart and hold back what belonged to God. Peter states, "You have not lied to man but to God" (Acts 5:3–4). Lying to God, others, and to ourselves will only bring us suffering. Instead, God calls us to show godly remorse (2 Corinthians 7:10) for our sin and take responsibility for actions (Psalm 51:3–4), and even to confess to one another (James 5:16) when we have failed. In so doing, we remain humble before the God of the universe. Will we challenge ourselves to look at honestly facing our depravity as a real opportunity for growth? It is through the power and blood of Jesus that we can courageously face our own depravity and stop using lies to hide or conceal our sinful nature. Instead, we can choose to confront and acknowledge our own depravity while simultaneously choosing to repent, show godly remorse/grief and watch our feet, so we stay on the path toward righteousness through our relationship with Christ.

Application Exercises and Questions for Truth-telling

As we conclude this section on truth-telling, I challenge each of us to spend time honestly answering the following questions.

1. Have you ever asked yourself what you tend to lie about? Do you tend to lie to avoid consequences or protect your own self-image or maintain a godly image?

2. Have you ever considered when you tend to lie or at least not fully disclose the truth to your friends, family, or spouse? Have you considered how that could negatively impact the nature of those relationships? Are you avoiding conversations that need to happen for the health of your marriage and for your own spiritual development? Have you considered what covering up the "necessary suffering" is doing and what lessons are being lost that God could teach you in these scenarios?
3. As you reflect on your own depravity, have you asked how lying or not disclosing parts of yourself has worked for you? Where are you hiding from God and others? If you are hiding, are you struggling to believe that if you repent and show godly remorse, God's grace is sufficient for you?

Speaking Truth at Church

Pastor Knute Larson

Truth is one of the major issues of our faith. God is the source of truth. Jesus is its personification, "I am the truth," He assures us. We believe His revelation of His eternal salvation plan, that it is all true. And so, in the church body formed by the Holy Spirit of truth, we must tell the truth. We must trust each other. We must be worthy of that trust. The church is one place where you meet with people from many different backgrounds and immediately trust each other. Or at least, it should be that way. It certainly follows that a person who claims, even humbly, to be linked spiritually to the One true God, the source of all truth, will be a person who tells the truth and even lives in a general way according to the truth revealed in Scripture. And we could say the same for the local church as a family of people committed to truth and God. Proverbs is clear about this, calling for an act of faith that does not merely salute these commands of Scripture but, in a noble way, obeys what God says.

We are to be known as people who believe and obey God's truth and as a body of believers who preach, teach, and model truth. People who believe in Jesus Christ the truth will also believe in and obey the Proverbs as truth, not just because we fear punishment assigned to lying, but because we care about how God feels. He hates falsehood (Proverbs 6:16–19). If "steadfast love and truth preserve the king" (Proverbs 20:28), it is not too big a stretch to say they will also uphold the pastor and other leaders of the church. The people of the church will have confidence in their leadership and in church communications. They will hear the truth of Scripture in sermons and lessons, not just human ideas. While any teacher has the right at times to say, "I think," he or she is also obligated to preach and teach the Word of truth. "I think" will be replaced most often by "The Bible says." And the leaders and the church will model that. Allowing for unforeseen circumstances, of course, when someone from the church says he will do something, you can take it to the bank. You can count it as true.

Why Truth and Truth-telling Is So Important

Christians, church people, follow the Master/Savior who said, "I am the way, the truth"—let's stop there this time. Jesus is the source of what is right. If He says something, it is so. He is the source of the systems that make the universe function. And we say we are intertwined with Him, which would imply we tell the truth and live it. The apostle Paul called the Ephesians and all believers to be growing in their faith and to stop living as unbelievers do, "in the futility of their minds. They are darkened in their understanding, alienated from the life of God because of the ignorance that is in them, due to the hardness of heart" (Ephesians 4:17–18). The way we are to live looks like "speaking the truth in love, we are to grow in every way into him who is the head, into Christ" (Ephesians 4:15), a strong contrast between a person who lives for self and one who lives in combination with Jesus Christ.

"A lying tongue hates its victims," a phrase already referred to in this commentary (Proverbs 26:28), shows that a group of people who love their Savior and each other must tell the truth.

In a sense, all we have from each other is our word. It is what brings trust and, therefore, confidence. It is hard to like someone whose word you cannot trust or even listen to them. And without all that, the church falls to weakness. It becomes a shamble of hypocrisy for its members and observers. It defames instead of exalts the name of its Savior. Our LORD is the source of facts and the revelation of reality. All that He says or has written in His Word is accurate and dependable. So, it is only right that we represent Him with truth. We hold to the truth and tell the truth. We do not deceive each other in any way. We live in the way defined in the truths of the Bible. It is, in one sense, what the church is about. We are the body of Christ, the temple of the living God, the family of those living in combination with God the Spirit.

Proverbs is clear: "Lying lips are an abomination to the LORD" because they divide and cripple His Church. Lies keep us from trusting each other or entrusting our children to another person for the Sunday school class or youth trip. We certainly would not want someone who lies counting the offering money of the church or keeping confidential records or working in the church office or giving the sermon or group lesson! As much as any organization in the world, or more, the Church is built on truth.

Why Truth and Truth-telling Don't Always Show Up

We do not need surveys from Barna to prove that lying often goes to church. We have all been deceived by a fellow believer who has exaggerated or disguised the truth, or we have done it to someone else. Proverbs calls leaders of the church and all of us to tell the truth to the people of the church. But we sometimes want to look better than the truth might imply. And we all know the temptation to color the truth, so we do look better, or the church does. We humans easily fudge and fib and make up other euphemisms that do not sound like lies. It just comes easily, especially if our ego is at stake or if we need an excuse for missing an assignment. Most of the verbal scuffles I have tried to mediate as a pastor or coach of pastors have involved a fib here, a slight change there, an exaggeration over here—and soon you have a church that is hurting related to unity. The ministry suffers.

What We Can Do Personally to Hold to the Truth

Wisdom calls out in Proverbs 8:7, "for my mouth will utter truth; wickedness is an abomination to my lips." And we must listen to her if our lives and churches are to be headed in the right direction. Sometimes this may mean sharing the truth with someone who states a false self-made claim about the life of faith. When it is held by someone we love or connected with a church, it is only loving to remind that person of what Scripture really says. We can, of course, only take care of ourselves. Tell the truth, always with love. People who do that influence groups and whole churches and help to make the body of Christ strong. So much of life and media and entertainment avoids the truth, neglecting the One who is the truth. It seems weird and hurts so many people. And the church is one place where we are committed to helping each other, and that would include sharpening others to tell and live the truth. The church is meant to be a center of such a lifestyle. We cannot change everything, but we can represent truth in our world and the places we go, and with the people we know. At appropriate times and with love, we can insist that our friends and also our church leaders tell the truth without exaggerating it or slanting it. How much has gossip hurt church unity and taken our focus off our mission?

A Personal Prayer for Truth and Truth-telling

Praise: Honor Him as our Creator and LORD, who is truthful in all His ways. Thank God for His Word of truth!

Repent: Take a quiet moment to reflect on the words you've said over the last few days. Is there any time you have misled others? Or skipped facts, so you look better?

Ask: Surely this is a good time to pray for your pastor and other leaders at church that they will teach the Word of Truth, the Scriptures, and model its truth in life and as they speak. Ask for courage to "truth it in love," as Ephesians 4:15 implies.

Yield: To the truth of Scripture you have read today, and to read and study the Word of truth on a very consistent basis.

CHAPTER 9

Speaking Kindly

The Wise Speak Kindly

Dr. Tiberius Rata

When I was young, I used to admire intelligent people.
Now I admire kind people.
—Abraham Herschel

Speaking Kindly in the Old Testament

One might find it odd that a whole chapter is dedicated to speaking kindly. And while we all appreciate Paul's exhortation about speaking the truth in love (Ephesians 4:15), can the Old Testament really help this matter? Isn't the God of the Old Testament full of wrath and fury?

In his book *The God Delusion,* famed atheist Richard Dawkins said this about Yahweh, the Father of our LORD Jesus Christ. "The God of the Old Testament is arguably the most unpleasant character in all fiction: jealous and proud of it; a petty, unjust, unforgiving control-freak; a vindictive, bloodthirsty ethnic cleanser; a misogynistic, homophobic, racist, infanticidal, genocidal, filicidal, pestilential, megalomaniacal, sadomasochistic, capriciously malevolent bully."[275] It's almost as if Richard Dawkins never opened a Bible. The Bible portrays God as righteous and just; He must punish sin. But He is also portrayed as loving and merciful.

275 Richard Dawkins, *The God Delusion* (Boston: Mariner Books, 2006), 51.

After Adam and Eve yielded to temptation and sinned, God asked them kindly, "Where are you?" (Genesis 3:9). This is not a geographical question as though God does not know His creation's whereabouts. Rather, this is a theological question rooted in God's kindness. "Where are you?" is God's invitation to confess and repent of sin. A chapter later, God's question to Cain, "Where is Abel your brother?" is not rooted in God's jealousy but His kindness. As He did with his parents, God is inviting Cain to confess and repent of anger and murder.

There is an interesting expression in Hebrew that is translated literally "to speak to the heart" or "to speak upon the heart" that is generally translated to speak tenderly or kindly. It is the expression used by Ruth to describe how Boaz spoke to her. "I have found favor in your eyes, my lord, for you have comforted me and spoken kindly (lit., spoke to the heart) to your servant" (Ruth 2:13).[276] After David mourns for Absalom, he is encouraged to speak to the heart of the servants who stood with him and protected him while Absalom sought to kill David (2 Samuel 19:5–7). Hezekiah speaks to the heart of the Levites, encouraging them after God healed him (2 Chronicles 30:20–22). As God looks to the restoration of Israel, He instructs Isaiah to speak to the heart of Jerusalem and enjoy God's forgiveness (Isaiah 40:2).

When Elijah is discouraged to the point of death while running away from the evil queen Jezebel, God does not point a vindictive finger in the prophet's face. Rather, God speaks to him in a "still, small voice."[277] God steps in Elijah's cave of despondency and kindly asks him, "What are you doing here, Elijah?" (1 Kings 19:13). Ronald Wallace writes, "Neither the whirlwind that rent the side of the mountains, nor the earthquake that seemed to shake the foundations of the earth, nor the fire that fell from the heavens, splendid and marvelous, forced Elijah to his knees in worship. It was the awe of the stillness that overwhelmed the

---

276 The expression appears for the first time in Genesis 34:1–3 when Shechem speaks to Dinah.

277 What the KJV translates as the "still, small voice," the ESV translates as "a low whisper," and the NIV translates as "a gentle whisper."

man and made him cover his face as if he were afraid to look upon the glory of God."[278]

Even though David commits adultery and tries to cover it up with murder, God sends the prophet Nathan to stir up his conscience. And while David's sins will have consequences (2 Samuel 12:1–15), David recognizes Yahweh's kindness. Psalm 51:1 is David's prayer that, for millennia, has been teaching sinners to pray, "Have mercy on me, O God, according to your steadfast love; according to your abundant mercy blot out my transgression." God's kindness is supposed to drive us into His loving arms. Paul writes to the church in Rome, "Or do you presume on the riches of His kindness and forbearance and patience, not knowing that God's kindness is meant to lead you to repentance?" (Romans 2:4). Through the prophets, God kindly called His idolatrous people back to Himself. "Return to me, for I have redeemed you," God implores His people through the prophet Isaiah (Isaiah 44:22). The message continues through Jeremiah, "If you return, O Israel, declares the LORD, to Me you should return" (Jeremiah 4:1). In His kindness, God wants to mend the broken relationship with His people. God's forgiveness leads to reconciliation. "If you return, I will restore you" (Jeremiah 15:19). Through the prophet Hosea, God is calling them back to Himself, promising to bring Israel back by speaking tenderly to her (Hosea 2:14). In Joel, God kindly continues pursuing His people. "Return to me with all your heart, with fasting, with weeping, and with mourning; and rend your hearts and not your garments. Return to the LORD your God, for he is gracious and merciful, slow to anger, and abounding in steadfast love; and he relents over disaster" (Joel 2:12–13).

Because God speaks kindly, He wants His people to do the same. Even though Joseph's brothers sold him into slavery, he "spoke kindly" to them after their father's death (Genesis 50:21). Boaz speaks kindly to Ruth, even though she is not even his servant, but a simple stranger gleaning leftovers. She realizes that grace is feeding Boaz's kindness, "Then she said, 'I have found favor in

278 Ronald Wallace, *Elijah and Elisha: Expositions from the Book of Kings* (Eugene, OR: Wipf and Stock, 2013), 48.

your eyes, my lord, for you have comforted me and spoken kindly to your servant, though I am not one of your servants'" (Ruth 2:13). God's expectation of His people includes not just loving kindness but exercising it through word and speech. "He has told you, O man, what is good; and what does the LORD require of you but to do justice, and to love kindness, and to walk humbly with your God?" (Micah 6:8). The same message is given through the post-exilic prophet Zechariah, "Thus says the LORD of hosts, Render true judgments, show kindness and mercy to one another" (Zechariah 7:9). Thus, a gracious God who speaks kindly wants His people to do the same. Speaking the truth in love is not a New Testament development but God's plan since the beginning.

Speaking Kindly in the New Testament

Jesus started His public ministry with the words, "Repent, for the kingdom of heaven is at hand" (Matthew 4:17). Is this an example of kind speech? It is truth, but is it kind? The answer is a very firm, "Yes!" The most loving and kind thing we can do is to tell people the truth. We are reminded by the apostle Paul that we need have love in our hearts as we have truth on our lips (Ephesians 4:15), but truth is what we are called to proclaim. Jesus is our great example when it comes to speaking kindly, thus, speaking the truth in love. To the paralytic who is brought to Him by four anonymous men, He kindly says, "Take heart, my son; your sins are forgiven" (Matthew 9:2). To the woman with the issue of blood who is healed after touching the hem of His garment, He kindly says, "Take heart, daughter; your faith has made you well" (Matthew 9:22). To the dismayed and frightened disciples after they see Jesus walk on water, He kindly says, "Take heart; it is I. Do not be afraid" (Matthew 14:27). "Take heart; I have overcome the world," Jesus kindly says to the disciples as He is setting out for Jerusalem to die for our sin (John 16:33).

We see Jesus's kindness, especially in dealing with the outcast of society. When the leper kneels before Jesus saying, "LORD if you are willing You can make me clean," Jesus kindly stretched out His hand, touched the leper, and said, "I will; be clean" (Matthew 8:1–3). Jesus is moved by compassion and that is why He speaks and acts kindly. "Out of the abundance of the heart the mouth speaks," is the timeless truth Jesus lays out in Scripture (Matthew 12:34). Speaking kindly then comes out of a kind heart that is transformed by the power of the Gospel. No amount of secular teaching or therapy can change a sinful heart. But the transformed heart of the one who surrenders their life to Christ will produce kind words. As Calvin Miller beautifully said, "The lips know only shallow tunes. The heart is where great symphonies are born."[279] The Gospels record how Jesus was moved with compassion before He healed the sick (Matthew 14:14), before He fed them (Matthew 15:32), before He healed two blind men (Matthew 20:34), and before He healed the leper (Mark 1:41). Jesus had compassion on the widow whose son died (Luke 7:13), and so does the loving father in the parable of the loving father and his two lost sons (Luke 15:20).

The only harsh words Jesus has in the Gospels are reserved for the religious authorities. "Woe to you, scribes and Pharisees, hypocrites! For you are like whitewashed tombs, which outwardly appear beautiful, but within are full of dead people's bones and all uncleanness" (Matthew 23:27). The apostle Paul instructs the believers in Colossae to be gracious in their speech. "Let your speech always be gracious, seasoned with salt, so that you may know how you ought to answer each person" (Colossians 4:6).

Speaking Kindly in the Book of Proverbs

Stylistically speaking, when the book of Proverbs addresses speaking, it uses terms like "tongue," "lips," and "words." Proverbs 10:19–21 contains all these words to communicate the importance of one's speech. Verse 19 focuses on wise and truthful speech, "When words are many, transgression is not lacking, but whoever restrains his lips is prudent." Talking a lot is not a spiritual gift; rather, talking a lot is associated with sin. We could extrapolate that talking a lot is not kind for those who are listening. The wise, prudent person, on the other hand, is kind in that they

279 Calvin Miller, *A Symphony in Sand* (Dallas: Word, 1990), 94.

exercise self-control. There are blessings associated with being kind, while the cruel one pays the penalty for his evil. "A man who is kind benefits himself, but a cruel man hurts himself" (Proverbs 11:17). One with gracious speech is even found in the company of kings, "He who loves purity of heart, and whose speech is gracious, will have the king as his friend" (Proverbs 22:11).

We are reminded of the words of Jesus when He connects someone's speech with the content of their heart. He doesn't hold back when rebuking the religious leaders. "You brood of vipers! How can you speak good when you are evil? For out of the abundance of the heart the mouth speaks" (Matthew 12:34).[280] The same idea is developed in Proverbs 15:26, "The thoughts of the wicked are an abomination to the LORD, but gracious words are pure." The word "abomination" is a strong word that comes from legal literature. The expression "abomination to the LORD" appears eighteen times: seven times in Deuteronomy and eleven times in Proverbs. In Deuteronomy, abomination is correlated to idolatry, offering blemished animals as sacrifices, child sacrifice, divination, magic, trans dressing, income from immoral sources, and acting dishonestly.[281] Solomon's audience would have been well acquainted with this language to understand the gravity of the use of "abomination" language in relation to one's thoughts. Abominable thoughts are contrasted with the pure and gracious words of the wise. The word translated "pure" is used in legal literature to describe the pure gold used on the ark of the covenant (Exodus 25:11), the pure incense (Exodus 30:35), a cultically clean man (Leviticus 14:57), and a cultically clean animal or bird (Genesis 7:2). Most interestingly, the word "pure" is used to describe God's eyes as being too pure to look upon evil (Habakkuk 1:13) and to describe God's words (Psalm 12:6).

Words have power. One of the greatest lies we learn as children is that "sticks and stones may break my bones, but words will never hurt me." Words can hurt, and rash words spoken as one blurts

---

280 See also Luke 6:45.

281 Deuteronomy 7:25; 17:1; 18:10–12; 22:5; 23:18; 25:13–16; 27:15. Proverbs 3:32; 11:1, 20; 12:22; 15:8–9, 26; 16:5; 17:15; 20:10, 23.

out hurtful words are compared to wounds produced by a sword. "There is one whose rash words are like sword thrusts, but the tongue of the wise brings healing" (Proverbs 12:18). The healing power of words cannot be overestimated. "The tongue of the wise" is a figure of speech where the author substitutes the tongue of the wise for what the tongue says. A kind word is better than medicine, "Anxiety in a man's heart weighs him down, but a good word makes him glad" (Proverbs 12:25).[282] A kind word, a wise word, has the ability to prevent a quarrel that a harsh word might start. "A soft answer turns away wrath, but a harsh word stirs up anger" (Proverbs 15:1). Wise words heal. "A gentle tongue is a tree of life, but perverseness in it breaks the spirit" (Proverbs 15:4). Solomon uses Genesis 2 and 3 language here to show that kind speech is as powerful as the fruit from the garden of Eden's tree of life. On the other hand, just as the serpent deceived Eve and broke her and her relationship with God, a perverse and deceitful tongue breaks people's spirits and, consequently, their relationships.

Kind words are sweet. "Gracious words are like a honeycomb, sweetness to the soul and health to the body" (Proverbs 16:24). The word translated "gracious" is used of God Himself in Psalm 90:17 and of wisdom in Proverbs 3:17. Before affirming that kind words are sweet, Solomon affirms that "the heart of the wise makes his speech judicious" (Proverbs 16:23). This points to the important principle that "the condition of the heart is of prime importance. If all be right there, the words of the lips will accord therewith; so that in place of the speculative vaporings of the worldly pedant there will be the counsel of the wise, who knows how to give forth what is profitable as well as pleasant and cheering. Note the characteristics of the wisdom that is from above in James 3:17, and see the confession of the queen of Sheba (1 Kings 10:6–9)."[283]

Like a wise investment, wise and kind words pay dividends. "Whoever pursues righteousness and kindness will find life, righteousness, and honor" (Proverbs 21:21). Kind speech will

282 The word ṯôḇ is generally translated "good," but in this case, it can be safely translated "kind" (as in the NIV).

283 Ironside, *Notes on the Book of Proverbs*, 200.

be rewarded with life, righteousness, and honor. This is the only place in the Old Testament where "life, righteousness, and honor" appear together as reward. The one who pursues righteousness will be rewarded with righteousness, and the one pursuing lovingkindness will be rewarded with life and honor. We could apply this to kind speech as well. Someone who speaks kindly will be rewarded with life and honor. Even if that is not the case in this life, the reward will come in the form of the crown of life in the afterlife.[284] Lastly, the woman of noble character who fears the LORD described in chapter 31 has kindness on her tongue (Proverbs 31:26). Spence observes that "her language to those around her is animated and regulated by love. As mistress of a family, she has to teach and direct her dependents, and she performs this duty with gracious kindness and ready sympathy."[285]

A Lesson from Church History

Mother Teresa said, "Kind words can be short and easy to speak, but their echoes are truly endless." Those working with Mother Teresa at the Loreto House in Calcutta remember her as "a very kind and charitable sort of person even as a young nun."[286] Her whole life was characterized by being kind to the poor and the needy. In 1950, she founded "Missionaries of Charity," and in 1957, she started working with lepers in the slums of Calcutta. After her death, she was remembered as "the saint of the gutters," "the hero of the poor," and "the angel of mercy."[287] But most notable, she was known for her kind speech to those whom she showed the love of God. "The dying, the cripple, the mental, the unwanted, the unloved—they are Jesus in disguise…speak tenderly to them. Let there be kindness in your face, in your eyes, in your smile, in

---

284 The crown of life is given to those who are faithful unto death (Revelation 2:10).

285 Spence-Jones, ed., *Proverbs*, 601.

286 Kathryn Spink, *Mother Teresa: An Authorized Biography* (New York: HarperOne, 2011), 14.

287 Harold J. Sala, *Heroes: People Who Made a Difference in Our Word* (Uhrichsville, OH: Promise Press, 1998), 36.

the warmth of your greeting. Always have a cheerful smile. Don't only give your care, but give your heart as well."[288]

A Christological Reading

Jesus spoke harshly and He spoke kindly. He reserved His harshest words for the hypocrites, the religious leaders of the day, and even His disciples. "You hypocrite(s)," or "Woe to you," are the two expressions that point to Jesus's righteous anger. He directs these words to the hypocrites who judge others but commit the same sins (Matthew 7:4), to the hypocrites who worship God with their lips and not their hearts (Matthew 15:7–9), to the "blind guides," the scribes and Pharisees who "shut off the kingdom of heaven from men" (Matthew 23:13). Most harshly, Jesus calls the scribes and Pharisees "you serpents, you brood of vipers" (Matthew 23:33).

But to the sinners and tax collectors, Jesus spoke kindly. It's evident from His ministry that the sinners and tax collectors were more willing to listen to Jesus than the religious leaders of the day. The beginning of Luke 15 shows this clearly. "Now the tax collectors and sinners were all drawing near to hear him. And the Pharisees and the scribes grumbled, saying, 'This man receives sinners and eats with them'" (Luke 15:1–2). A classic example of Jesus speaking kindly is the encounter with the woman caught in adultery, as recorded in John 8. While the scribes and the Pharisees want to stone the woman to death, Jesus tells her, "Neither do I condemn you; go and sin no more" (John 8:11). As followers and imitators of Christ, we are also to be kind to one another in both act and speech (Ephesians 4:32).

288 Dale A. Johnson, *The Authentic Life: Compassion, Hospitality, and Gratitude* (Sinai Press, 2013), 58.

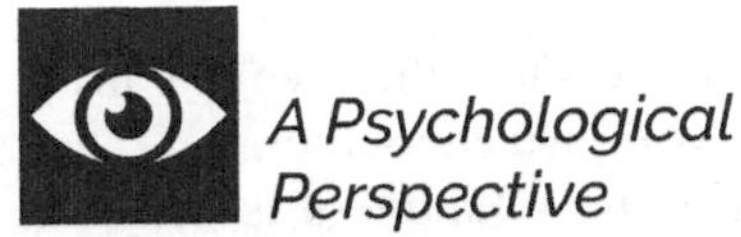

Reflections on Kindness

Dr. Kevin Roberts

He has told you, O man, what is good; and what does the LORD require of you but to do justice, and to love kindness, and to walk humbly with your God?
—Micah 6:8

Kindness is the language which the deaf can hear and the blind can see.
—Unknown

Have you ever really tried to define kindness? Can I encourage you to take a minute and write down just a few words about how you would define this somewhat elusive construct? The research around kindness has produced some powerful results that point us toward the value and virtue of kindness. But it remains a difficult construct to separate from other key terms in psychological research, including empathy, altruism, social responsibility, agreeableness, love, moral reasoning, and being nice. We all know kindness when we see it and experience the kindness of others, but it is often hard to describe. In reading the Scriptures, we see the kindness of Christ in dozens of examples throughout the New Testament, whether it is speaking to the woman at the well, healing the leper, or dining with sinners. Therefore, Scripture serves as a compass for demonstrating how we are to show the love of Christ in the way we show kindness to everyone we encounter.

This chapter will set out to describe how kindness is defined, how it develops, and how it impacts others and ourselves psychologically. Showing how kindness can be displayed to our larger world and how we may model it will also be covered. We will also explore the idea of being kind to ourselves.

Defining Kindness

But love your enemies, and do good, and lend, expecting nothing in return, and your reward will be great, and you will be sons of the Most High, for he is kind to the ungrateful and the evil. (Luke 6:35)

Have you ever met a truly kind person? The one who seems to always be thinking of others, takes a genuine interest in what you have to say, and has scores of friends? Have you ever considered how their kindness is so freely given to others? The psychological literature has found that terms like love, altruism, and empathy are often closely correlated with kindness. Of note, altruism and kindness have a shared orientation that is focused away from the self and toward others. Altruism is more closely linked with selfless interest and the behaviors that originate from having a kind heart. For the purposes of this chapter, we will use altruism and kindness interchangeably. From this perspective, one looks at his or her fellow man as being worthy of his or her time, effort, and attention. The ability to separate our own needs and conscientiously choose to put the needs of others higher than our own is an essential skill on the road to Christian maturity. This may, at times, create genuine internal dissonance because we are sinful beings who, more often than not, look to satisfy our own wants before others. However, showing kindness when it is inconvenient requires a choice to practice an unselfish and accepting form of love that early Christians described as *agape.*[289] Agape love is an action-first type of love, like what Christ showed us on the cross. After all, what demonstrates selfless love more than being willing to sacri-

289 Peterson and Seligman, *Character Strengths and Virtues: A Handbook and Classification.*

fice your own life (Romans 5:8)? This type of love and kindness leads mankind toward the saving grace of God (Romans 2:4).

The theory of Positive Psychology tends to place the virtue of kindness under a broader character list known for being in relation to humanity. Kindness fits solidly under this heading because it involves selfless acts like being compassionate, nurturing, and caring for others. Individuals make difficult decisions by putting aside their personal agendas and listening patiently to a friend who is suffering. This type of kindness requires the surrender of personal goals, along with deep compassion for your fellow man. This is where we often see an overlap in the research between love and kindness. As Neimiec and McGrath stated, "Kindness can be distinguished from love in that the character strength of love has more to do with intimate relationships, whereas kindness is more general strength, involving reaching out to positively impact people beyond your close circle. Unlike love, the goal of kindness is not necessarily to achieve intimacy and security; it is to make others feel cared for."[290] Therefore, kindness is more likely to be tuned in to the needs and ideas of others. Here core concepts like generosity, nurturance, care, compassion, and the act of being nice to others are the behavioral aspects of this definition. This type of kindness requires a shift in our perspective to be less focused on our own needs and more on the needs of others.

Developing Kindness

Be kind to one another, tenderhearted, forgiving one another, as God in Christ forgave you. (Ephesians 4:32)

Is all kindness motivated from a perspective to serve others? Or can kindness toward others be motivated from a self-serving or sinful perspective? Have you ever met a person whose kindness felt like a subtle manipulation? If a person uses kindness to pursue their own wants and needs first, it is nothing more than a tool of manipulation and control. This type of manipulative kindness might be seen when you are impatient with those close to you but always kind to those you are first meeting in order to make a good impression and win the approval of others. This is why un-

290 Niemiec and McGrath, *The Power of Character Strengths*, 142.

derstanding the motives of our kindness and making sure we are doing things for the right reasons is essential. In examining the Scriptures, we quickly find kindness as a desire to serve another human being without receiving an explicit reward. We see this in Paul's letter to the church in Corinth (1 Corinthians 13:4–7) and in Philippi when he states,

> So if there is any encouragement in Christ, any comfort from love, any participation in the Spirit, any affection and sympathy, complete my joy by being of the same mind, having the same love, being in full accord and of one mind. Do nothing from selfish ambition or conceit, but in humility count others more significant than yourselves. Let each of you look not only to his own interests, but also to the interests of others. Have this mind among yourselves, which is yours in Christ Jesus, who, though he was in the form of God, did not count equality with God a thing to be grasped, but emptied himself, by taking the form of a servant, being born in the likeness of men. (Philippians 2:1–7)

Christian kindness, listed as one of the fruits of the Spirit (Galatians 5:22–23), does not use kindness as a means to get what we want but instead is done out of the heart of serving others and deep empathy. Weinstein and Ryan found that those who offered help to others, known as autonomous help (choice to freely give to another), had significantly higher scores in well-being.[291] In fact, the less formal types of volunteering and helping behaviors were linked to great physical health in both young and older adults.[292] Kindness is similarly the willingness to stop staring in the mirror, looking at the world from another's perspective, and then the

291 Netta Weinstein and Richard M. Ryan, "When Helping Helps: Autonomous Motivation for Prosocial Behavior and Its Influence on Well-Being for the Helper and Recipient," *Journal of Personality and Social Psychology* 98, no. 2 (2010): 222–24. https://doi.org/10.1037/a0016984.

292 Oliver Scott Curry et al., "Happy to Help? A Systematic Review and Meta-Analysis of the Effect of Performing Acts of Kindness on the Well-Being of the Actor, "*Journal of Experimental Social Psychology* 76 (2018): 320–29. https://doi.org/10.1016/j/jesp.2018.02.014.

willingness to freely give to another without any possible reward. However, the benefits of helping appear to be mitigated by one's motive for helping. Konrath et al. found that helping motivated by a desire to gain personal benefit resulted in no gains in well-being or physical health.[293]

If kindness is an active concept that requires gaining the perspective of another, then what better way to demonstrate this than in purposeful listening to others? The idea of really listening to others is a concept that is frequently lost in a multitasking world. I find it ironic that the same letters that spell "listen" are also used in the word "silent." We must be willing to silence our minds as we listen in order to understand the thoughts, feelings, and behaviors of another. This means we shouldn't be thinking of grocery lists, ballgame scores, or household duties in the midst of being fully present with another person. These moments when people are sharing their hearts with you need to be held dearly as an opportunity to show the kindness and love of God. Take a moment and think about the people in your life who are great listeners. What is it that makes them do this so well? It's almost as if the world stops around them, and they are just present with you in a responsive and kind manner. This is active kindness: seeking to put one's own needs aside and be fully present with another. In doing so, we become more understanding, empathetic, loving, and patient, demonstrating the love of Christ.

Impact of Kindness

Whoever pursues righteousness and kindness will find life, righteousness, and honor. (Proverbs 21:21)

Is gaining the perspective of another, serving without the hope of a reward, and being willing to subjugate our own needs all we have to look forward to in demonstrating the kindness of Christ? Or are there some benefits that we receive from developing kindness and altruism? Interestingly, as indicated in Proverbs 11:17, "A man who

293 Sara Konrath et al., "Motives for Volunteering Are Associated with Mortality Risk in Older Adults," *Health Psychology* 31, no. 1 (2012): 87–96. https://doi.org/10.1037/a002522.

is kind benefits himself, but a cruel man hurts himself." The clear message in kindness is that we must be motivated out of concern for our fellow man and not for ourselves. In taking that approach, we actually do receive an extrinsic reward. Rowland and Curry found that by performing acts of kindness, people benefited by seeing their own happiness scores increase, as well.[294] The recipients of the acts of kindness also appeared to have significant gains.

The psychological literature is quite extensive as it pertains to kindness and the potential benefits. Individuals who score high on kindness scales also are strongly correlated with higher overall mental and physical health as well as longevity of life. The concept that kindness could actually produce improved physical and mental health outcomes has remained consistent in the literature.[295] Those individuals who score higher in kindness tend to better connect with peers and demonstrate higher peer acceptance scores.[296] Furthermore, kindness seems to show a strong correlation with positive emotions and an improved sense of well-being. These two characteristics seem to contribute to larger social networks. As a result, those who demonstrate higher kindness scores tend to be healthier and happier individuals as Niemiec and McGrath found.[297] Conversely, it only makes sense that lowered scores in kindness also correlate with increased depression and

---

294 Lee Rowland and Oliver Scott Curry, "A Range of Kindness Activities Boost Happiness," *The Journal of Social Psychology* 159, no. 3 (2018): 340–43. https://doi.org/10.1080/00224545.2018.1469461.

295 Christopher Peterson and Martin E. P. Seligman, *Character Strengths and Virtues: A Handbook and Classification* (Oxford: Oxford University Press, 2004); Ryan M. Niemiec, "VIA Character Strengths: Research and Practice (The First 10 Years)," in *Well-Being and Cultures: Perspectives from Positive Psychology,* ed. Hans Henrick Knoop and Antonella Delle Fave (Dordrecht: Springer Science + Business Media, 2013), 11–30; Ryan M. Niemiec, *Mindfulness and Character Strengths: A Practical Guide to Flourishing* (Boston, MA: Hogree Publishing, 2014); Ryan M. Niemiec and Danny Wedding, *Positive Psychology at the Movies: Using Films to Build Character Strengths and Well-Being,* 2nd ed. (Boston MA: Hogrefe Publishing, 2014).

296 Niemiec and McGrath, *The Power of Character Strengths: Appreciate and Ignite Your Positive Personality.*

297 Niemiec and McGrath, *The Power of Character Strengths: Appreciate and Ignite Your Positive Personality.*

anxiety scores.[298] Therefore, what we learn about kindness is that developing kindness from the perspective of genuine concern for others and empathetic response results in improved social connection, happiness, lowered rates of depression and anxiety, and overall higher rates of mental and physical health.

Is it easy for you to show kindness to others, yet difficult to show yourself the same level of kindness? Is there such a thing as self-kindness? The concept of self-kindness from the psychological literature is the ability to direct inward some self-compassion. We know as believers in Christ that we were born as sinful human beings. But how do we respond to our sinful nature and the guilt and shame we all experience? Do we ruminate on our mistakes and sinful behaviors, or can we learn to show self-compassion? What is the balance between turning away from sinful behaviors, yet learning to accept the kindness of God? To understand this, we must first understand the nature of our guilt and shame. We all know that shame is a powerful experience. Like Adam and Eve in the garden, when we feel shame, we often fear being exposed in front of others and being rejected. Individuals often demonstrate this even in their body language. When people fear rejection from others, they often dip their heads, avoid eye contact, or choose to hide away just as Adam and Eve did. Shame is often tied to human relationships whereas guilt is often tied more to breaking the law. Edgington stated, "Shame without a state of guilt is the essence of illegitimate shame. We can be ashamed of our appearance, our age, our gender, our best efforts, our legitimate longings, etc. These things should not produce shame, yet they may depend on our own thinking and possibly on being shamed for one or more of these in the past. Legitimate shame involves our sinfulness, or moving in an ungodly direction with our lives. …We are to feel ashamed if we have sinned, and the God-given emotion of shame is designed to move us toward confession and repentance."[299]

---

298 Niemiec and McGrath, *The Power of Character Strengths: Appreciate and Ignite Your Positive Personality.*

299 Thomas J. Edgington, *Healing Helps from the Bible: For Hurting People Seeking Help from Scripture* (Evangel Press, 1995), 188.

The problem is that we often feel illegitimate shame and are unable to show self-compassion for failures that are not sin issues. Our sin is supposed to produce guilt and shame that moves us toward godly repentance. The experience of receiving God's grace instead of condemnation when we confess and repent should produce humility as we experience the kindness of God. But we often choose to ruminate negatively on our traits, failing to recognize that this line of thinking is not from God. Scripture calls us to have wholesome thoughts that focus on what is noble, right, pure, admirable, and praiseworthy (Philippians 4:8). Self-compassion involves embracing our faults and should produce humility and gratitude for a God who does not reject us but instead accepts and loves us in the midst of our messes. Niemiec and McGrath found that self-compassion actually correlates with less anxiety and depression and higher life satisfaction and self-esteem.[300] But we must be willing to ask ourselves a few hard questions. Are you exempt from receiving the kindness of God? If self-compassion is merely redirecting our thinking to align with Scripture, then why is God's grace good enough for others and not you?

In the healthcare and behavioral health fields, we often see people suffer from what is called compassion fatigue. A life and profession of kindness and pouring into others comes at a cost. The result is compassion fatigue, where people show signs of stress such as weight loss, irritability, self-contempt, and chronic fatigue, both emotionally and physically. There are entire seminars devoted to this topic, and it requires counselors or healthcare professionals to learn to recognize their symptoms and understand and learn how to improve their self-care and coping skills.[301] In Scripture, we see that even Christ had moments of fatigue and would set aside time to be alone and pray. These moments are essential for anyone in the helping profession and serve to recharge their emotional or kindness batteries. This recharging allows one

300 Niemiec and McGrath, *The Power of Character Strengths: Appreciate and Ignite Your Positive Personality.*

301 Moshe Zeidner et al., "Personal Factors Related to Compassion Fatigue in Health Professionals," *Anxiety, Stress, & Coping* 26, no. 6 (2013): 595–609. https://doi.org/10.1080/10615806.2013.777045.

to continue to serve in the midst of people's suffering and yet demonstrate the love of Christ day in and day out.

Application Exercises and Questions for Demonstrating and Modeling Kindness

So how do we model kindness in an everyday way? I have included an application section of ideas to make kindness a bigger part of your daily life. This section will involve personal questions and to-do lists to increase your demonstration of kindness.

1. To engage in kindness, we must first be willing to really listen to others. Practice listening to people and not being distracted so you can really hear another person and identify what needs, desires, or wishes they are trying to express. Listen by remaining silent and only respond with deeper, reflective questions about themselves. Avoid trying to bring yourself more into the conversation with things like "me too" or "that reminds me of" or switching the topic to yourself in some way.
2. Ask yourself the hard questions about whether you can accept kindness from others. Can you accept the grace and kindness of God? If you cannot, kindness will be very difficult for you to model in your life. So, list the kind things you do each week and be purposeful with your kindness. Be honest with yourself about your shortcomings but do so without ruminating on negative traits. This means letting go of your perfectionism and your desire to control.
3. Ask yourself the question, what is motivating you to be kind to certain people and not to others? Remember that kindness is sometimes about winning the approval of others or subtle forms of manipulation, and this type of kindness cannot be what motivates us. We must accept that in being kind to others there is little chance of reward. An extrinsic reward should not be tied to our kindness. We want our kindness (autonomous helping) to be driven by a godly and compassionate part of us.
4. Can you be kind to those who annoy you or to someone you simply do not like? Can you do acts of kindness anonymously

for this individual? Find a way to pour into the life of another or give generously with your time, talents, or resources.

5. Find ways to pour into others by taking someone to coffee with the sole purpose of letting them feel fully heard and appreciated. Or even showing kindness by paying for a stranger's meal or finding a way to help someone in the cubicle next to you get a project done. Could you mow your neighbor's yard or find ways to show kindness? You will have your own list when you really listen because you will hear their struggles and needs. You will then know how to better show kindness to those around you.

Speaking Kindly at Church

Pastor Knute Larson

Kindness does not seem like a major issue at first. Creation of the world—yes, that's a big issue! The sovereignty of God plus human responsibility is another big topic. Somehow both are true and that has to rank high on our study list. But speaking kindly? That seems, well, not as varsity. But all of us who have attended church very religiously know how significant are the words people say to each other. Words edify and encourage or hurt and divide; thus, the clear Proverbs teaching calls us to kindness in what we say and how we say it. Indeed, it is a major issue. And anyone who has watched a mean-spirited church business meeting, where people were making up their minds whether to stay or split, knows how important kindness is. Anyone who is the child of divorce, who has stepped between his parents as their unkind yelling grew unkinder (I write from experience), wishes they would have listened more at church, and that the church would have had kinder words to help and heal instead of just waving goodbye. In the halls, in class or home group discussions, even about controversial subjects, on social media, phone calls, emails or text, by the grace of God's Spirit within us, there should be kindness. The Church is the body of Jesus Christ, who is the kindest of all.

True, there are many church people who enjoy a good argument about how much kindness should show from the pulpit. For some, maybe it would be more accurate to say they like to be "put in their place" as they listen to a sermon. "Tell it like it is" is the way one of them put it to me in a rather forceful way. "Speaking the truth in love" was my New Testament logic with him, as I recall. And I could have quoted quite a few verses from Proverbs. Many churches have "Grace" in their given names, and all believers in and followers of Jesus Christ are called to a life of grace, which by definition must include a new and strong manner of kindness. While the church is not a place for cheap talk or even sweet talk that is superficial, kindness is to be predominant. By all means and at all board or committee meetings and in the hallways and from the pulpit, the people of the King love "purity of heart," and their "speech is gracious" (Proverbs 22:11). We can believe the Bible, which speaks candidly of damnation or eternal judgment, without being unkind or judgmental in our teaching or leading. Even leaders who might be unkindly, called "fire and brimstone" people, can be kind by Proverbs standards in their sharing of truth.

Churches, like people, are known by their words and their actions. And while those of us who have been churched for a long time might describe a church as evangelical or liberal, Calvinist or Arminian, informal or formal, people on the street probably think of a particular church more in terms of being caring or separatist, kind or harsh, or accepting or judgmental. If "the tongue of the wise brings healing," and it does, and "gracious words are like a honeycomb, sweetness to the soul and health to the body" (Proverbs 12:18; 16:24), then a kind church will have a reputation over time as being a place of kindness and charity and a light of caring love in the community. Its people will be respected for their humble servanthood and the way they do business, treat their neighbors, and give to others.

Why Kindness Is So Important

Reckless words pierce like a sword, but the tongue of the wise brings healing. (Proverbs 12:18)

A gentle answer turns away wrath, but a harsh word stirs up anger. (Proverbs 15:1)

Anyone who loves the church of our Lord knows how important such warnings are from the above verses. In one sense, people know a church by the words of that church, how the pastor preaches, how the teachers teach, and what we all say or don't say in the halls and our neighborhoods and workplaces. The church can get a reputation for being fiery and judgmental or of being truthful and kind. And if we honestly follow Jesus, the wisest of all, we will emulate something of His manner: "I am gentle and lowly in heart, and you will find rest for your souls"—the one time He described Himself, adding, "For my yoke is easy and my burden is light" (Matthew 11:28–30). Church relationships are meant to be rather extraordinary. We are to love each other, and that would include the absence of gossip and mean words. Even people who shy away from the truth about Jesus Christ as to their personal spiritual needs ought to see that there is something different about a church where people speak kindly.

I was a teenager in the back row of our church's Wednesday evening business meeting when a few were arguing over what color the walls in the new addition to our church building would be—green or blue. (Yes, I remember the colors.) One man's face was red as he argued for blue, and the responses of a few green advocates were equally unkind. I remember thinking then that I would never want to be a pastor in charge of such things, and I wish I had suggested aqua, a combination of blue and green.

Why Kindness Does Not Always Show Up

"Wise and truthful speech"—the theme of the Proverbs teaching is associated, theologically, with our spiritual connection to God's Holy Spirit of grace and truth. And kindness often does not show up because we who are speaking unkindly are, at least for the moment, living as if we are unattached from Christ the Lord and His Spirit. That, of course, ought not to be. Those among us who run after loving-kindness will be honored, Proverbs promises (21:21). But someone who uses unkind remarks about those who differ in order to gain attention and look good to others may find a following. And it may even feel good for the time being. And churches have mistakenly honored church "tribal chiefs"—sometimes called "church bosses"—who selfishly try to win an audience at the expense of pastoral leadership. It should not be so, but it does show up.

At times in my work as a church coach, I have pointedly told church leaders in a meeting that they "cannot speak that way to each other," at least if we are to be caring about our Savior and His Church more than about ourselves. Kindness should show up, even when we are seeking to handle differences and a variety of opinions. Could it be that some people, without thinking, speak as if God does not hear and write on social media as if He does not read?

What We Can Do Personally to Be Kind

Practice kindness. Speak kindly. With holy nerve and kindness, urge others to do that too. Do not receive gossip—often, you can tell when it is starting.

Pray the pointed prayer, "May the words of my mouth, and the meditation of my heart, be pleasing in your sight, O Lord, my Rock and my Redeemer" (Psalm 19:14).

Thank your pastor and other leaders when they handle a difficult text or church situation with truthful and kind words—do not take it for granted. And pray for the peace of Jerusalem and your church also.

A Personal Prayer for Kindness

Praise: To God for giving us truth with love and modeling patience with all of us.

Repent: It will not be hard for any of us to think of times when we spoke selfishly or unkindly. And if there is such a need, pray for God's strength and love to go to any offended person.

Ask: Pray Psalm 19:14 for yourself. Pray for the mood of family love to be present in your church. Pray for your leaders as they shepherd and often deal with unkindness.

Yield: If you noted the commentary about Proverbs carefully, it should not be hard to embrace verses about speaking kindly as a way of life.

CHAPTER 10

Lifelong Learning

A Theological Perspective

The Wise Are Lifelong Learners

Dr. Tiberius Rata

If I have seen further, it is by standing on the shoulders of giants.
—Isaac Newton

Lifelong Learning in the Old Testament

Learning is a lifelong process that starts in the cradle and ends in the grave. While we associate learning with educational institutions, learning first takes place in the home. As God reveals Himself to His people, He establishes the learning process.

God reveals Himself to His people, and His people are to pass on what they learn to their children. Moses recalls God's communication on Mount Horeb. "The Lord said to me, 'Gather the people to me, that I may let them hear my words, so that they may learn to fear me all the days that they live on the earth, and that they may teach their children so'" (Deuteronomy 4:10). The lifelong aspect of learning is particularly targeting the king. "And when he sits on the throne of his kingdom, he shall write for himself in a book a copy of this law, approved by the Levitical priests. And it shall be with him, and he shall read in it all the days of his life, that he may learn to fear the Lord his God by keeping all the words of this law and these statutes, and doing them, that his heart may not be lifted up above his brothers" (Deuteronomy 17:18–20).

Learning, then, is not done for learning's sake but for the character development of the one learning. Learning is humbling because the more we learn, the more we realize how little we actually know. The Law instructs us, and we learn from it in order to keep the God-given commandments. The king's obedience is directly connected to the longevity of his kingdom, "so that he may continue long in his kingdom, he and his children, in Israel" (Deuteronomy 17:20). The learning process is not limited to the Israelites, but also concerns the foreigners who "may hear and learn to fear the LORD" (Deuteronomy 31:12). It is a lifelong process since they are to learn "as long as you live in the land that you are going over the Jordan to possess" (Deuteronomy 31:13).

After the death of Joshua's generation, "there arose another generation after them who did not know the LORD or the work that he had done for Israel" (Judges 2:10). What a tragic statement. A generation that stops learning becomes a godless generation. This was true then and is true today. The German philosopher Georg Hegel said that what we learn from history is that we do not learn from history. "But what we experience and history teaches is this – that peoples and governments never have learned anything from history, or acted on the teaching to be drawn from it."[302] Is our generation learning from past generations that have lost their vision of God?

I grew up in Romania when a communist government led the socialist country. My dad risked his life to defect and come to the United States because it was considered to be a modern-day Promised Land. As I studied American history, I realized that America was indeed founded on Christian principles. In his classic work *Democracy in America,* Tocqueville notes that "Americans combine the notions of Christianity and of liberty so intimately in their minds that it is impossible to make them conceive the one without the other."[303] He continues to affirm that "there is no country in

302 G. W. F. Hegel, *Lectures on the Philosophy of History,* translated by Ruben Alvarado (Aalten, the Netherlands: WordBridge, 2011), 6.

303 Alex de Tocqueville, *Democracy in America,* trans. Henry Reeve (London: Saunders and Otley, 1835), 233–34.

the whole world in which the Christian religion retains a greater influence on the souls of men than in America…Upon my arrival in the United States, the religious aspect of the country was the first thing that struck my attention."[304]

American presidents such as Dwight D. Eisenhower, Franklin D. Roosevelt, and Harry S. Truman affirmed in their public addresses that America was a Christian nation. Sadly, our nation has shifted toward agnosticism and atheism. George Barna combines atheists and agnostics in one group called "skeptics" and concludes that they represent 25 percent of all unchurched adults.[305] Is America of today in danger of becoming like post-Joshua Israel? Not if we learn from history and teach our children and our children's children to be lifelong learners of God, His Word, and His world. And we need to lead by example. As parents and grandparents, we need to be lifelong learners in order to instill a love of learning in our children and grandchildren. May it be said of our generation and the generations to come what was said about the sons of Issachar, "men who had understanding of the times, to know what Israel ought to do" (1 Chronicles 12:32).

Waiting on God could be part of the psalmist's lifelong-learning attitude. "Make me to know your ways, O Lord; teach me your paths. Lead me in your truth and teach me, for you are the God of my salvation; for you I wait all the day long" (Psalm 25:4–5). We don't know how old the psalmist is when he writes the contents of Psalm 71, but he remembers that his learning started when he was young. "O God, from my youth you have taught me, and I still proclaim your wondrous deeds" (Psalm 71:17). Part of the lifelong-learning process is the generational aspect of learning. One generation must impart to the other teachings about who God is and what He has done.

---

304 Alex de Tocqueville, *Democracy in America*, 237. See also, David Barton and Tim Barton, *The American Story: The Beginnings* (Aledo, TX: WallBuilders: 2020).

305 https://www.barna.com/research/2015-state-of-atheism-in-america/. 31% of skeptics have never attended a church service, 18% are under thirty years old, 43% are women, and 50% are college educated. These 2013 numbers are higher than the 1993 survey.

> We will not hide them from their children, but tell to the coming generation the glorious deeds of the LORD, and his might, and the wonders that he has done. He established a testimony in Jacob and appointed a law in Israel, which he commanded our fathers to teach to their children, that the next generation might know them, the children yet unborn, and arise and tell them to their children, so that they should set their hope in God and not forget the works of God, but keep his commandments. (Psalm 78:4–7)

We know that the author of Psalm 119 is a lifelong learner because the psalm reads like a diary with "different stanzas or groups of stanzas are conjectured to have been written during different periods in the psalmist's life."[306] Zemek's insights point to the psalmist being a lifelong learner because his testimonies "are predicated upon his actual experience of walking with God from the time of his youth up to and including however old he might have been at the time of composition."[307] Learning the word of God when young helps keep one's way unpolluted while living in a sinful world. "How can a young man keep his way pure? By guarding it according to Your word" (Psalm 119:9).

The exile was proof that the Israelites did not learn from previous generations about taking God seriously. They did not take the prophets' messages to heart, and that is why they went into the Assyrian and Babylon exiles. But God, in His grace and mercy, brought them back to the Promised Land and gave them godly leaders like Ezra and Nehemiah.

Lifelong Learning in the New Testament

The word "disciple" is synonymous with the word "learner." Jesus, the disciple-maker, invites us to learn from Him. Jesus always leads by example; He never asks us to do something He does not. "Come to me, all who labor and are heavy laden, and I

---

306 George J. Zemek, *The Word of God in the Child of God: Exegetical, Theological, and Homiletical Reflections from the 119th Psalm* (Eugene, OR: Wipf and Stock, 2005), 10.

307 George J. Zemek, *The Word of God in the Child of God.*

will give you rest. Take my yoke upon you, and learn from me, for I am gentle and lowly in heart, and you will find rest for your souls" (Matthew 11:28–29). In His humanity, Jesus shows a love of learning when, at the age of twelve is at the temple "sitting among the teachers, listening to them and asking them questions" (Luke 2:46). If Jesus listened and asked questions, how much more should we resolve to be lifelong learners? Of the Son of God is said that He "increased in wisdom and in stature and in favor with God and man" (Luke 2:52). If the One who spoke the cosmos into existence increased in wisdom, how much more should we strive to increase in the wisdom that is available to us through the One "who became to us wisdom from God" (1 Corinthians 1:30).

The believers of the first-century church understood the importance of being lifelong learners and "devoted themselves to the apostles' teaching" (Acts 2:42). Paul and Barnabas spent a whole year in Antioch teaching. "And when [Barnabas] had found [Paul], he brought him to Antioch. For a whole year they met with the church and taught a great many people. And in Antioch the disciples were first called Christians" (Acts 11:26). Lifelong learning is accompanied by lifelong teaching. God is faithful, so in every generation, He raises up teachers to teach because, in every generation, there is a flock to be taught. Warren Wiersbe writes,

> What Barnabas did for Saul needs to be practiced in our churches today. Mature believers need to enlist others and encourage them in their service for the Lord. It was one of D. L. Moody's policies that each new Christian be given a task soon after conversion. At first, it might be only passing out hymnals or ushering people to their seats, but each convert had to be busy. As previously mentioned, he said, "It is better to put ten men to work than to do the work of ten men." Many of Mr. Moody's "assistants" became effective Christian workers in their own right and this multiplied the witness.[308]

---

308 Warren W. Wiersbe, *The Bible Exposition Commentary*, vol. 1 (Wheaton, IL: Victor Books, 1996), 449–50.

Moody took a page from the apostle Paul's proverbial play book. To the church at Corinth, the apostle Paul writes that believers are given different gifts, and some of these gifts are for the purpose of learning. "For you can all prophesy one by one, so that all may learn and all be encouraged" (1 Corinthians 14:31).

Teaching and learning start at home. Paul writes to Timothy in his first letter, "But if a widow has children or grandchildren, let them first learn to show godliness to their own household and to make some return to their parents, for this is pleasing in the sight of God" (1 Timothy 5:4). Paul employs a present active imperative verb to encourage people to learn how to do good (1 Timothy 5:4; Titus 3:14).

But learning should be the means to an end, not the end in itself, and should always be grounded in truth. In his second letter to Timothy, Paul writes about false teachers "who creep into households and capture weak women, burdened with sins and led astray by various passions, always learning and never able to arrive at a knowledge of the truth" (2 Timothy 3:6–7). We see here a potential danger in learning. If learning is solely intellectual and does not make its way to the heart, one will never arrive at the ultimate goal of learning, to know God. There are many members of the Society of Biblical Literature who do not believe the Bible is the inerrant Word of God, and yet they "teach" it to others.[309] If knowing God or even believing could be an intellectual endeavor, the demons would be saved. But they are not saved, yet they tremble (James 2:19).

Lifelong Learning in the Book of Proverbs

The book of Proverbs is clear that learning is active and not passive. Learning must be pursued. Since one's learning can increase, that means that it is not achieved at one point in time. From the

309 Some papers read at the 2021 Society of Biblical Literature conference include "Ambiguity as a Bridging Identity: The Role of Semitic Ambiguity in Forming the Prophetic Identity of Muhammad," "Reading Ezekiel as a Jewish Lesbian Biblicist: A Thirty Year Relationship," and "Love and Eunuchs: Esther and Ishtar as Queer Queens."

beginning of the book, Solomon teaches his pupils that the wise will listen to instruction and increase in learning. "Let the wise hear and increase in learning, and the one who understands obtain guidance" (Proverbs 1:5).

The lifelong process of learning starts with hearing and listening to truth. The verb translated "hear" can be translated "hear," "listen," or "obey," depending on the context.[310] Learning is not just reserved for the young and those in need of wisdom but also for the wise who still have the potential to grow in learning. As Garrett correctly points out, "Those who are already mature and learned (v. 5) also have a great deal to learn from this book, and they should not shun it as unworthy of their time."[311]

The reward for wisdom is more wisdom. The riches of God's Word are so deep that we could spend the rest of our lives digging and still not get to the bottom of it. The reason the Word is always fresh to us is that as we go through different seasons of life, the Holy Spirit uncovers new insights that fit the particular season we are navigating.

The fact that learning must be a lifelong endeavor can also be gleaned from the use of the verbs "to keep hold" and the jussive "do not let go" in Proverbs 4:13. "Keep hold of instruction; do not let go; guard her, for she is your life." The volitional "do not let go" has the strength of the imperative.[312] But the verb employed can also be translated "do not even loosen your grip." Why? Because your life depends on it. "She is your life!" Three other times we have the contrast between life and death in Proverbs.

---

310 The verb is always translated obey if it is followed by the preposition lamed (ל).

311 Garrett, *Proverbs, Ecclesiastes, Song of Songs*, 67.

312 In Hebrew, a jussive (volitional) preceded by an imperative takes the force of the imperative.

LIFE	DEATH
The teaching of the wise is a fountain of life	that one may turn away from the snares of death (13:14)
The fear of the LORD is a fountain of life	that one may turn away from the snares of death (14:27)
Life is in the power of the tongue; those who love it will eat its fruits	Death is in the power of the tongue; those who love it will eat its fruits (18:21)

Figure 10.1 Life and death in Proverbs[313]

In Proverbs 9:9, Solomon connects wisdom with righteousness. "Give instruction to a wise man, and he will be still wiser; teach a righteous man, and he will increase in learning." The parallel parts are wise man//righteous man, and wiser//add to his learning.[314] Both the wise and righteous are teachable because they understand the need to be lifelong learners. Warren Wiersbe is right in that "Fools, scoffers, and the simple like to have their own way and be told they're doing fine, but wise men and women want the truth. Teach wise people, and they'll accept the truth and become wiser; try to teach fools and they'll reject the truth and become even greater fools."[315] O, LORD, give us a hunger and thirst for wisdom and righteousness, and forgive us for the times when we thought we knew it all!

Proverbs 19:25–29 deals with the scoffer or mocker who dishonors his parents, puts a pause in the learning process, and has no respect for truth. In contrast with the scoffer and mocker is the wise person who will continue gaining knowledge after being rebuked. "Strike a scoffer, and the simple will learn prudence;

313 The words "life" and "live" occur more than fifty times in the book of Proverbs. These are just the instances where life and death appear together and they are contrasted.

314 The language is very similar to Proverbs 1:5, "Let the wise hear and increase in learning, and the one who understands obtain guidance."

315 Warren Wiersbe, *Be Skillful,* (Wheaton, IL: Victor Books, 1995), 32.

reprove a man of understanding, and he will gain knowledge" (Proverbs 19:25). There are consequences associated with pausing the learning process. "Cease to hear instruction, my son, and you will stray from the words of knowledge" (Proverbs 19:27). The way of the LORD is the way of knowledge that is a stronghold (Proverbs 10:29), and departing from it means straying from knowledge. The one listening to instruction is portrayed as being on the path of life, while the one who rejects reproof not only is lost but leads others astray (Proverbs 10:17). The person who ignores the learning process harms himself. "Whoever ignores instruction despises himself, but he who listens to reproof gains intelligence" (Proverbs 15:32). If learning is associated with the fear of the LORD, then lack of learning can be associated with not caring about who God is or what He says. "The fear of the LORD is instruction in wisdom, and humility comes before honor" (Proverbs 15:33). May the LORD grant us the humility to always fear Him in order to gain wisdom to follow Him on the path of life and righteousness.

Some practical ways to be lifelong learners include generation and reflection.[316] Brown et al. suggest that "you don't engage the mind by reading a text over and over again or by passively watching PowerPoint slides. Generation takes place when 'you engage it by making the effort to explain the material yourself, in your own words—connecting the facts, making it vivid, relating it to what you already know...when you want to master something new, delete the whimpering and go wrestle the bear.'"[317] In the act of reflection, we ask some important questions, such as "What did I do? How did it work? How could I do it better next time?" Captain Sullenberger, the pilot who successfully landed US Airways flight 1549 on the Hudson River in 2009, "refined his understanding of flight and the control of his aircraft through training, personal experience, and the close observation of others."[318]

316 Adapted from Peter C. Brown et al., *Make It Stick: The Science of Successful Learning* (Boston, Harvard University Press, 2014), 220–25.

317 Brown et al., *Make It Stick,* 222.

318 Brown et al., *Make It Stick,* 223.

A Lesson from Church History

Though he held a doctor's degree, Luther was no mere member of the learned guild of scholastic theologians. His theology grew out of his anguished quest for a gracious God. For Luther, theology was not simply the academic study of religion. Rather, it was a lifelong process of struggle and temptation. As Luther never tired of saying, only experience makes a theologian. "I did not learn my theology all at once," he said, "but I had to search deeper for it, where my temptations took me.... Not understanding, reading, or speculation, but living—nay, dying and being damned—make a theologian."[319]

319 Timothy George, "Dr. Luther's Theology," *Christian History 34* (2/1992): 18–22.

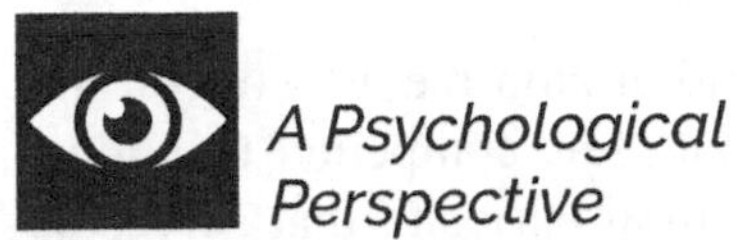

Reflections on Lifelong Learning

Dr. Kevin Roberts

A wise man will hear and increase in learning,
And a man of understanding will acquire wise counsel.
(Proverbs 1:5)

It is made clear throughout all of Scripture that our God is everlasting and His ways unsearchable (Isaiah 40:28). This leaves an extraordinary gap between finite human wisdom and that of our God. It is in this gap that we human beings often find our sense of awe, wonder, curiosity, and a desire to both know and understand. In this chapter, we will seek to discuss the role of our innate human curiosity and how it serves as the engine for the love of learning. Furthermore, we will discuss the psychological literature surrounding human curiosity, motivation, and the love of learning. We will also seek to consider Solomon's advice in the book of Proverbs around the many benefits of becoming a lifelong learner.

A Lifelong Learner

Give instruction to a wise man, and he will be still wiser; teach a righteous man, and he will increase in learning. (Proverbs 9:9)

What does it mean to become a lifelong learner? A lifelong learner is someone who is systematically seeking to deepen their knowledge and understanding of the world around them.[320] He or she has an inquisitive, curious mind that feels compelled to understand. The lifelong learner has a natural curiosity that serves as the engine to drive lifelong learning. However, for the engine to run well, the fuel, or the intrinsic motivation, is required to make it happen. Our intrinsic motivation provides the energy over the course of our life to continually seek knowledge (Proverbs 18:15). Intrinsic motivation is best described as, "motivation to perform an activity because of the value or pleasure associated with that activity, rather than for an external goal or purpose."[321] In other words, our intrinsic motivation serves as fuel for our curiosity if we inherently see the value and enjoy the task of learning.

Lifelong Learning Means "Seeking Knowledge"

An intelligent heart acquires knowledge, and the ear of the wise seeks knowledge. (Proverbs 18:15)

In the Old Testament, we often see the instruction to wait on the Lord (Psalm 25:4–6; 27:14; 31:24; 37:7; 130:5). It is through this waiting on the Lord, who is our source for knowledge, understanding, and wisdom, that we can humbly receive instruction regarding His paths. We serve an omniscient, omnipotent God, and we His servants are finite, fallible, and sinful human beings. This *gap* between an all-knowing God and His finite created human beings makes each one of us become acutely aware of our inferiority in the presence of a holy God! Alfred Adler, a famous psychiatrist practicing in the early 1900s, was keenly aware of man's finite limitations. Adlerian Psychology also known as Individual Psychology, readily acknowledges these feelings of inferiority. "In some ways, we all feel we are less than others and less than what we want to be. These feelings of inferiority may be well based in fact. If we feel in awe of the universe, less than its totality, there is a good reason for feeling this way. Mankind

---

320 Niemiec, *Mindfulness and Character Strengths: A Practical Guide to Flourishing.*

321 Elizabeth A. Phelps, Elliot Berkman, and Michael Gazzaniga, *Psychological Science*, 7th ed. (W. W. Norton & Company, 2022), 396.

has spent forever coming up with myths, rituals, and other devices for coming to grips with our essential inferiority which is the existential task."[322]

These inferiority feelings that all humans experience drive us toward growth, according to Adler.[323] In (Adlerian) Individual Psychology, this growth drive is pushing us toward perfection, whereas other personality theorists have come to very similar conclusions but describe this growth with terms like self-actualization, need for perfection, and competency.[324] For those of us in the Christian faith, we see perfection in the life of Christ. This innate growth perspective has been further connected to positive mental health outcomes when taught to people who had a fixed mindset.[325]

The idea of pursuing this growth has been further explored in a recent bestselling book *Mindset* by Stanford professor Carol Dweck.[326] In her book, she illustrates the differences between having a growth or a fixed mindset. The fixed mindset sees people as having to set abilities and aptitudes, which lends to their constant desire to prove themselves and their value to the world. This is in direct contrast to the growth mindset described as such, "In this mindset, the hand you're dealt is just the starting point for development. The growth mindset is based on the belief that your basic qualities are things you can cultivate through your efforts. Although people may differ in every which way—in their initial

---

322 Manaster and Corsini, *Individual Psychology,* 63.

323 Manaster and Corsini, *Individual Psychology*.

324 Kurt Goldstein, *The Organism: A Holistic Approach to Biology Derived from Pathological Data in Man* (New York: American Book Co., 1939); Karen Horney, *Neurosis and Human Growth* (W. W. Norton, 1950); Robert W. White, "Motivation Reconsidered: The Concept of Competence," *Psychological Review* 66, no. 5 (1959): 297–333.

325 Jessica L. Schleider and John R. Weisz, "Reducing Risk for Anxiety and Depression in Adolescents: Effects of a Single-Session Intervention Teaching That Personality Can Change," *Behaviour Research and Therapy* 87 (2016): 170–81. https://doi.org/10.1016/j.brat.2016.09.011.

326 Carol S. Dweck, *Mindset: The New Psychology of Success: How We Can Learn to Fulfill Our Potential* (New York: Random House, 2006).

talents and aptitudes, interests, or temperaments—everyone can change and grow through application and experience."[327]

This idea of ongoing growth is illustrated in the opening verses of Proverbs, "A wise man will hear and increase in learning, and a man of understanding will acquire wise counsel" (Proverbs 1:5 NASB). As we see in this verse, growth is an active thing whereby we "hear" and we "learn." If the wise man or woman does not know the answer, then they are compelled to go "acquire wise counsel." We know that the lifelong learner must be willing to receive instruction and seek it out if it is not readily available. He or she must be willing to pursue this wisdom, and this is where our intrinsic motivation and curiosity come into play.

The Role of Curiosity

Several classic studies dating back to Harlow's experiments in the 1950s show that human beings and primates have a strong exploratory drive once their basic social, attachment, and physical needs are being met. Harlow found that human beings and primates essentially have an innate drive that pushes them toward difficult tasks.[328] Interestingly, this exploratory or growth drive includes difficult tasks, even when there is no reward at the end of the task. We even see this in our children when they get a new toy and play with it, and then casually disregard the toy and move on to the next toy. But is this natural curiosity a good thing for children and our mental health?

In a number of studies, curiosity is strongly correlated with individuals who successfully build confidence, develop autonomy, and achievement.[329] Curiosity also appears to be important for the development of creativity, personal relationships, spirituality, and for meeting our needs for belonging.[330] This would indicate that

327 Dweck, *Mindset: The New Psychology of Success,* 7.

328 H. F. Harlow and M. K. Harlow, "Learning to Love," *American Scientist* 54, no. 3 (1966): 244–72.

329 Shannon Polly, Kathryn Britton, and Senia Maymin, *Character Strengths Matter: How to Live a Full Life* (Charleston, SC: Positive Psychology News, LLC, 2015).

330 Polly, Britton, Maymin, *Character Strengths Matter.*

encouraging the development of curiosity is essential for overall human wellbeing. However, this level of curiosity does not happen for everyone. Are there things that each of us does that interfere with the cultivating of the innate quality of curiosity?

Can We Do Things to Discourage Others from Wanting to Be Curious or to Become Lifelong Learners?

As parents, we often do things unintentionally that discourage our kids from following their curious and inquisitive nature. For example, we all want our children and grandchildren to be strong readers, so we do things to incentivize kids to read by giving them money or other rewards. However, the messages we send to these children is that reading and the process of exploration was not, in and of itself, rewarding enough. Lepper conducted now-classic research with drawing and found that by rewarding children for creative activities, they make activities like reading and drawing into transactions.[331] Once we turn these activities into extrinsic rewards, the child no longer looks upon those activities as potential enjoyment. In essence, we ruin these activities for kids because they now view drawing or reading as unenjoyable tasks and, consequently, discourage their future interest in these activities.

Does Curiosity Have a Downside?

Because I have called and you refused to listen, have stretched out my hand and no one has heeded, because you have ignored all my counsel and would have none of my reproof. (Proverbs 1:24–25)

Since the garden of Eden, we have seen Adam and Eve's curiosity for knowing more and understanding more about God's creation (Genesis 3). Satan desired to take this innately human quality and subvert it by getting us to try eating the forbidden fruit. However, God also gave us the wise the ability to learn and grow in knowl-

331 Mark R. Lepper, David Greene, and Richard E. Nisbett, "Undermining Children's Intrinsic Interest with Extrinsic Reward: A Test of the 'Overjustification' Hypothesis," *Journal of Personality and Social Psychology* 28, no. 1 (1973): 129–37. https://doi.org/10.1037/h0035519.

edge, understanding, and wisdom. But at what point can trust in our own learning become problematic?

The problem that we all face is our tendency to trust in our own learning. We can take a prideful position as we continue to grow and learn because we often get reinforcement from our environment. This reinforcement encourages us to trust in our own intelligence, believing we are more clever than we are. Solomon, in all his wisdom, eventually strayed into seeking out hedonistic pleasures rather than remaining tied to the source of all wisdom (Ecclesiastes 2). Solomon developed for himself a mighty kingdom and was likely receiving all kinds of praise for his performance as the leader of Israel. In all of Solomon's wisdom, though, he seemed to lose sight of the humility he had as a young man when he prayed for wisdom in leading God's people. As we see in Proverbs 16:2, "All the ways of a man are pure in his own eyes, but the LORD weighs the spirit." But one wonders, at what point did Solomon lose his fear of the LORD and begin to trust and take pride in his own ways? As we learn and grow, we must maintain a sense of humility and stay true to our purpose, as outlined in 1 Corinthians 10:31, which indicates that we are to glorify God in all that we do. Did Solomon lose this vision? Although we cannot know for certain, it is clear that trusting in our own wisdom and knowledge leads us down dangerous paths. Are there any traits that we can develop that can push back against our pride?

Curiosity Involves Being Open and Flexible

The psychological literature maintains that openness and flexibility are strongly correlated with curiosity.[332] If we are going to remain humble in our learnings and stay curious about God's creation, then we must always be challenging the limitations of our knowledge. To be open-minded, we must be willing to challenge our points of view and use critical thinking to examine if we are being wise or not.[333] The literature supports the notion that open-mindedness improves our judgment and critical thinking

332 Polly, Britton, Maymin, *Character Strengths Matter.*

333 Polly, Britton, Maymin, *Character Strengths Matter.*

skills and thus positively impacts problem-solving.[334] This willingness to critically examine ourselves appears to help us make better decisions and develop a more comprehensive and wise view of the world. In contrast, we see the fool described in Proverbs as someone who hates instruction and often displays ignorance (Proverbs 1:7; Ecclesiastes 2:14). The fool contrasts the wise in their refusal to remain open to new learning because of their resistance to instruction.

Application Exercises and Questions for the Love of Learning

Get wisdom; get insight; do not forget, and do not turn away from the words of my mouth. Do not forsake her, and she will keep you; love her, and she will guard you. (Proverbs 4:5–6)

1. What is one thing you have learned in the last month that you had no idea about one month ago? Are you consuming at least one book a month? If you are a leader of any kind, what books on leadership are you reading?
2. What is an area of your life where you've refused to fall humbly before God? Where do you have insight or intellectual knowledge of your problems but refuse to act on changing this behavior? What is holding you back?
3. What is an aspect of God that you want to know more about? Have you researched it?
4. What is your plan for personal growth? Do you have goals for growth? If you do not have a plan, then what are you striving toward?

334 Polly, Britton, Maymin, *Character Strengths Matter.*

Lifelong Learning at Church

Pastor Knute Larson

Before we talk about sermons, small groups, discipleship-accountability groups, and the electives and functions of the church, let's talk about why we exist—to glorify God with our love and obedience and to enjoy Him forever. And, we add, because we are so fallen, to learn how to do that for all our lives. We are not about conversion only, though the emphasis can seem that way at times. We are not about meetings and Sundays alone, though they get a lot of publicity. Church is about converting from our fallen ways to receiving Jesus Christ into our spirits by His Spirit, then living to do all things in obedience to His ways and bringing Him acclaim and pleasure. This purpose of the church takes a lifetime of learning. And anything else is shallow church.

The first emphasis for all of us should be our own personal and spiritual growth. We ought to be getting stronger in our faith and better in our obedience so that we can help others do the same. That could be called lifelong learning because, in spite of snappy titles for courses and books, there is no shortcut—we all have much to convert and learn. When Proverbs tells us to "keep hold of instruction; do not let go; guard her, for she is your life," we should hear that with sober reaction (Proverbs 4:13). Good truths can easily get away from us. We can stop and become proud and stall in our growth.

Witness the headlines about disaster and pride explosions in churches, proof that some have rejected reproof and ended up leading others astray (Proverbs 10:17). The wisdom principles are for people in positions of leadership, for sure, since even they can stop growing as they admire themselves in the mirror of pride with the lusty feelings of power.

All of us who are believers in our LORD, the same God of the Old Testament and incarnate Word of the New, should be getting stronger in our faith and more obedient in our love. Church should look like a group of people seeking to sharpen each other in the graces of godliness and growing in their action love toward people not yet convinced that Jesus is LORD.

Solomon had to be thinking of himself when he wrote, "whoever ignores correction leads others astray" (Proverbs 10:17 NIV). Surely, he could look back on his "vanity of vanities" experiences with wine, women, and song as very damaging to the glory of God and the shining of God's kingdom. For a time, he stopped learning, and we must learn from that.

A strong church is a pleasant place of love and learning. Its times of worship are meaningful, causing our spirits to look up to God and rejoice in Him. Its times of group or classroom interaction are not a waste, for there are strong points made about commitment and unselfish devotion to the ways of our Savior. There is truth applied to everyday, common allegiance to do what is right, and encouragement to serve others. There we learn together how the presence of Christ—believers live in combination with our LORD—will show through our actions and decisions.

It is a good look.

Why Lifelong Learning Is So Important

No one who knows the wisdom and challenges of Scripture thinks conversion to Christ is a destination. Rather, it is a new birth to a way of learning and serving, and loving. It is a beginning rather than a conclusion. In one of the most poignant Proverbs, the writer is pretty straightforward: "O simple ones, learn prudence; O fools, learn sense" (Proverbs 8:5). And none of us can actually "knock some sense into each other," as the old expression goes. We must desire it for ourselves. We must want to learn.

A church of believers is a body that shines in the community with unity, service, and love for outsiders, as well as humble servanthood to each other. People who gather there are, in one sense of the expression "at church," but in another, more biblical sense, this church is a group of people who represent the body of Christ where they work as priests to serve God, something like Jesus did when He made cabinets. And at home, where they grow together in love. They fail at times, but they also grow to forgive and go on to lift each other up with love and good works.

Why Lifelong Learning Does Not Always Show Up

In his informal preface to the thirty-one chapters of Proverbs—one for each day of most months, perhaps—Solomon gives a straightforward warning: "The fear of the LORD is the beginning of knowledge; fools despise wisdom and instruction" (Proverbs 1:7). Enough said about why wisdom shown in continual learning does not always show up. We can be foolish in our selfishness and pretend we have arrived.

Life is about many facts, giant truths: God created us. We are not inclined on our own to obey Him and seek Him. He chases us, as He did Israel, His chosen, in the Old Testament. In a planned and miraculous move, God came down here as the only divine-human person ever and "the Word became flesh" (John 1:14). Wisdom took on a human body. Jesus of Nazareth, whom John 1:14 speaks of, lived a perfect and godly life as a true child and man, and then, in accord with an eternal plan, He died a death that defied the wisdom of all the ages and sages and men on the street. He was judged in a holy way for all our sins. "The LORD has laid on him the iniquity of us all" (Isaiah 53:6).

"He was delivered over to death for our sins and was raised to life for our justification" (Romans 4:25). Our being declared righteous in God's sight because the perfect righteousness of Jesus is accredited to us as a covering simply because of our faith in Jesus, God's Son (Romans 4:6–8). We are to begin a life while here on earth where we "keep hold of instruction; do not let go," and where we "guard her, for she is your life" (Proverbs 4:13). A life of obeying and loving and learning, yes. But also a life of learning, for we have so far to go from our selfish inclinations.

Lifelong learning may not always show up if we think that faith in Christ is the end rather than the beginning and a very important part of the journey. And many churches and leaders and individual believers have decided, with no backing from Proverbs or any other wisdom in the Bible, that "being saved," a good phrase indeed, is the end or goal rather than the step that leads to living in Christ with a lifetime of learning and obeying. Conversion, the act of faith, is not the whole story.

Yes, what has been called "make a decision" is final if it means to place faith in the person and incarnate work of Jesus Christ. But that faith, by the strength of God, should also be shaping us into what a new creation looks like at home, work, and church. It is the start of something new. The whole New Testament is about how the church is to believe and behave, clearly growing and staying with the good news for everyday learning and growing. It shows us how our LORD changes a life or a whole crowd of people.

Growth in learning will not show up for another reason—if the family relinquishes its responsibility to the church or to no one. "My son" in Proverbs is often followed by the clear instruction to learn. "Keep at it," is frequently commanded. "Hear, O sons, a father's instruction" (Proverbs 4:1). And so the church tries to help parents know God's truth and also pass it on. Much of that comes through sermons and lessons and groups, or seminars that help motivate and give ideas for parental skills, but then it must show up at home.

What Each of Us Can Do Personally to Be Lifelong Learners

One of the main things we can do is model growth. Also, fear the LORD, for that is "instruction in wisdom" (Proverbs 15:32, 33). Enjoy the spiritual growth that comes through God's Word and the life joined to His Spirit. Celebrate that this walking with the

Lord is the prudent and sensible way to live, given what we are like when left to ourselves (Proverbs 8:5).

Pray for your family and church that by learning and growing, they will experience "every good path" and live a life that is pleasant to their souls (Proverbs 2:9, 10).

Get in a small group where there is true Bible study with candid application to life, where people love each other and sharpen each other, not just have an ice cream social.

Decide to be a lifelong learner.

A Personal Prayer for Lifelong Learning

Praise: Thank God for His wisdom and truths and ways of truth that indeed take a lifetime to learn. His ways and secrets are amazing.

Repent: Decide if you have any neglect to confess about daily and regular growth in God's truth and the practice of it.

Ask: For areas of life where you need to improve in spirit and for help for those you love.

Yield: To the call to run after wisdom and to "grow in the grace and knowledge of our Lord and Savior Jesus Christ" (2 Peter 3:18).

Bibliography

Ainsworth, M. D. S. et al. *Patterns of Attachment: A Psychological Study of the Strange Situation*. Erlbaum, 1978.

Alcoholics Anonymous: The Big Book–4th Ed. New York City, NY: Alcoholics Anonymous World Services, Inc.

Arnold, Bill T., and Bryan E. Beyer. *Readings from the Ancient Near East*. Grand Rapids: Baker, 2002.

Ashton, Michael C., Kibeom Lee, and Reinout E. de Vries. "The Hexaco Honesty-Humility, Agreeableness, and Emotionality Factors." *Personality and Social Psychology Review* 18, no. 2 (2014).

Bandura, Albert. *Social Learning Theory*. Englewood Cliffs, NJ: Prentice-Hall, 1977.

Bartholomew, Craig G., and Ryan P. O'Dowd. *Old Testament Wisdom Literature: A Theological Introduction.* Downers Grove, IL: InterVarsity Press, 2011.

Barton, David, and Tim Barton. *The American Story: The Beginnings*. Aledo, TX: WallBuilders, 2020.

Batson, C. Daniel. "How Social an Animal? The Human Capacity for Caring." *American Psychologist* 45, no. 3 (1990). https://doi.org/10/1037/0003-066x.45.3.336.

__________. "Where Is the Altruism in the Altruistic Personality?" *Journal of Personality and Social Psychology* 50, no. 1 (1986).

__________. *The Altruism Question: Toward a Social-Psychological Answer.* Hilldale, 1991.

Baumeister, Roy F., and Todd F. Heatherton. "Self-Regulation Failure: An Overview." *Psychological Inquiry* 7, no. 1 (1996). https://doi.org/10.1207/s15327965pli0701_1.

Beard, John R. et al. "Predictors of Mental Disorders and Their Outcome in a Community Based Cohort." *Social Psychiatry and Psychiatric Epidemiology* 42, no. 8 (2007).

Berkman, Elliot T., Alice M. Graham, and Philip A. Fisher. "Training Self-Control: A Domain-General Translational Neuroscience Approach." *Child Development Perspectives* 6, no. 4 (2012). https://doi.org/10.1111/j.1750-8606.2012.00248.x.

Berkowitz, Leonard, and Kenneth G. Lutterman. "The Traditional Socially Responsible Personality." *Public Opinion Quarterly* 32, no. 2 (1968).

Bierhoff, Hans Werner, Renate Klein, and Peter Kramp. "Evidence for the Altruistic Personality from Data on Accident Research." *Journal of Personality* 59, no. 2 (1919).

Blakemore, Sarah-Jayne, and Kathryn L. Mills. "Is Adolescence a Sensitive Period for Sociocultural Processing?" *Annual Review of Psychology* 65, no. 1 (March 2014). https://doi.org/10.1146/annurev-psych-010213-115202.

Bond, Lyndal et al. "Social and School Connectedness in Early Secondary School as Predictors of Late Teenage Substance Use, Mental Health, and Academic Outcomes." *Journal of Adolescent Health* 40, no. 4 (2007).

Bowlby, John. "Attachment and Loss; Retrospect and Prospect." *American Journal of Orthopsychiatry* 52, no. 4 (1982).

Bridges, Jerry. *Respectable Sins: Confronting the Sins We Tolerate*. Colorado Springs: NavPress, 2007.

Brooks, Arthur C. "Religious Faith and Charitable Giving." *Policy Review* 121 (2003).

Brown, Peter C., Henry L. Roediger, and Mark A. McDaniel. *Make It Stick: The Science of Successful Learning*. Cambridge, MA: Belknap Press of Harvard University Press, 2014.

Brown, W. M., N. S. Consedine, and C. Magai. "Altruism Relates to Health in an Ethically Diverse Sample of Older Adults." *The Journals of Gerontology Series B: Psychological Sciences and Social Sciences* 60, no. 3 (January 2005).

Bullard, Maurice L. "Logical and Natural Consequences." *Alfred Adler: His Influence on Psychology Today*, ed. Harold H. Mosak. Park Ridge: Noyes Press, 1973.

Bullinger, E. W. *Figures of Speech Used in the Bible*. Grand Rapids: Baker, 2003.

Bultmann, R. *Πιστεύω*. *Theological Dictionary of the New Testament*, vol. VI. Grand Rapids, MI: Eerdmans, 2006.

Chou, Kee-Lee. "The Rushton, Chrisjohn, and Fekken Self-Report Altruism Scale: A Chinese Translation." *Personality and Individual Differences* 21, no. 2 (1996).

Ciampa, Roy E., and Brian S. Rosner. *The First Letter to the Corinthians*. Pillar New Testament Commentary. Grand Rapids, MI: Eerdmans, 2010.

Clements, Ronald E. *Wisdom in Theology.* Grand Rapids, MI: Eerdmans, 1992.

Collins, Kenneth J. *A Real Christian: The Life of John Wesley*. Nashville: Abingdon, 1999.

Costa, Paul T., Robert R. McCrae, and David A. Dye. "Facet Scales for Agreeableness and Conscientiousness: A Revision of the NEO Personality Inventory." *Personality and Individual Differences* 12, no. 9 (1991).

Crenshaw, James L. *Old Testament Wisdom: An Introduction.* Louisville, KY: Westminster John Knox, 1998.

Curry, Oliver Scott et al. "Happy to Help? A Systematic Review and Meta-Analysis of the Effect of Performing Acts of Kindness on the Well-Being of the Actor." *Journal of Experimental Social Psychology* 76 (2018). https://doi.org/10.1016/j/jesp.2018.02.014.

Dawkins, Richard. *The God Delusion.* Boston: Mariner Books, 2006.

DePaulo, Bella M. et al. "Lying in Everyday Life." *Journal of Personality and Social Psychology* 70, no. 5 (1996).

Diagnostic and Statistical Manual of Mental Disorders: DSM-5, 5th edition. Arlington, VA: American Psychiatric Association, 2013.

Diamond, Adele. "Activities and Programs That Improve Children's Executive Functions." *Current Directions in Psychological Science* 21, no. 5 (2012). https://doi.org/10.1177/0963214124537 22.

Dickinson, Anthony, Andrew Watt, and W. J. H. Griffiths. "Free-Operant Acquisition with Delayed Reinforcement." *Quarterly Journal of Experimental Psychology Section B* 45, no. 3b (1992). https://doi.org/10/1080/14640749208401019.

Dreikurs, Rudolf. *Fundamentals of Adlerian Psychology.* Chicago: Alfred Adler Institute, 1953.

Duckworth, A. L., and M. E. P. Seligman, "Self-Discipline Outdoes IQ in Predicting Academic Performance of Adolescents." *Psychological Science* 16, no. 12 (January 2005). https://doi.org/10.1111/j.1467-9280.2005.01641.x.

Dumas, Jean E. et al. "Home Chaos: Sociodemographic, Parenting, Interactional, and Child Correlates." *Journal of Clinical Child & Adolescent Psychology* 34, no. 1 (2005). https://doi.org/10.1207/x15374424.jccp30401_9.

Dumbrell, W. J. ענו. *The New International Dictionary of Old Testament Theology and Exegesis,* vol. 3. Grand Rapids, MI: Zondervan, 1997.

Dweck, Carol S. *Mindset: The New Psychology of Success: How We Can Learn to Fulfill Our Potential.* New York: Random House, 2006.

Easton, M. G. *Illustrated Bible Dictionary and Treasury of Biblical History, Biography, Geography, Doctrine, and Literature.* New York: Harper & Brothers, 1893.

Edgington, Thomas J. *Healing Helps from the Bible: For Hurting People Seeking Help from Scripture.* Evangel Press, 1995.

Ejiri, Manami et al. "'Predictors of Older Adults' Objectively Measured Social Isolation: A Systematic Review of Observational Studies." *Archives of Gerontology and Geriatrics* 94 (2021): 104357.

Erikson, Erik H. *Childhood and Society.* New York: Norton, 1950.

__________. *Identity and the Life Cycle: Selected Papers.* International Universities Press, 1959.

Exline, J. J., B. Bushman, J. Faber, and C. Phillips. "Pride Gets in the Way: Self-Protection Works Against Forgiveness." In *Ouch! Who Said Forgiveness Was Easy? Symposium Presented at the Annual Meeting of the Society for Personality and Social Psychology,* ed. J. J. Exline. Nashville, TN.

Fox, Claire L., and Michael J. Boulton. "Friendship as a Moderator of Relationship between Social Skills Problems and Peer Victimization." *Aggressive Behavior* 32, no. 2 (2006). https://doi.org/10.1002/ab.20114.

Fredericks, Daniel C., and Daniel J. Estes. *Ecclesiastes and The Song of Songs*. Downers Grove, IL: InterVarsity Press, 2010.

Fretheim, Terrence E. "חנן." *The New International Dictionary of Old Testament Theology and Exegesis*, vol. 2, ed. Willem A. VanGermeren. Grand Rapids, MI: Zondervan 1997.

__________. "חנן." *The New International Dictionary of Old Testament Theology and Exegesis*, vol. 2. Grand Rapids, MI: Zondervan 1997.

Garrett, Duane A. *Proverbs, Ecclesiastes, Song of Songs*. The New American Commentary, vol. 14. Nashville: Broadman & Holman Publishers, 1993.

George, Timothy. "Dr. Luther's Theology." *Christian History 34* (2/1992).

Glasser, William. *Choice Theory: A New Psychology of Personal Freedom*. New York, NY: Harper Collins, 1998.

Goff, Matthew. "Hellish Females: The Strange Woman of Septuagint Proverbs and 4QWiles of the Wicked Woman (4Q184)." In *Journal for the Study of Judaism* 39 (2008).

Goldstein, Kurt. *The Organism: A Holistic Approach to Biology Derived from Pathological Data in Man*. New York: American Book Co., 1939.

Goleman, Daniel. *Emotional Intelligence*. New York: Bantam Books, 1995.

Gordon, Amie M. et al. "The Dark Side of the Sublime: Distinguishing a Threat-Based Variant of Awe." *Journal of Personality and Social Psychology* 113, no. 2 (2017).

Gottman, John M. *The Science of Trust: Emotional Attunement for Couples.* New York: W. W. Norton, 2011.

Grison, Sarah, and Michael Gazzaniga. *Psychology in Your Life*. W. W. Norton & Company, Inc., 2022.

Hansen, Walter. *The Letter to the Philippians*. Pillar New Testament Commentary. Grand Rapids, MI: Eerdmans, 2009.

Harbaugh, William T., Ulrich Mayr, and Daniel R. Burghart. "Neural Responses to Taxation and Voluntary Giving Reveal Motives for Charitable Donations." *Science* 316, no. 5831 (2007).

Hardy, Sam et al. "Dynamic Associations between Religiousness and Self-Regulation across Adolescence into Young Adulthood." *Developmental Psychology* 56, no. 1 (2020). https://doi.org/10.1037/dev0000841.

Harlow, H. F., and M. K. Harlow. "Learning to Love." *American Scientist* 54, no. 3 (1966).

Hawks, Annie S., and Robert Lowry. "I Need Thee Every Hour." 1872.

Hegel, G. W. F. *Lectures on the Philosophy of History*. Translated by Reuben Alvarado. Aalten, the Netherlands: WordBridge, 2011.

Hook, Joshua N. et al. "Intellectual Humility and Forgiveness of Religious Leaders." *The Journal of Positive Psychology* 10, no. 6 (February 2015).

Horney, Karen. *Neurosis and Human Growth*. W. W. Norton, 1950.

Horton, Robert F. "The Book of Proverbs." *The Expositor's Bible: Psalms to Isaiah*, ed. W. Robertson Nicoll, vol. 3. Hartford, CT: S.S. Scranton Co., 1903.

Inesi, M. Ena et al. "Power and Choice." *Psychological Science* 22, no. 8 (2011).

Ironside, H. A. *Notes on the Book of Proverbs*. Neptune, NJ: Loizeaux Brothers, 1908.

Johnson, Dale A. *The Authentic Life: Compassion, Hospitality and Gratitude*. New Sinai Press, 2013.

Kelley, Harold H. et al. "An Atlas of Interpersonal Situations." (2003).

Kempis, Thomas á. *The Imitation of Christ*. New York: Vintage Books, 1998.

Khanna, Rajesh, Poonam Singh, and J. Philippe Rushton. "Development of the Hindi Version of a Self-Report Altruism Scale." *Personality and Individual Differences* 14, no. 1 (1993).

Kidner, Derek. *Psalms 1–72 : An Introduction and Commentary*. Tyndale Old Testament Commentaries, v. 15. Downers Grove, IL: InterVarsity Press, 1973.

__________. *Proverbs: An Introduction and Commentary*. Tyndale Old Testament Commentaries, vol. 17. Nottingham, England, Downers Grove, IL: InterVarsity Press, 2008.

Kitchen, John. *Proverbs: A Mentor Commentary*. Ross-Shire, Scotland: Christian Focus, 2006.

Knight, David C. et al. "Amygdala and Hippocampal Activity during Acquisition and Extinction of Human Fear Conditioning." *Cognitive, Affective, & Behavioral Neuroscience* 4, no. 3 (2004).

Konrath, Sara et al. "Motives for Volunteering Are Associated with Mortality Risk in Older Adults." *Health Psychology* 31, no. 1 (2012). https://doi.org/10.1037/a002522.

Kosfeld, Michael et al. "Oxytocin Increases Trust in Humans." *Nature* 435, no. 7042 (2005).

Kovacs, Brian W. "Sociological-Structural Constraints Upon Wisdom: The Spatial and Temporal Matrix of Proverbs 15:28–22:16." PhD Diss., Vanderbilt University, 1978.

Lange, John Peter et al. *A Commentary on the Holy Scriptures: Proverbs*. Bellingham, WA: Logos Bible Software, 2008.

Lee, Jia Ying, and Kana Imuta. "Lying and Theory of Mind: A Meta-Analysis." *Child Development* 92, no. 2 (2021).

Lee, Kibeom, and Michael C. Ashton. "Psychopathy, Machiavellianism, and Narcissism in the Five-Factor Model and the HEXACO Model of Personality Structure." *Personality and Individual Differences* 38, no. 7 (2005). https://doi.org/10.1016/j.paid.2004.09.016.

Lepper, Mark R., David Greene, and Richard E. Nisbett. "Undermining Children's Intrinsic Interest with Extrinsic Reward: A Test of the 'Overjustification' Hypothesis." *Journal of Personality and Social Psychology* 28, no. 1 (1973). https://doi.org/10.1037/h0035519.

Longman III, Tremper. *The Fear of the Lord is Wisdom: A Theological Introduction to Wisdom in Israel.* Grand Rapids, MI: Baker, 2017.

__________. *Proverbs.* Baker Commentary on the Old Testament Wisdom and Psalms. Grand Rapids, MI: Baker, 2006.

Manaster, Guy J., and Raymond J. Corsini. *Individual Psychology: Theory and Practice*. F. E. Peacock, 1982.

Matthews, Timothy et al. "Social Isolation and Mental Health at Primary and Secondary School Entry: A Longitudinal Cohort Study." *Journal of the American Academy of Child & Adolescent Psychiatry* 54, no. 3 (2015).

Mayer, J. D., and P. Salovey. "What is emotional intelligence?" (1997).

McCullough, Michael E., and Brian L. Willoughby. "Religion, Self-Regulation, and Self-Control: Associations, Explanations, and Implications." *Psychological Bulletin* 135, no. 1 (2009). https://doi.org/10.1037/a0014213.

McNeely, Bonnie L., and Bruce M. Meglino. "The Role of Dispositional and Situational Antecedents in Prosocial Organizational Behavior: An Experimentation of the Intended Beneficiaries of Prosocial Behavior." *Journal of Applied Psychology* 79, no. 6 (1994).

Merrill, Eugene H. *Deuteronomy*. The New American Commentary, vol. 4. Nashville: Broadman & Holman, 1994.

Midlarsky, Elizabeth et al. "Altruistic Moral Judgment among Older Adults." *The International Journal of Aging and Human Development* 49, no. 1 (1999).

Mischel, Walter. *The Marshmallow Test: Mastering Self-Control*, 1st edition. Little, Brown, and Company, 2015.

Miller, Calvin. *A Symphony in Sand*. Dallas: Word, 1990.

__________. *Until He Comes*. Nashville: Broadman & Holman, 1998.

Moberly, R. W. L. "!ma." *The New International Dictionary of Old Testament Theology and Exegesis,* vol. 1. Grand Rapids, MI: Zondervan, 1997.

Moo, Douglas J. *The Letters to the Colossians and to Philemon*. Pillar New Testament Commentary. Grand Rapids, MI: Eerdmans, 2008.

Morris, Leon. *The Gospel According to Matthew*. Pillar New Testament Commentary. Grand Rapids, MI: Eerdmans, 1992.

Murphy, Roland E. *Proverbs.* World Biblical Commentary, vol. 22. Nashville: Thomas Nelson, 1998.

Muraven, Mark, and Roy F. Baumeister. "Self-Regulation and Depletion of Limited Resources: Does Self-Control Resemble a Muscle?" *Psychological Bulletin* 126, no. 2 (2000). https://doi.org/10.1037/0033-2909.126.2.247.

Murray, Andrew. *Humility and Absolute Surrender*. Peabody, MA: Hendrickson, 2005.

Niemiec, Ryan M., and Robert E. McGrath. *The Power of Character Strengths: Appreciate and Ignite Your Positive Personality*. VIA Institute on Character, 2019.

Niemiec, Ryan M., and Danny Wedding. *Positive Psychology at the Movies: Using Films to Build Character Strengths and Well-Being,* 2nd ed. Boston MA: Hogrefe Publishing, 2014.

Niemiec, Ryan M. *Mindfulness and Character Strengths: A Practical Guide to Flourishing*. Boston, MA: Hogree Publishing, 2014.

__________. "VIA Character Strengths: Research and Practice (The First 10 Years)." In *Well-Being and Cultures: Perspectives from Positive Psychology,* ed. Hans Henrick Knoop and Antonella Delle Fave. Dordrecht: Springer Science + Business Media, 2013.

Northrup, Chrisanna, Pepper Schwartz, and James Witte. *The Normal Bar: The Surprising Secrets of Happy Couples and What They Reveal about Creating a New Normal in Your Relationship.* New York: Crown Archetype, 2012.

Oden, Thomas C., ed. *Ancient Christian Commentary on Scripture: Proverbs, Ecclesiastes, Song of Solomon,* vol. IX. Downers Grove, IL: InterVarsity Press, 2005.

Olson, L. "The Assessment of Moral Integrity Among Adolescents and Adults." *Dissertation Abstracts International* 60, no. 6 (1998).

Omoto, Allen M., and Mark Snyder. "Sustained Helping without Obligation: Motivation, Longevity of Service, and Perceived Attitude Change among AIDS Volunteers." *Journal of Personality and Social Psychology* 68, no. 4 (1995).

Our Daily Bread. 1996 May. Our Daily Bread. © 1996 by Our Daily Bread Ministries. All rights reserved.

Peters, Annette Susanne, Wade Clinton Rowat, and Megan Kathleen Johnson. "Associations between Dispositional Humility and Social Relationship Quality." *Psychology* 2, no. 03 (2011). https://dx.doi.org/10.4236/psych.2011.23025.

Peterson, Christopher, and Martin E. P. Seligman. *Character Strengths and Virtues: A Handbook and Classification.* Oxford: Oxford University Press, 2004.

Phelps, Elizabeth A., Elliot Berkman, and Michael Gazzaniga. *Psychological Science*, 7th ed. W. W. Norton & Company, 2022.

Piper, John. *This Momentary Marriage: A Parable of Permanence*. Wheaton, IL: Crossway Books, 2009.

Polly, Shannon, Kathryn Britton, and Senia Maymin. *Character Strengths Matter: How to Live a Full Life*. Charleston, SC: Positive Psychology News, LLC, 2015.

Prosise, Ronald V. *Preaching Illustrations from Church History*. The Woodlands, TX: Kress Christian Publications, 2016.

Rata, Tiberius, and Kevin Roberts. *Fear God and Keep His Commandments: A Practical Exposition of Ecclesiastes*. Winona Lake, IN: BMH, 2016.

Reeves, Michael. *What Does it Mean to Fear the LORD?* Wheaton: Crossway, 2021.

de Ridder, Denise T. et al. "Taking Stock of Self-Control." *Personality and Social Psychology Review* 16, no. 1 (2012). https://doi.org/10.1177/1088868311418749.

Robson, Davina A., Mark S. Allen, and Steven J. Howard, "Self-Regulation in Childhood as a Predictor of Future Outcomes: A Meta-Analytic Review." *Psychological Bulletin* 146, no. 4 (2020). https://doi.org/10.1037/bu10000227.

Rohr, Richard. *Falling Upward: A Spirituality of the Two Halves of Life*. San Francisco: Jossey-Bass, 2013.

Ross, Allen P. *Proverbs*. Expositor's Bible Commentary, vol 5. Grand Rapids: Zondervan, 1991.

Rowland, Lee, and Oliver Scott Curry. "A Range of Kindness Activities Boost Happiness." *The Journal of Social Psychology* 159, no. 3 (2018). https://doi.org/10.1080/00224545.2018.1469461.

Rushton, J. Philippe, G. Cynthia Fekken, and Roland D. Chrisjohn. "The Altruistic Personality and the Self-Report Altruism Scale." *Personality and Individual Differences* 4, no. 3 (1981).

Tangney, June Price. "Humility: Theoretical Perspectives, Empirical Findings and Directions for Future Research." *Journal of Social and Clinical Psychology* 19, no. 1 (2000).

Tankersley, Dharol, C. Jill Stowe, and Scott A. Huettel. "Altruism is Associated with an Increased Neural Response to Agency." *Natural Neuroscience* 10, no. 2 (2007).

Sala, Harold J. *Heroes: People Who Made a Difference in Our World*. Uhrichsville, OH: Promise Press, 1998.

Salovey, P., and D. Sluyter (eds.) *Emotional Development and Emotional Intelligence: Implications for Educators.* New York: Basic Books, 1997.

Schleider, Jessica L., and John R. Weisz. "Reducing Risk for Anxiety and Depression in Adolescents: Effects of a Single-Session Intervention Teaching That Personality Can Change." *Behaviour Research and Therapy* 87 (2016). https://doi.org/10.1016/j.brat.2016.09.011.

Setoh, Peipei et al. "Parents with Greater Religiosity Lie Less to Their Children." *Psychology of Religion and Spirituality* 14, no. 1 (2022).

Spence-Jones, H. D. M., ed. *Proverbs.* The Pulpit Commentary. London: Funk & Wagnalls Company, 1909.

Spidel, Alicia et al. "'Wasn't me!' A field study of the relationship between deceptive motivations and psychopathic traits in young offenders." *Legal and Criminological Psychology* 14, no. 2 (2011).

Spink, Kathryn. *Mother Teresa: An Authorized Biography*. New York: HarperOne, 2011.

Spinka, Matthew. *John Hus: A Bibliography*. Princeton, NJ: Princeton University Press, 2017.

Spurgeon, C. H. *The Treasury of David: Psalms 111–119,* vol. 5. London: Marshall Brothers, 1881.

Steinmann, Andrew. *Proverbs*. Concordia Commentary. Saint Louis, MO: Concordia, 2009.

Stellar, Jennifer E. et al. "Awe and Humility." *Journal of Personality and Social Psychology* 114, no. 2 (2018). https://doi.org/10/1037/pspi0000109.

Storbeck, Justin, Jessica Dayboch, and Jordan Wylie. "Fear and Happiness, but Not Sadness, Motivate Attentional Flexibility: A Case for Emotion Influencing the Ability to Split Foci of Attention." *Emotion* 19, no. 4 (2019).

Stuart, Douglas K. *Exodus*. The New American Commentary, vol. 2. Nashville: Broadman & Holman, 2006.

Thielman, Frank. *Philippians*. New International Version Application Commentary. Grand Rapids: Zondervan, 1995.

Thomas, Robert L. *Revelation 8–22: An Exegetical Commentary*. Chicago: Moody Publishers. 1995.

Tocqueville, Alex de. *Democracy in America*. Translated by Henry Reeve. London: Saunders and Otley, 1835.

Tripp, Paul. *Parenting: The 14 Gospel Principles That Can Radically Change Your Family*. Wheaton: Crossway, 2016.

Tripp, Tedd. *Shepherding a Child's Heart*. Wapwallopen, PA: Shepherd Press, 1995.

Urry, Heather L. et al. "Prefrontal Cortical Activation During Emotion Regulation: Linking Religious/Spiritual Practices with Well-Being." (2012).

Waite, Linda, and Maggie Gallagher. *The Case for Marriage: Why Married People are Happier, Healthier and Better off Financially.* New York: Broadway Books, 2002.

Wallace, Charles, ed. *Susanna Wesley: The Complete Writings.* Oxford: OUP, 1997.

Wallace, Ronald. *Elijah and Elisha: Expositions from the Book of Kings*. Eugene, OR: Wipf and Stock, 2013.

Waltke, Bruce K. *The Book of Proverbs: Chapters 15–31*. The New International Commentary on the Old Testament. Grand Rapids: Eerdmans, 2005.

Waltke, Bruce K. and Ivan D. V. de Silva. *Proverbs: A Shorter Commentary.* Grand Rapids: Eerdmans, 2021.

Ward, Mary J., Shelley S. Lee, and Evelyn G. Lipper. "Failure-to-Thrive Is Associated with Disorganized Infant-Mother Attachment and Unresolved Maternal Attachment." *Infant Mental Health Journal* 21, no. 6 (2000): 428–42.

Warren, Lerner, and Phelps (Eds.). *Thriving and Spirituality Among Youth: Research Perspectives and Further Possibilities* (2012).

Wegner, Daniel M. et al. "The Suppression of Exciting Thoughts." *Journal of Personality and Social Psychology* 58, no. 3 (1990). https://doi.org/10/1037/0022-3514.58.3.409.

Weinstein, Netta, and Richard M. Ryan. "When Helping Helps: Autonomous Motivation for Prosocial Behavior and Its Influence on Well-Being for the Helper and Recipient." *Journal of Personality and Social Psychology* 98, no. 2 (2010). https://doi.org/10.1037/a0016984.

Wellman, Henry M., David Cross, and Julanne Watson. "Meta-Analysis of Theory-of-Mind Development: The Truth about False Belief." *Child Development* 72, no. 3 (2001).

White, Robert W. "Motivation Reconsidered: The Concept of Competence." *Psychological Review* 66, no. 5 (1959).

Wiersbe, Warren. *Be Skillful*. An Old Testament Study. Proverbs. Wheaton, IL: Victor Books, 1995.

Wiersbe, Warren. *The Bible Exposition Commentary,* vol 1. Wheaton, IL: Victor Books, 1996.

Wiersbe, Warren. *The Bible Exposition Commentary,* vol 2. Wheaton, IL: Victor Books, 1996.

Wilson, Gerald H. "חכם." Pages 130–134 in *New International Dictionary of Old Testament Theology and Exegesis,* vol 2. Grand Rapids: Zondervan, 1997.

Woodruff, Elissa et al. "Humility and Religion: Benefits, Difficulties, and a Model of Religious Tolerance." In *Cross-Cultural Advancements in Positive Psychology,* ed. C. Kim Prieto (Dordrecht, Springer Netherlands, 2014).

Wright, J. Robert. *Proverbs, Ecclesiastes, Song of Solomon*, Ancient Christian Commentary on Scripture IX. Downers Grove, IL, InterVarsity Press, 2005.

Zak, Paul J. "Trust: A Temporary Human Attachment Facilitated by Oxytocin." *Behavior and Brain Sciences* 28, no. 3 (2005).

Zeidner, Moshe et al. "Personal Factors Related to Compassion Fatigue in Health Professionals." *Anxiety, Stress, & Coping* 26, no. 6 (2013). https://doi.org/10.1080/10615806.2013.777045.

Zemek, George J. *The Word of God in the Child of God: Exegetical, Theological, and Homiletical Reflections from the 119th Psalm.* Eugene, OR: Wipf and Stock, 2005.

Diagnostic and Statistical Manual of Mental Disorders: DSM-5, 5th edition. Arlington, VA: American Psychiatric Association, 2013.